# Models of Simon

Herbert Simon (1916–2001) is mostly celebrated for the theory of bounded ratio-nality and satisficing. This book of essays on *Models of Simon* tackles these topics that he broached in a professional career spanning more than 60 years. Expository material on the fundamental concepts he introduced is re-interpreted in terms of the theory of computability.

This volume frames the behavioural issues of concern for economists, such as hierarchy, causality, near-diagonal linear dynamical systems, discovery, the con-trasts between the notion of *Heuristics*, and *the Church–Turing Thesis* of Comput-ability Theory. There is, consistently, an emphasis on the historical origins of the concepts Simon worked with, in emphasizing Human Problem Solving and Deci-sion Making – by rational individuals and institutions (like organizations). The main feature of the results in the book is its emphasis on the procedural aspects of human problem solving, decision making, and the remarkable way Simon harnessed many tools of mathematical logic, mathematics, cognitive sciences, economics, and econometrics.

This long-awaited volume is an important read for those who study economic theory and philosophy and microeconomics and political economy, as well as those interested in the great Herbert Simon's work.

**Kumaraswamy Vela Velupillai** is a retired emeritus professor, living in Stock-holm, Sweden. He was, formerly the John E. Cairnes Professor of Economics at NUI Galway, Ireland, a Professore di Chiara Fama in the department of econom-ics at the University of Trento, Italy – from both tenured posts he opted for early retirement. He was, for a very short period, also (a non-tenured) Distinguished Professor of Economics at NSSR, in New York.

# Models of Simon

**Kumaraswamy Vela Velupillai**

Routledge
Taylor & Francis Group

LONDON AND NEW YORK

First published 2018
by Routledge

2 Park Square, Milton Park, Abingdon, Oxfordshire OX14 4RN
52 Vanderbilt Avenue, New York, NY 10017

*Routledge is an imprint of the Taylor & Francis Group, an informa business*

First issued in paperback 2020

*British Library Cataloguing-in-Publication Data*
A catalogue record for this book is available from the British Library

*Library of Congress Cataloging-in-Publication Data*
A catalog record for this book has been requested

ISBN: 978-0-415-31158-8 (hbk)
ISBN: 978-0-367-59393-3 (pbk)

Typeset in Times New Roman
by Apex CoVantage, LLC

**To:** *Viveka Lalitha*

Med manga kulörta lyktor
Jag gick mej i världen ut.
De slocknade – ljudlöst och oförmärkt
Och så tog det vackra slut.

Jag stannade – högst förlägen,
– Allt hade ju mist sin glans!
Men nu har jag gått på vägen,
Som kommer från Ingenstans

Och ringlar till Ingenstädes,
i många de långa år
förutan kulörta lyktor.
Det är ganska svårt – men det går
                    **Nils Ferlin, 1944**

# Contents

# Figures

# Preface

My greatest indebtedness, in the preparation of this manuscript, is to my sometime collaborator, Dr Ying-Fang Kao (referred to as *Selda Kao*, in this volume), once a valued research student and now a friend. In particular, during the two-year period, 2011–2012, prior to my ill-fated departure to take up a fixed-term professorship at the New School for Social Research (NSSR), in New York, Selda and I worked intensively, discussed incessantly and developed various aspects of Herbert Simon's research program, not only in *Behavioural Economics* but also in evolutionary dynamics due to near-decomposability, what Simon referred to as 'the sweet peas, Drosophila and E. coli of cognitive science' (Simon, 1989a, p. 394), that is, 'the metaphor of chess, cryptarithmetic and the Tower of Hanoi' (*ibid.*; see also Newell & Simon, 1972, Parts 2 & 4), extending those 'metaphors to constructing implementable *heuristics* for *Weiqi* (in Chinese; *GO* in Japanese, the word that is used in this text).

Chapters 2, 3 and 10 represent joint work, suitably amended by this author singly and with Selda, over this intensive period of collaboration (Kao & Velupillai, 2012; Velupillai & Kao, 2014, 2016); in addition, there was also Kao and Velupillai (2012).

In these joint works, after much discussion and many trials and tribulations, we defined and characterized *Classical* – or *Cognitive* – *Behavioural Economics* (**CBE**), as that which Herbert Simon single-handedly defined, fostered and worked with; we contrasted this with a characterization – based on extensive historical and doctrine-historical studies – of *Modern Behavioural Economics* (**MBE**) as that which emanates from the works of Ward Edwards (almost simultaneously with Simon's pioneering writings on **CBE**). We traced the origins of currently fashionable work on behavioural economics, without any model of computation at its basis or a coherent model of probability in its foundations, to the kind of *expected utility maximization* models of Ward Edwards, who had tried to incorporate Leonard Savage's ideas on *subjective probability* within the traditional expected utility framework of orthodox economic and game theories. This led us to refer to the actual practice of the Modern Behavioural Economists as attempting to run a '*bicycle repair shop*' for orthodox economic theory.

I am almost as grateful for the sterling support, intellectual and otherwise, of my other – that is, 'other than' Dr Selda Kao – active founder-members of the

*Algorithmic Social Sciences Research Unit* (**ASSRU**) – Professor Stefano Zambelli, Dr Navaneethakrishnan Dharmaraj and Dr Venkatachalam Ragupathy.

With Stefano Zambelli I was able to show that Simon's notion of problem solving, procedural rationality and simulation required the framework of computability and computational complexity theory of understanding dynamical systems by means of simulation on digital computers in the spirit of the Fermi-Pasta-Ulam problem. Some of this research is reported in Velupillai and Zambelli (2015).

Ragupathy and I worked on the claims of constructivism by those who advanced the view that agent-based modelling (ABM) of aggregate dynamics, based on simple rules of interactions at a variety of 'micro' levels of agents and institutions. Among the 'simple rules' that these ABM modellers invoked was the 'bounded rationality' of agents, formalized in a way that had nothing to do with any of Herbert Simon's lifelong work in defining this notion in a rich and layered way. This work, together with our joint work on algorithmic dynamical systems was a pathway to completing one kind of circle towards a vision of discovery as a search outcome in the space of alternatives, explored with a repertoire of *heuristics*. Some of this work is represented in Ragupathy and Velupillai (2012, 2016).[1]

However, the most relevant joint work with Ragupathy, in relation to this monograph, was our contribution on Frank Ramsey (Velupillai & Ragupathy, 2016, especially the last part). My own attempt at a unified framework for approaching the many-faceted visions of Simon, in terms of computability theory, was decisively influenced by an epistemological – especially – interpretation of the *Ramsey Theorem* (Ramsey, 1930, chapter 13). A recursion theoretic study, and understanding, of *Ramsey's Theorem*, in particular, is what made it possible for me, invoking the crucial distinction between *Recursively Enumerable* and *Recursive* sets, on one hand, and that between *Recursive Separability* and *Recursive Inseparability*, to view Simon's *Human Problem Solving* from the point of view of *computational rules* Smullyan, 1993; Dowek, 2015).

When the idea of **ASSRU** was first mooted, there was unanimous agreement among the five[2] of us, the 'founder-members', that its intellectual heritage was spanned by the works of *Alan Turing, Herbert Simon, Luitzen Brouwer, Richard Goodwin, Piero Sraffa* and *Maynard Keynes*.

The **ASSRU** logo which took thought and time to conceive, design and implement, therefore, was as shown in Figure 0.1.

'They', as intellectual 'patrons' of **ASSRU**, defined the scope and nature of the kind of quantitative economics we – as members of the research unit – hoped to develop, using computability theory (Turing), constructive mathematics based on intuitionistic logic (Brouwer), Behavioural Economics (Simon), Macrodynamics (Goodwin & Keynes) and a Multisectoral Theory of Production Systems (capable of self-reproduction, an extension of the ideas of Sraffa). The parallel idea of productive and reproductive thought processes, human problem solving based on them (following the work of Otto Selz and Karl Duncker in European continental research on the psychology of cognitive processes), was an important part of Simon's research program. Understanding – however imperfectly and

*Figure 0.1* The ASSRU Logo; clockwise: Turing, Simon, Bouwer, Goodwin, Sraffa, Keynes and a Medieval COUNTING Table.

inadequately – this helped me rethink the role of *heuristics* in human problem solving, in contrast to *algorithmic thinking* in machine-based approaches to problem solving.

Alas, this 'understanding' dawned on me only very recently. This belated understanding is reflected in the contents of Chapter 5.

It is hoped that this manuscript is a partial realization of the larger **ASSRU** vision. This is the part for which **ASSRU** work is determined by aspects of what is called, here, the *Classical* (or *Cognitive*) *Behavioural Economics* (**CGE**) of Herbert Simon, interpreted mathematically, where possible, in the language of computability theory, based on Turing's Model of Computation or Brouwerian constructivism underpinned by intuitionistc logic.

Although the various chapters were conceived and completed at different times, during the decade and a half – and more – during which, off and on, I wrote them for different audiences, it was sometimes based on a variety of *secondary sources*. However, in the completion of this manuscript I have relied exclusively on many (alas, *not all*) writings by Herbert Simon, primarily his series of books with the praenomen *Models* in the titles (see the Appendix to this Preface).

Thus, although I am well aware of the many and enlightening contribution to various aspects of Herbert Simon's scholarship, and references to some of them do appear in some of the chapters (particularly Chapters 2, 3 and 10 as well as Appendices 1 and 2), on the whole I avoid any discussion, critical or otherwise, of this derived (or secondary) literature.

The book itself is dedicated to my eldest daughter, **Viveka Lalitha**, who is now *almost* as old as I was when first acquainted with Herbert Simon (as the architect of the *Hawkins-Simon Conditions for Stability*, which was first introduced to me, during the doctoral course on Microeconomics in the department of economics at the University of Lund, in 1972 – four decades and a half ago, by my beloved teacher and mentor, the late professor Björn Thalberg).

The manuscript is being completed more than a decade and a half after it was first conceived, during my tenure as a visiting fellow at Peterhouse, in Cambridge, now, in my retired, reclusive years in Stockholm.

*K. Vela Velupillai*
*Solna, Sweden*
*15 July 2017*

## Notes

1 It is a melancholy, yet *observable, fact* – in the sense in which Simon used these two (italicized) words – that all this collaborative work at **ASSRU** was done either in the period *before* my ill-fated sojourn at NSSR or *after* it! I am sure there is lesson to be learned from this *factual observation*!

2 Dr Navaneethakrishnan Dharmaraj, although he has, now, left the academic world, remains an active contributor to the *ASSRU Discussion Paper* series. My own collaboration with Dharmaraj, of relevance to the notion of *rationality in disequilibrium* and out-of-equilibrium dynamics, applied – albeit implicitly – to Simon's ideas on learning discrete dynamical behaviour by means of simulation is reported in Velupillai and Dharmaraj (2017).

## References

Dowek, Gilles (2015), *Computation, Proof, Machine: Mathematics Enters a New Age*, translated from the French by Pierre Guillot & Marion Roman, Cambridge University Press, Cambridge.

Kao, Ying-Fang & K. Vela Velupillai (2012), Origins and Pioneers of Behavioural Economics, *Interdisciplinary Journal of Economics and Business Law*, Vol. 1, No. 3, pp. 47–73.

Kao, Ying-Fang & K. Vela Velupillai (2015), Behavioural Economics: Classical and Modern, *The European Journal of the History of Economic Thought*, Vol. 22, No. 2, pp. 236–271.

Newell, Allen & Herbert A. Simon (1972), *Human Problem Solving*, Prentice-Hall, Inc., Englewood Cliffs, New Jersey.

Ragupathy, V. & K. Vela Velupillai (2012), Origins and Early Development of the Nonlinear Endogenous Mathematical Theory of the Business Cycle, *Economia Politica*, Vol. 29, No. 1, April, pp. 45–79.

Ragupathy, V. & K. Vela Velupillai (2016), Notes on a 'Constructive Proof of the Existence of a Collateral Equilibrium', *Computational Economics*, Vol. 48, No, 1, pp. 179–181.

Ramsey, Frank P. (1930), On a Problem of Formal Logic, chapter 3, pp. 82–111, in: *The Foundations of Mathematics, and other Logical Essays*, edited with an Introduction by R.B. Braithwaite and a Preface by G. E. Moore, Kegan Paul, Trench, Trubner and Company, Ltd., London.

Simon, Herbert A. (1989a), The Scientist as Problem Solver, chapter 14, pp. 375–398, in: *Complex Information Processing: The Impact of Herbert A. Simon*, edited by David Klahr & Kenneth Kotovsky, Lawrence Erlbaum Associates, Publishers, Hillsdale, New Jersey.

Smullyan, Raymond M. (1993), *Recursion Theory for Metamathematics*, Oxford University Press, Oxford.

Velupillai, K. Vela & N. Dharmaraj (2017), Out-of-Equilibrium Traverse Dynamics: The Time-to-Build Tradition, *The International Journal of Computational Economics and Econometrics*, Vol. 7, No. 3, pp. 213–224.

Velupillai, K. Vela & V. Ragupathy (2016), Frank Plumpton Ramsey, in: *The Handbook of the History of Economic Analysis*, edited by Gilbert Faccarello & Heinz Kurz, Edward Elgar Publishing.

Velupillai, K. Vela & Ying-Fang Kao (2014), Computable and Computational Complexity Theoretic Bases for Herbert Simon's Cognitive Behavioral Economics, *Cognitive Systems Research*, Vol. 29/30, September, pp. 40–52.

Velupillai, K. Vela & Ying-Fang Kao (2016), Herbert A. Simon, in: *The Handbook of the History of Economic Analysis*, edited by Gilbert Faccarello & Heinz Kurz, Edward Elgar Publishing.

Velupillai, K. Vela & Stefano Zambelli (2015), Simulation, Computation and Dynamics in Economics, *Journal of Economic Methodology*, Vol. 22, No. 1, March, pp. 1–27.

# Appendix to the Preface

I have relied mostly on the following **MODELS** books by Herbert Simon, in the completion of this manuscript:

- **Models of Man: Social and Rational**, John Wiley & Sons, Inc., New York, 1957.
- **Models of Discovery – and Other Topics in the Methods of Science**, D. Reidel Publishing Company, Dordrecht, Holland, 1977.
- **Models of Thought, Volume I**, Yale University Press, New Haven, 1979.
- **Models of Thought, Volume II**, Yale University Press, New Haven, 1989.
- **Models of Bounded Rationality, Volume 1: Economic Analysis and Public Policy**, The MIT Press, Cambridge, Massachusetts, 1982.
- **Models of Bounded Rationality, Volume 2: Behavioral Economics and Business Organization**, The MIT Press, Cambridge, Massachusetts, 1982.
- **Models of Bounded Rationality, Volume 3: Empirically Grounded Economic Reason**, The MIT Press, Cambridge, Massachusetts, 1997.
- **Models of my Life**, Basic Books, New York, 1991.

In addition, the following five *Non-MODELS* books by Herbert Simon that have decisively influenced me include the following:

- **Administrative Behaviour:** *A Study of Decision-Making Processes in Administrative Organizations* (Fourth Edition), The Free Press, New York.
- **Organizations** (Second Edition), by James March & Herbert Simon, Blackwell Publishers, Oxford.
- **The Shape of Automaton: For Men and Management**, Harper & Row, Publishers, Inc., New York, 1965.
- **Human Problem Solving** by Allen Newell & Herbert Simon, Prentice-Hall, INC., Englewood Cliffs, New Jersey, 1972.
- **Reason in Human Affairs**, Basil Blackwell, Oxford, 1983.
- **The Sciences of the Artificial** (Third Edition), The MIT Press, Cambridge, Massachusetts, 1996.
- **An Empirically Based Microeconomics: The Raffaele Mattioli Lectures**, Cambridge University Press, Cambridge, 1997.

Finally, two articles which I have not succeeded in locating in any of the preceding MODELS volumes, have also been very important for my (obviously limited) understanding of the fascinating world of Herbert Simon:

- *The Scientist as Problem Solver*, chapter 14, pp. 375–398, in: **Complex Information Processing: The Impact of Herbert Simon**, edited by David Klahr & Kenneth Kotovsky, Lawrence Erlbaum Associates, Publishers, New Jersey, 1989a.
- *Machine as Mind*, chapter 5, pp. 81–102, in: **Machines and Thought: The Legacy of Alan Turing, Vol. 1**, Oxford University Press, Oxford, 1996a.

# Acknowledgements

Chapters 2, 3, 6, 7, Appendix 1 & 3 are revised versions of chapters, articles and an obituary published earlier in, respectively, **Handbook of the History of Economic Analysis**, the **European Journal of the History of Economic Thought**, **Cognitive Systems Research, Economia Politica**, an **OECD** booklet, the **Interdisciplinary Journal of Economics and Business Law** and **The Independent**. I am greatly indebted to the editors of these publications for permission to republish (revised) versions of articles appearing first in them.

# 1 Introduction

> *My economist friends have long since given up on me*, consigning me to psychology or some other distant wasteland. If I cannot accept the true faith of expected utility maximization, it is not the fault of my excellent education in economics. . . . .
> . . . .
>
> My traumatic exposure in 1935 to the budgeting process un the Milwaukee recreation department had immunized me against the idea that human beings maximize expected utility, and had *made me an incorrigible satisficer*. . . . [T]he theory of scientific discovery to which my study . . . has led me . . . is not a theory of global rationality, but *a theory of human limited computation in the face of complexity.*
>
> $\qquad\qquad\qquad\qquad\qquad$ – Simon (1989a, pp. 394–395; italics added)

It is, therefore, important to recall that a few years earlier Simon (1986, p. S.223; italics added) had clarified this notion of *complexity* and its implication for *deductive prediction*:

> In this kind of *complexity*, there is *no* single sovereign principle for *deductive prediction*.

My own precept for Simonian *Human Problem Solvers* was thus (Rustem & Velupillai, 1990, p. 432; italics added):

> The *search* for simplicity in the growth of complexity is the *exercise of reason*

Simon was the quintessential *Reasonable Man*, whose task was to *search systematically* for *solutions* to problems, even in the absence of any 'single sovereign principle of deductive prediction'. Searching systematically, in my interpretation, was an act of procedural rationality. Hence, human problem solvers were procedurally implementing systematic search procedures. The space over which a solution was systematically searched for was complex; simplifying it was an act of the reasonable human problem solver. It is here that the reasonable human problem solver was characterized by boundedly rational systematic search, which led to (often but not always) a satisficing solution.

This 'incorrigible satisficer', the self-confessed 'closet-engineer since the beginning of [his] career (Simon, 1991, p. 109), the monomaniacal (Simon, 1957, p. vii) rational artificer, the compelling storyteller traversing *Mazes without Minotaurs* (*ibid.*, chapter 15 & Simon, 1991, chapter 11), the renaissance man *par excellence*, master applied mathematician, founding father of cognitive behavioural science, with a supreme mastery of the methodology of scientific method and processes of discovery and much else, was said to have 'had it put together at least 40 years ago [i.e., in 1939!]' (Newell, 1989, p. 400). 'The central idea', in putting it all together, being '*bounded rationality*' (*ibid.*, p. 400).

It would be a very foolish person, or one who is outrageously audacious, who would contradict Allen Newell's characterization of the central theme of Herbert Simon's lifelong research program. I hope I am not 'foolish', nor do I think of myself as 'outrageously audacious'. Yet, the central theme that informs my interpretation of **Models of Simon** is *not bounded rationality*; it is *Human Problem Solving*. I emphasize the **Human** aspect of *Problem Solving* to draw parallels with Alan Turing's Computability (*Machine*) approach to *Solvable and Unsolvable Problems* (Turing, 1954) – a parallelism, bordering on similarity, emphasized in Simon's *Machine as Mind* in **The Legacy of Alan Turing** (Simon, 1996a), explored in Velupillai (2013, pp. 339–341). The contrast should be with the (partially) intuitionistic, constructive, Brouwer–Heyting–Kolmogorov (BHK) approach to proof procedures (Brouwer, 1923, 1925; Heyting, 1930 a, 1930b; Kolmogorov, 1932).

In the rest of this Introduction I try to explain – even, at times, justify – my (peculiar) stance, which goes 'against the stream' of current and standard interpretations of Simon's construction of his vision (which was in constant flux on many fronts, but not all). In addition, this Introduction tries, also, to *summarize* the contents of each of the chapters and the various appendices. It is doubtful that the summaries are a surrogate for the actual contents of the different chapters and appendices, where their contexts are also made reasonably clear.

Without a uniform point of view that I can adopt, it would be impossible to tell a coherent story of Simon's vision. For such a uniform approach it is necessary that I interpret Simon's theories, the methods with which he formed, developed, implemented and experimented with them from some unified stance. If not it will be a patchwork quilt, which has its own charm, even usefulness, but it is not one that I think Simon would approve. I am, of course, not trying to develop a unified stance to satisfy (*sic*!) Simon's (posthumous) approval, even if only in spirit. However, it – the unified stance – impressed upon me, as I read, reread, worked with, worked over and tried to understand the many-faceted world that Simon strode with a mastery of diverse tools, concepts, methods and theories.

Thus, in may seem at odds with any unified stance when one views his work on the Hawkins–Simon conditions for stability, on causality, identification and aggregation, on evolution due to semi- (or near-)decomposability, to a variety of aspects of organization and administrative theories, to empirical microeconomics, even to game theory and macrodynamics, to discovery, creativity, axiomatics and the philosophy of science, to artificial intelligence and the weird and wonderful world of cognitive – or classical – behavioural social sciences. Without exception, Simon's contributions to social, human, natural and pure sciences, both in their theoretical and empirical aspects, are absolutely original. If a second-rate (perhaps, actually, third-rate) intellectual like myself tries to interpret and summarize these outstandingly original visions and contributions it can only lead to third- (or fourth-)rate results and less than worthy stories of the work of a – I choose this word deliberately – magician, one who wrought, out of the material available to all and sundry, a world of possibilities that enriched experience, both theoretically and from a policy point of view.

But if I am able to find a convincing and unified theoretical stance, to tell the story of Simon's many-faceted visions, then it might – at least – mitigate the narrative's potential low status and, who knows, may even contribute to a development of one (or more) of the many frontiers he broached, and created.

Thus, my search – I nearly qualified it by using 'sic'! – for a unified (theoretical) stance, at least one that is consistent with his explicitly expressed visions of the many-faceted world he created and strode, like the colossus he was.

My first attempt at formulating a unified theoretical vision was to begin and end chronologically, to begin at the beginning with bounded rationality, (henceforth, **BR**) refined around the end of the first third of his professional life with the addition of satisficing (hereafter referred to as **SAT**) embellished with the pioneering of cognitive behavioural science (**CBE**, where the 'C' could refer, interchangeably, to 'Cognitive' or 'Classical') and artificial intelligence; then, in that properly fertile professional time of 'half-life', came the monumental *Human Problem Solving*, summarizing, essentially, the novel approach to problem solving as a dynamic process, underpinned by a model of computation that was peopled by solvers who were procedurally rational.

This first attempt led to my 'unified theoretical stance' in terms of a model of computation – in particular, the Turing Machine but also using the Church–Turing Thesis as I then understood it, interpreting heuristics as algorithms in the sense of computability theory – and buttressed by computational complexity theory. This enabled me to embed BR and SAT as elements defining procedural rationality and use the idea of the duality between computational processes and dynamical systems.

One important observation must be made at this point. I do not think, or ascribe to, Simon's world, peopled by procedurally rational agents, indulging in problem solving in diverse domains, was stochastic or probabilistic in any *ad hoc* sense; any probabilistic underpinning came from an algorithmic information stance, which was also the foundation on which randomness was based, and this was embraced wholeheartedly by Simon, all the way from the time of the Dartmouth conference, where artificial intelligence – AI, henceforth, in the Turing tradition was enunciated – to the end of his life (but especially so in Simon (1989a, 1996a)).

This was the first attempt helped me organize my thoughts and interpretations of Simon's contributions fairly adequately, but was, I felt, inadequate from many theoretical and empirical points of view. It was, however, a rereading of Section 6 of **Models of Discovery** (henceforth, **MoD**) that led to my current unified theoretical stance. To this must be added the influence of a serious ('nth') reading of

Martin Davis's classic **Computability and Unsolvability** (in its Dover version as Davis, 1982).

My current unified theoretical stance, to interpret the many-faceted world of Simon is based *entirely* on computability theory because I am able to interpret mathematical logic from a recursion theoretic point of view (Davis, *ibid.*, chapter 8) and understand the interplay between the underpinnings of *predicate logic in axioms and inference rule*s and *computation rules*, for the way *Human Problem Solving* leads to search for *proofs* of the discovery of structures with some notion of order, by creative, procedurally rational agents (or organizations or processes of evolution), in a dynamically evolving environment. It is as if Simon was trying to tame an *evolving pattern of a jigsaw puzzle, pro tempore*, which is why chess played in important role in his research (and time eluded his obvious path towards **GO**, or *Weiqi*,[1] where the *surprise* element in an evolutionary process plays an important part in the thought processes implemented by Human Problem Solvers playing this game, when pitted against Machine-based strategies).[2]

But above all, it is the inspiration of the *Ramsey Theorem*, and *Ramsey Theory*, in general, together with a particular uncomputability between the former and Busy Beaver functions that were instrumental in disciplining my unified stance of Simon's world of Human Problem Solving. The duality I discovered, between $R(k, l)$[3] in Ramsey Theory and $S(m, n)$[4] in the theory of *Busy Beavers*, together with the recursive graph theorem of Brattka (2008), was instrumental in understanding the essentially constructive nature of human problem solving in chess, Cryptarithmetic and (Recreational) Games that form the backbone of Newell and Simon (1972).

Essentially, five precepts form the backdrop against which I formulate the unified vision to tell this story of **Models of Simon** (stated in the chronological sequence, which does not imply that it is the way my approach was disciplined – for example, Ramsey Theory and the Ramsey Theorem became familiar to me only after the other four became part of my intellectual 'armory'):

1    Ramsey (1931, p. 82; italics added)

> This paper [Ramsey, 1928] is primarily concerned with a special case of one of the leading problems of mathematical logic, the problem of finding *a regular procedure* to determine the truth or falsity of any given logical formula.[5]

The *regular procedure* turned out to be, at the hands of Church and Turing, *algorithmic decidability*. The mathematical tools and the formalization of the mind's repertoire with which Simon underpinned his approach to heuristic problem solving, were disciplined by a mastery of the foundations of algorithmic decidability in computability and computational complexity theories.

2    Turing (1954, p. 23; italics added)

> These, and some other results [on the unsolvability of the *decision problem*] *of mathematical logic* may be regarded as going some way towards a

demonstration, within mathematics itself, of *the inadequacy of 'reason' unsupported by common sense.*

Simon's lifelong advocacy of procedural rationality was because of the 'inadequacy of 'reason' unsupported by common sense', in orthodox, formal, economics, and hence his development of boundedly rational agents, satisficing, in heuristically searching for solutions of decision problems.

3    Simon (1996a, p. 101)

If we hurry, we can catch up to Turing on the path he pointed out to us so many years ago.

Simon followed 'the path [Turing] pointed out to us', even before he became familiar with the important contributions by Alan Turing in computability theory, oracle computation, artificial intelligence and much else.

4    Day (1993, p. 39; italics added)

*[V]iability creating mechanisms are the analogue of equilibrium 'existence' proofs, but in the out-of-equilibrium setting.* They are required to guarantee the existence of a continuing 'solution' to the system in terms of feasible actions for all of its constituent model components. When they are explicitly represented, then not only the population of production processes evolve, but also the population of agents, organizations, and institutions.

In all his dynamic formulations – whether of problem solving by procedurally rational agents, of evolving systems due to semi-decomposability, or of causal dynamics due to unilateral coupling – it was always a case of seeking and building viability creating mechanisms in every kind of behavioural decision making in Simon's visions.

5    Simon (in Sieg, 2001)

Proceed, as if you were proving a theorem!

It was a piece of advice Simon gave Sieg, and the latter continued (*ibid.*; italics added):

I followed his advice and, lo and behold, it worked: *proving a theorem requires,* after all, *to look at the problem from a variety of perspectives and to expend lots of patience.*

To understand, and appreciate Simon's cognitive behavioural economics, it was necessary, I found, to 'proceed as if I was proving theorems' – but proving them in the sense of automated theorem proving (**ATP**), as in the Appel–Hagen proof of Guthrie's conjecture, which became the *four-colour theorem.*

My interpretations of Simon's vision depend almost decisively on the preceding five precepts. Because of this I have been perplexed by the absence, in Simon's work (at least that which I know and am familiar with, which is of relevance to the heuristic problem-solving approach by procedurally rational agents and institutions, processing information algorithmically) of any discussion of the *Entsheidungsproblem*; this also is true of my perplexity regarding the Ramsey Theorem and its intuitive formulation as a 'party problem', as well as a *Busy Beaver*' approach to discovery and creativity, especially for devising chess strategies and algorithms for the Tower of Hanoi problem.

The four-colour theorem, and its computer-aided proof by Appel–Haken, is, surely, a natural consequence of the Newell–Simon work on cryptarithmetic and the machine-based proofs of the theorems in the first part of volume 1 of the monumental work by Whitehead and Russel; so, why is there no mention of the four-colour theorem in at least the later work by Herbert Simon?

In the case of the *Entsheidungsproblem*, I am most puzzled by the absence of any mention of Hilbert's Tenth Problem in any of Simon's writings; this is especially so, because I have always believed that the famous resolution of this problem by Matiyasevich (Davis, *op. cit.*, Appendix 2) can easily be viewed as a 'parlour game', in the sense of the Tower of Hanoi.

I do not pretend to have answers – coherent, cogent or whatever – to any of these perplexities. On the other hand, I invoke some of the techniques used in tackling these problems – especially since I work with the five previously listed precepts in fashioning my vision of Simon's work – in my work in this manuscript.

## Notes

1 If chess plays the role of *sweet peas,* in the Mendelian sense, then – surely – **GO** (or **Weiqi**) must correspond to the source of classificatory ambiguities and nightmares of all latter-day Linnaeists: the *duck-billed playtipus*! This analogy allows (recursive) incompleteness and undecidability to become part of the way human problem solvers face the difficulties of computational complexity in search processes. How, and when, can stopping rules come into play, if the search is for a duck-billed platypus?

2 I have no doubts whatsoever that Simon would have approved of the structure of Google's AlphaGo, and its successes against the 9-dan Lee Sodol – and the way it was thwarted from completely overwhelming thought processes implemented by human players who, intuitively, employed 'surprise' move strategies, to which the machine-learning, neural-networked AI model of AlphaGO had no patterned response.

3 **R (k, l)** is the *minimum number* N, called the **Ramsey Number**, s.t., for any colouring c of the set of edges $K_N$ of a *Complete Graph*, G, it contains a red $K_k$ or a yellow $K_l$ as a *subgraph*.

4 $S(m, n)$ is the *shift function* of a *Turing Machine* (TM) with m *states* and n *symbols* in a *Busy Beaver 'Game'* between all such TMs, s.t., the 'winner' is that machine which can 'write' the '*most*' symbols on a two-way, indefinitely extendable tape (cf. Rado, 1962). The question posed by the Busy Beaver 'Game', intuitively, is that of searching in the space of *m*-state, *n*-symbol, TMs for the location of the *smallest* – that is, *minimal* – Universal machine.

5 To this Ramsey adds the following footnote: 'Called in German the *Entsheidungsproblem*; see Hilbert und Ackermann, *Grundzüge der Theoretischen Logik*, pp. 72–81.' This was fully four years *before* Max Newman lectured on the *Entsheidungsproblem*

and a *further* three years before Turing began his work which culminated in that path-breaking paper of his of 1936, which settled the *Entsheidungsproblem* forever!

## References

Brattka, V. (2008), Plottable Real Number Functions and the Computable Graph Theorem, *SIAM Journal on Computing*, Vol. 38, pp. 303–328.

Brouwer, Luitzen E. J. (1923; 1998), Intuitionist Splitting of the Fundamental Notions of Mathematics, translated from the Dutch by Walter P. van Stigt, chapter 18, pp. 286–289, in: *From Brouwer to Hilbert: The Debate on the Foundations of Mathematics in the 1920s*, edited by Paolo Mancosu, Oxford University Press, Oxford.

Brouwer, Luitzen E. J. (1925; 1998), Intuitionist Splitting of the Fundamental Notions of Mathematics, translated from the German by Walter P. van Stigt, chapter 19, pp. 290–292, in: *From Brouwer to Hilbert: The Debate on the Foundations of Mathematics in the 1920s*, edited by Paolo Mancosu, Oxford University Press, Oxford.

Davis, Martin (1982), *Computability and Unsolvability* (Dover edition, with a new Preface and an Appendix on Hilbert's Tenth Problem), Dover Publications Inc., New York.

Day, Richard H. (1993), Nonlinear Dynamics and Evolutionary Economics, chapter 3, pp. 18–41, in: *Nonlinear Dynamics and Evolutionary Economics*, edited by R. H. Day & P. Chen, Oxford University Press, Oxford.

Heyting, Arend (1930a; 1993), On Intuitionistic Logic, translated from the French by Amy L. Rocha, chapter 23, pp. 306–310, in: *From Brouwer to Hilbert: The Debate on the Foundations of Mathematics in the 1920s*, edited by Paolo Mancosu, Oxford University Press, Oxford.

Heyting, Arend (1930b; 1993), The Formal Rules of Intuitionistic Logic, translated from the German by Paolo Mancosu, chapter 24, pp. 311–327, in: *From Brouwer to Hilbert: The Debate on the Foundations of Mathematics in the 1920s*, edited by Paolo Mancosu, Oxford University Press, Oxford.

Kolmogorov, Andrei (1932; 1993), On the Interpretation of Intuitionistic Logic, chapter 25, pp. 328–334, in: *From Brouwer to Hilbert: The Debate on the Foundations of Mathematics in the 1920s*, edited by Paolo Mancosu, Oxford University Press, Oxford.

Newell, Allen (1989), Putting It All Together, chapter 15, pp. 399-440, in: *Complex Information Processing – The Impact of Herbert A. Simon*, edited by David Klahr & Kenneth Kotovsky, Lawrence Erlbaum Associates, Publishers, Hillsdale, New Jersey.

Rado, Tibor (1962), On Non-Computable Functions, *The Bell Systems Technical Journal*, Vol. 41, No. 3, pp. 877–844.

Ramsey, Frank P. (1931), *The Foundations of Mathematics*, Routledge, London.

Rustem, Berc & Kumaraswamy Velupillai (1990), Rationality, Computability, and Complexity, *Journal of Economic Dynamics and Control*, Vol. 14, No. 2, May, pp. 419–432.

Sieg, W. (2001), *Remembrances of Herbert Simon*, accessed 27 December, 2015 at www.cs.cmu.edu/ simon/all.html.

Simon, Herbert A. (1957), *Models of Man: Social and Rational*, John Wiley & Sons, Inc., New York.

Simon, Herbert A. (1986), Rationality in Psychology and Economics, *Journal of Business*, Vol. 59, No. 4, Pt. 2, October, pp. S.209–S.224.

Simon, Herbert A. (1989a), The Scientist as Problem Solver, chapter 14, pp. 375–398, in: *Complex Information Processing: The Impact of Herbert Simon*, edited by David Klahr & Kenneth Kotovsky, Lawrence Erlbaum Associates, Publishers, Hillsdale, NJ.

Simon, Herbert A. (1991), *Models of My Life*, Basic Books, New York.

Simon, Herbert A. (1996a), Machine as Mind, chapter 5, pp. 81–102, in: *Machines and Thought: The Legacy of Alan Turing*, Vol. 1, edited by Peter Millican & Andy Clark, Oxford University Press, Oxford.

Turing, Alan (1954), Solvable and Unsolvable Problems, *Science News*, edited by A. Haslett, Vol. 31, February, pp. 7–23.

Velupillai. K. Vela (2013), Turing on 'Solvable and Unsolvable Problems' and Simon on 'Human Problem Solving', pp. 339–341, in: *Alan Turing: His Work and Impact*, edited by S. Barry Cooper & Jan Van Leeuwen, Elsevier, Amsterdam.

# 2 Herbert Simon
## A life[1]

[S]cientific knowledge is *not* the Philosopher's Stone that is going to solve *all* . . . *problems*.

—Simon (1983, p. 105; italics added)

The cognitive sciences, Human Problem Solving, heuristics, procedural rationality, causal ordering, (deterministic) identifiability and eliminability, near decomposability, aggregation and dynamical systems, bounded rationality, artificial intelligence, satisficing, discovery, creativity and information processing systems, all these concepts implemented in decision processes by reasonable human beings and feasible institutions, in administrative, political, scientific and economic environments, characterized the work and life of the remarkable man that was Herbert Simon. It is not possible for an ordinary mortal like me – as I pointed out earlier – to even begin the process of adequately summarizing the life of a *Renaissance man*. Thus, this cannot be anything other than an inadequate story of some aspects of the rich repertoire Simon created by his many-faceted contributions.

No other single person has won the Nobel Memorial Prize in Economics (1978), the Turing Award of the Association for Computing Machinery (Newell & Simon, 1972), the Orsa/Tims John von Neumann Theory Prize (1988), the Distinguished Scientific Contribution Award of the American Psychological Association (1969) and the National Medal of Science (1986). Perhaps this Renaissance man's outlook on the scientific spirit he nurtured can be summarized in his characterization of 'the central task of natural science' to be (Simon, 1996, pp. 1–2; italics added):

[T]o make the wonderful commonplace: to show that *complexity*, correctly viewed, is only a mask for *simplicity*; to find pattern hidden in apparent chaos . . . . . . . This is the task of natural science: to show that the wonderful is not incomprehensible, to show how it can be comprehended – but not to destroy wonder. For when we have explained the wonderful, unmasked the hidden pattern, a new wonder arises at *how complexity was woven out of simplicity*. The aesthetics of natural science and mathematics is at one with the aesthetics of music and painting – both inhere in the *discovery* of a partially concealed pattern.

In an academic life spanning more than six decades, Simon managed, almost single-handedly, to create the wholly new disciplines of behavioural economics,[2] cognitive sciences, Artificial Intelligence, computer aided proofs, a particular kind of evolutionary theory, a notion of causality, theories of discovery, creativity and (non-stochastic) identifiability and, at the same time, nurture through to growth and prosperity one of the great academic institutions, the *Graduate School of Industrial Administration* (GSIA) at the *Carnegie Institute of Technology* (now the *Carnegie Mellon University* – CMU) in Pittsburgh, where these disciplines were fostered with immense dedication. The eminent proof theorist, metamathematician and philosopher Wilfried Sieg recalled during a memorial event that Simon was also instrumental in the creation of a department of philosophy at CMU and went on to observe (Sieg, 2001; italics added),

> How intimately theoretical issues and practical affairs were intertwined for Herb! Having discussed some difficult administrative problems with him, he remarked without further explanation: *Proceed, as if you were proving a theorem*! I followed his advice and, lo and behold, it worked: proving a theorem requires, after all, to look at the problem from a variety of perspectives and to expend lots of patience.

Of course, Simon would not have suggested this metaphor to a Bourbakist or an Hilbertian Formalist, but only to a proof-theorist like Sieg, who would have thought of a proof as a procedure, in the same sense in which Simon extolled the virtues of procedural decision making – that is, underpinned by procedural rationality – in all aspects of administrative and economic life. Incidentally, Sieg's colleague in the philosophy department at CMU, Teddy Seidenfeld, is the current holder of the *Herbert Simon Professorship of Philosophy and Statistics*.

Herbert Simon was the second son of Arthur Carl Simon, a German émigré electrical engineer, inventor and patent lawyer, and Edna Marguerite Merkel, pianist and a second-generation descendant of immigrants from Prague and Cologne. He was wholly Jewish on his father's side and partly Lutheran on his mother's. His brother Clarence was five years older. He was introduced to Dorothea Isabel Pye by William W. Cooper (of 'Charnes–Cooper' fame and coincidentally the man who helped establish the School of Urban and Public Affairs at CMU, serving also as its dean from 1969 to 1975), and they married on Christmas Day in 1937. Their daughter Kathie was born in 1942, followed by a son, Peter, in 1944 and another daughter Barbara in 1946.

From the public elementary and high schools in Milwaukee, he won a full scholarship ($300 per year) to the University of Chicago, taking the examination in physics, mathematics and English. His maternal uncle, Harold Merkel, 'an ardent formal debater [whom] I followed in that activity too', who had died young, at the age of 30, in 1922, was an early intellectual influence. Uncle Harold had graduated with distinction in law from the University of Wisconsin, having also studied economics under the legendary John R. Commons and leaving behind copies of *The Federalist Papers* and William James's *Psychology* in the family library, both of which were devoured by the young Herbert, leaving indelible impressions on the future civil libertarian, behavioural economist, computer scientist and cognitive psychologist. His first publication was a letter to the Editor of the *Milwaukee Journal* defending atheism.

To buttress his debating skills, he began to read widely in the social sciences. Two books in particular were decisively influential: Richard T. Ely's *Outlines of Economics* (Ely, 1893) and Henry George's *Progress and Poverty* (George, 1879). By the time he was ready to embark on a university career, he had developed a clear sense of the general direction he intended to take in his studies. He would devote himself to becoming a 'mathematical social scientist'. We cannot imagine anyone else encapsulating and wearing this mantle with more grace and justification.

He obtained his BA in political science from Chicago in 1936 and a PhD in 1943 and decided to major in political science because his first choice of major, economics, required him to take an obligatory course in accounting, which he detested.

The undergraduate term paper, written for graduation, led to a research assistantship at the Milwaukee City government in the field of Municipal Administration, which in turn led to a firectorship at the Bureau of Public Measurement at the University of California, Berkeley, from 1939 to 1942. For Milwaukee he undertook a study of how the municipal employees made budget decisions, for example, when deciding between planting trees and hiring a recreation director. From this work grew his PhD thesis that, subsequently, became one of the fountainheads for the whole field of organization theory: *Administrative Behavior*, published first in 1947 and still in print.

Simon's main intellectual impulses during the Chicago years came from Henry Schultz in mathematical economics and econometrics, who was also a mentor; from Rudolf Carnap, in the philosophy of science; from Nicholas Rashevsky, in mathematical biophysics; and from Harold Lasswell and Charles Merriam, in political science.

Simon observed, when writing an appreciation of Allen Newell, that the four great questions of human intellectual endeavour are those on the nature of matter, the origins of the universe, the nature of life and the working of the mind. There is little doubt that he himself devoted the whole of his professional life to various aspects of the problem of the working of the mind. How does the mind perceive the external world? How does perception link up with memory? How does memory act as a reservoir of information and knowledge in interacting with the processes that are activated in human decision making, in individual and social settings? In short, *human problem solving* (the title of his 1972 book with Newell): in the face of internal constraints emanating from the working of the mind; and constraints, imposed on its workings, by the external, perceived, world.

Much is made these days of 'ecological rationality' and 'ecological cognitive computing', by which is meant that any internal constraints on the working of the mind should be taken in conjunction with the 'external constraints of the environment' in which the mind is situated for its interaction with the external world. Simon's definition of bounded rationality – the term, although not the concept, was introduced in the introduction to part IV of Simon (1957, p. 198), while the analytical content, together with its conceptual underpinnings, were fully developed by Simon (1955, 1956) – from the outset, was to encapsulate both of these aspects of the workings of the mind, in its rational, decision-making incarnation.

Nothing, and no one, in the burgeoning field of *Modern Behavioural Economics* (see also the next chapter) seem to have ever underpinned any of their theories on a model of computation. Thus, they are unable to comprehend the nature of the decision problem framework, intrinsically framed with an underlying algorithmic basis, within which Simon first advanced, and then developed, boundedly rational and satisficing decisions.

George Polya's influential little book *How to Solve It?* (Polya, 1945) introduced generations of students to *heuristics – the art of guided search*. Simon (1983) felt that the Polya framework provided a starting point for investigating, experimentally, the *creative aspects of the workings of the mind* in two formally and rigorously definable areas – *human problem solving* and in the *art of discovery*.[3] From lessons that could be learnt in understanding the formal aspects of human problem solving they felt they could move on to more ambitious tasks: to an understanding of human thinking, in general. From there it would be a natural step to a formal understanding of the underpinnings of human decision making in general.

The art of discovery, based on heuristics as guided search, led Simon to develop *Models of Discovery* (1977), resurrecting the Peirce–Hanson (Hanson, 1958) emphasis on retroduction (or abduction; thus, circumventing the tiresome dichotomy between induction and deduction) and, simultaneously, taking a well-aimed attack on the nihilism in Karl Popper's stance that there was no scientific basis for a 'logic of scientific discovery' (see, in particular, Simon, 1977: ch. 5.4).

Simon used "experimentally" in the sense of exploring by computer simulation, guided by *programmed heuristics*. These were, for Simon, algorithms that were not necessarily constrained by the *Church–Turing Thesis* of computability theory. In this sense, his lifelong adherence to heuristic methods in human problem solving, models of discovery, design of organizations and evolutionary dynamics had more in common with the notion of algorithms as proofs in constructive mathematics. A lack of appreciation of this subtle difference may have been the reason for even the great Hao Wang to be critical of the way Newell, Shaw and Simon automated proofs in *Principia Mathematica*, in contrast to the way he had done the same (Wang, 1970, p. 227; italics added):

> There is no need to kill a chicken with a butcher's knife. Yet the net impression is that Newell – Shaw – Simon failed even to kill the chicken with their butcher's knife. . . . To argue the superiority of '*heuristic*' over *algorithmic methods* by choosing a particularly inefficient algorithm seems hardly just.

What is a heuristic, if not a stunted algorithm – is what Hao Wang seems to be saying; it is easy to show that, conversely, there were elements of heuristic search in Wang and it was, if anything, a stunted heuristic search process that he was implementing for the same problem in *Principia Mathematica*. Newell and Simon, on the other hand, had a conception of heuristic that was more 'general' than an algorithm, subject to the Church–Turing Thesis. Surely, any reading of Brouwer (1923) or Bishop (1967) would convince even the great Hao Wang that there are processes not constrained by the strictures of the Church–Turing Thesis that can be used in the search for a proof in a complex space of propositions? It was not until many years later, after Martin-Löf's *Intuitionistic Type Theory* (Martin-Löf, 1972), that some of these conundrums of the differences between heuristics and algorithms began to be clarified.

Much of this becomes clarified in the literature that eventually led to the dethroning of the duo of the *axiomatic method* and *inference rules*; the duo was supplemented, almost to the extent of the demise of axioms, by *computation rules* – and, at least in this sense, Newell and Simon were pioneers of modern trend towards *Automated Theorem Proving* (ATP).

It is possible that part of the conflict between the methods employed by Newell and Simon and that by Wang was due to the lack of a precise definition of heuristics. Ira Pohl (1970) has done much to characterize, more precisely, the notion of heuristic, in terms of search path in a defined graph. However, it must be remembered that the notion of algorithm employed by Hao Wang depends for its 'rigorous definition', especially to discuss 'efficiency', depends on the acceptance, albeit implicitly, the Church–Turing *Thesis*. A thesis is not a theorem (of any sort – i.e., proved classically, constructively or computably); it is an attempt to show the equivalence between a formally defined concept – algorithm – and an intuitively accepted notion, (effective) calculation.

In my opinion, Simon – in particular – in advocating, almost passionately, the heuristic approach to selective search, in a suitably constrained complex space of possible proofs of problems (in the *Intuitionistic* sense of Kolmogorov, 1932) was, implicitly, allowing for one of Bishop's precepts (Bishop, *op. cit.*, p. 7; italics added):

> [I]t is impossible to consider *every possible* interpretation of our definition and say whether that is what we have in *mind*. There is *always ambiguity.* . . . The expositor himself can *never fully know all* the possible ramifications of his definitions, and he is subject to the same necessity of modifying his interpretations, and sometimes his definitions as well, *to conform to the dictates of experience.*

Simon was a member of the Cowles Foundation for Economic Research in its early Chicago days, before its move to Yale in New Haven; he was also a member of the Rand Corporation in its glory days, the early 1950s. The former nurtured, in Simon's own words, the econometric 'mafia'; the latter fostered the mathematical economics 'mafia'. He remained a gadfly inside these citadels of orthodoxy while enjoying the respect, perhaps even the envy, of his distinguished and eminent peers.

His contributions to formal and traditional economic theory – both to micro and macro variants – and to econometric theory were fundamental and path-breaking. At a very early stage in the mathematization of economics he deduced, in joint work with the mathematician David Hawkins (Hawkins & Simon, 1949), conditions for stability, which came to be known as the Hawkins – Simon conditions in the folklore of the subject, for linear multi-sectoral models of the economy. This led to an amusing episode with the House Un-American Committee hearings, during the 'McCarthy era', because Hawkins – whom Simon had never met and with whom he had written the famous paper entirely by correspondence – was a paid-up member of the Communist Party.

During the Great Depression, Simon had seen a chart on the walls of his father's study, tracking the dismal progress of a faltering American economy. This chart was constructed on the basis of a model of the macroeconomy and its flows built on the principles of servomechanism theory, using hydrodynamic analogies devised by an imaginative engineer, with a doctorate in sociology, A. O. Dahlberg. Inspired by the memories of the Dahlberg chart in his father's study, he began to look at the economy from the point of view of the theory of servomechanisms and feedback control. This line of research led him to his celebrated results on certainty equivalence in the devising of optimal policy in decisions on production scheduling in firms. He did not pursue the servomechanism metaphors for too long, because he felt, by then, that analogue simulations were a distinct second best to the digital possibilities he was pioneering.

The origins of the inspiration that led to the influential work with his eminent Japanese student Yuji Ijiri on the size distributions of the growth and decay of business firms and organizations are narrated with humour and candour in his charming autobiography, *Models of My Life* (Simon, 1991). It is also a tale of academic bloody-mindedness, recounted without rancour, and revisited with nostalgia and regrets on the fallibility of memory.

In 1946 Richard Goodwin (1947) had begun interpreting economic agents, markets and the economic system as (non-linear) oscillators, analysing markets as coupled oscillators with hierarchies of coupling strengths. All of them were linked by economy-wide, common expenditure impulses (and averaged expectations). In a series of papers, extending over half a century, Simon exploited this simple idea in many fertile ways: to study causality in economic models, to formalize causality and link it with identifiability in econometric models, to theorize about aggregation in economic models, to formalize the idea of the hierarchy of complexity utilizing near decomposability in hierarchical organizations (Simon, 1996, pp. 173–216) and to study counterfactuals in scientific theorizing, and on using the idea of near-decomposability to study evolutionary aspects of mind, thought, organizations and nature.

The idea of 'near-decomposability', extracted from Goodwin's notion of unilateral coupling in markets with production lags, was made mathematically rigorous by the idea of approximately decomposable (or indecomposable) matrices. It was in Goodwin's own pioneering work on multi-sectoral dynamic models (in the late 1940s and early 1950s) that both the link between indecomposability and the Perron–Frobenius theorem(s) and, indeed, the use and introduction of the Perron–Frobenius theorem(s) first appeared. The Goodwin–Simon analytical nexus straddled both inter-industrial and macroeconomic dynamics, in that Simon's work on applying servomechanism theory to the modelling of macroeconomic systems was also inspired by the former's classics on aggregate non-linear macrodynamics (see Goodwin, 1951, Simon, 1952).

In *Models of My Life*, he takes this particular example of the inspiration he got from Goodwin's attempt to represent markets interacting with delayed responses as hierarchically coupled oscillators to wonder about the kinds of representations scientists use in thinking about research problems: Where do the metaphors for scientific representations come from? How are they represented and retained in the human mind? How are they recalled – when, and why at that particular juncture? What are the triggering mechanisms and the catalysts? He had answers, tentative, testable and, as always, interesting and provocative.

In his *Raffaele Mattioli Lectures* of 1993 (Simon, 1997), he argued for a study of economies in terms of organizations as the basic unit rather than the traditional device of markets. This automatically dethroned the privileged position of perfect competition. His case was based on solid empirical and theoretical results. He felt – justified by empirical and experimental data and results – the reliance on markets led to the unnecessary and false claims for their optimality properties (true only in one of many possible mathematical worlds and false in all others), as well as the propagation of the false dichotomy between the virtues of decentralization and the vices of centralization, without forgetting the merits of the former and the disadvantages of the latter.

Finally, it is rarely recognized that Simon, in his imaginative experimental approach to human problem solving was one of the undisputed pioneers of so-called agent-based modelling. He always made clear, for example, in studying and automating chess, that understanding the difference between the rules determining the exact dynamics of an individual chessman, say, the rook, and its particular position in the configuration of a game, was formally – that is, algorithmically – indeterminate (without going as far towards claiming algorithmic undecidability for this 'aggregation' problem).

He was optimistic about the future of economics and even more so of computer science and the interaction between the two and psychology. In a letter written after reading Velupillai (2000), he wrote that 'the battle has been won, at least the first part, although it will take a couple of academic generations to clear the field and get some sensible textbooks written and the next generations trained'.

The precept that may have guided his astonishingly fertile scientific life may well have been, in his own words (Simon, 1996, p. 28; italics in the original):

What a person *cannot* do he or she *will not* do, no matter how strong the urge to do it.

## Notes

1  This chapter is a revised version of Velupillai and Kao (2016).
2  Since about a decade ago, I have been referring to this as *Cognitive* (or *Classical*) *Behavioural Economics* (see the next chapter for details).
3  I would *now* – in July 2017 – add Duncker's important work *On Problem Solving* (Duncker, 1945), in the context of human thought processes, as an equally important source for the Newell–Simon approach to *Human Problem Solving* – at least via De Groot (1978), with which both Newell and Simon were very familiar (in fact from about 1946).

## References

Bishop, Errett (1967), *Foundations of Constructive Analysis*, McGraw-Hill Book Company, New York.
Brouwer, Luitzen E. J. (1923; 1998), Intuitionist Splitting of the Fundamental Notions of Mathematics, translated from the Dutch by Walter P. van Stigt, chapter 18, pp. 286–289, in: *From Brouwer to Hilbert: The Debate on the Foundations of Mathematics in the 1920s*, edited by Paolo Mancosu, Oxford University Press, Oxford.
De Groot, Adriaan (1978), *Thought and Choice in Chess* (Second Edition), Mouton Publishers, The Hague.
Duncker, Karl (1945), On Problem Solving (translated by Lynne S. Lees), *Psychological Monographs*, Vol. 58, No. 5, pp. iii–114.
Ely, R. T. (1893), *Outlines of Economics*, Hunt and Eaton, New York.
George, H. (1879), *Progress and Poverty: An Enquiry into the Cause of Industrial Depressions, and of Increase of Want with Increase of Wealth: The Remedy*, K. Paul, Trench & Company, New York.
Goodwin, Richard M. (1947), Dynamical Coupling with Especial Reference to Markets Having Production Lags, *Econometrica*, Vol. 15, No. 3, pp. 181–204.
Goodwin, Richard M. (1951), The Nonlinear Accelerator and the Business Cycle, *Econometrica*, Vol. 19, No. 1, pp. 1–17.
Hanson, Norwood Russell (1958), *Patterns of Discovery*, Cambridge University Press, Cambridge.
Hawkins, David and Herbert A. Simon (1949), Note: Some Conditions of Macroeconomic Stability, *Econometrica*, Vol. 17, Nos. 3/4, pp. 245–248.
Kolmogorov, Andrei (1932), Zur Deutung der intuitionistischen Logik, *Mathematische Zeitschrift*, Vol.35, pp. 58–65.
Martin-Löf, Per Martin (1972), *An Intuitionistic Theory of Types*, Technical Report, University of Stockholm, Stockholm, Sweden.
Newell, Allen & Herbert A. Simon (1972), *Human Problem Solving*, Prentice-Hall, Englewood Cliffs.
Pohl, Ira (1970), Heuristic Search Viewed as Path Finding in a Graph, *Artificial Intelligence*, Vol. 1, pp. 193–204.
Polya, George (1945), *How to Solve It: A New Aspect of Mathematical Method*, Princeton University Press, Princeton, NJ.
Sieg, Wilfried (2001), *Remembrances of Herbert Simon*, accessed 27 December, 2015 at www.cs.cmu.edu/ simon/all.html.
Simon, Herbert A. (1952), On the Application of Servomechanism Theory in the Study of Production Control, *Econometrica*, Vol. 20, No. 2, pp. 247–68.

Simon, Herbert A. (1955), A Behavioral Model of Rational Choice, *Quarterly Journal of Economics*, Vol. 69, No. 1, pp. 99–118.

Simon, Herbert A. (1956), Rational Choice and the Structure of the Environment, *Psychological Review*, Vol. 63, No. 122, pp. 129–138.

Simon, Herbert A. (1957), *Models of Man: Social and Rational*, John Wiley & Sons, New York.

Simon, Herbert A. (1977), *Models of Discovery*, D. Reidel, Dordrecht.

Simon, Herbert A. (1983), *Reason in Human Affairs*, Basil Blackwell, Oxford.

Simon, Herbert A. (1991), *Models of My Life*, MIT Press, Cambridge, MA.

Simon, Herbert A. (1996), *The Sciences of the Artificial* (Third Edition), MIT Press, Cambridge, MA.

Simon, Herbert A. (1997), *An Empirically Based Microeconomics*, The Raffaele Mattioli Lectures, delivered on 18 and 19 March 1993, Cambridge University Press, Cambridge.

Velupillai, Kumaraswamy (2000), *Computable Economics*, Oxford University Press, Oxford.

Velupillai, K. Vela & Ying-Fang Kao (2016), Herbert A. pp. 669–674, in: *The Handbook of the History of Economic Analysis*, edited by Gilbert Faccarello & Heinz Kurz, Edward Elgar Publishing.

Wang, Hao (1970), *Logic, Computers and Sets*, Chelsea, New York.

# 3 Classical – or Cognitive – Behavioural Economics (CBE) versus Modern Behavioural Economics (MBE)[1]

## §0 Introduction

> Let us call [the bounded rationality] model of human choice the *behavioral model*, to contrast it with the Olympian model of SEU[2] theory.
>
> Within the behavioral model of human rationality, one *doesn't have to make choices that are infinitely deep in time*, that encompass the whole range of human values, in which each problem is interconnected with all the other problems in the world.
> . . . .
>
> Rationality of the sort described by the behavioral model *doesn't optimize*, of course. Nor does it even guarantee that our decisions will be consistent.
>
> —Simon (1983, pp. 19–23; italics added)

Behavioural economics may have, finally, come of age. It is part of the curricula of graduate schools in economics, finance and management, even one of the compulsory courses.[3] More than a decade ago, in a letter to Velupillai (Simon, 2000; italics added), Herbert Simon was optimistic enough to state, after a half century of tireless efforts to make behavioural economics a viable alternative to orthodox Neoclassical economics, that

> [t]he economists here [at Carnegie Mellon University] remain, for the most part, . . . backward . . . , but I am encouraged by the great upswell, in the US and especially in Europe, of experimental economics and various forms of bounded rationality. I think the battle has been won, at least the first part, although it will take a couple of academic generations to clear the field and get some sensible textbooks written and the next generations trained.

Yet, not much more than one year earlier, at the **84th Dalhem Workshop** on *Bounded Rationality: The Adaptive Toolbox*[4] (Gigerenzer-Selten, 2001, p. ix), two distinguished economists claimed:

> Bounded rationality, needs to be, but it is not yet, understood.

How, one may legitimately ask, can a 'battle [have] been won', with a crucial concept lying at the foundation of its 'armory', yet to be understood? We believe there is a case for Gigerenzer and Selten to feel that the notion of bounded rationality remains to be clarified. This is because they have been meticulous in having dissected the way the notion has been (ill) defined by varieties of orthodox theorists,[5] including those we shall shortly identify as some of the pioneers of Modern Behavioural Economics. Moreover, they have also understood, with impeccable perspicacity, that boundedly rational behaviour has nothing to do with either optimization, or irrationality (*ibid.*, p. 4).

Where I differ with Gigerenzer and Selten is their anchoring of bounded rationality and satisficing in 'fast and frugal stopping rules for search' without, however, providing this anchor a solid foundation in itself. Bounded rationality and satisficing, in the frame work of this chapter, is a natural outcome of replacing optimization with *decision problems* (in its *metamathematical* senses), whereby problem solving, in general, and human problem solving, in particular, lead to structured search in computationally complex spaces that are classified in terms of *solvability*, *decidability* and *computability*. Optimization becomes a very special case of the solvability of a decision problem, intrinsically coupled to algorithms, which are given measures of complexity that are capable of encapsulating the notions of 'fast and frugal' in precise ways.

Three important omissions, particularly from the point of view of contemporary *European History of Economic Thought* – the **'Present as History'** (Sweezy, 1953) – should be mentioned here. First, I have refrained from mentioning the impressive research programme of Ernst Fehr and his collaborators (e.g., Fehr & Krajbich, 2009; Fehr & Rangel, 2011; Camerer & Fehr, 2006); second, I have only taken up one particular aspect of the outstanding work of Reinhard Selten, which is also true of the third 'omission', that of the work of the 'Berlin Group' under the leadership of Gigerenzer. In particular, it is the absence of any reference to Fehr that may require some explanation. The reason for the absence is partly space, but mainly because I have concentrated on discussing a difference in two types of behavioural economics based on their bases in, on one hand (for CBE), computability and computational complexity theory and on the other (for MBE), an underpinning – from the very outset – in a particular variety of subjective probability (although later works in this genre was more *ad hoc* in the use of theories of probability).

Moreover, in Velupillai (2016) I have taken up Fehr's works as paradigmatic of what I call *Neuro-Behavioural Economics* and subject it to a searching critique from the point of view of the philosophy of neuroscience (Bennett & Hacker, 2003), experimental ethics (Appiah, 2008), computable economics (Velupillai, 2000) and the methodology and epistemology of mathematical modelling (Simon, 2002).[6]

Reinhard Selten's pioneering work in behavioural economics defies easy classifications, but I am happy to refer interested readers who wish to pursue this line of research to Sadrieh and Ockenfels (eds., 2010).

In many ways the work of Gigerenzer comes closest to my work on Classical Behavioural Economics, with one important caveat: I identify the notion of *heuristics* with the formal recursion theoretic concept of *algorithms* in this chapter and, hence, subject to the *Church–Turing Thesis* (cf. Velupillai, 2000).[7]

This chapter it structured as follows. A broad-brush discussion of the two kinds of behavioural economics is provided in the next section. Next, the analytical foundations of modern and Classical Behavioural Economics are discussed and dissected in section 2. Section 3 is devoted to a discussion of the special role played by Herbert Simon in forging, *ab initio*, Classical Behavioural Economics and its rich vein of characterizing subfields. The concluding section suggests ways of going forward with a research programme in Classical Behavioural Economics – eventually with the hope of exposing the lacunae in the foundations of Modern Behavioural Economics, and its *ad hockeries*.

## §1   *Emergence*[8] of behavioural economics

*Emergence* is a *Weaselword*[9]

Behavioural economics, which originated, almost fully developed, during the 1950s, can be classified into at least two streams – *Classical* and *Modern*. The former was pioneered by Herbert Simon and the latter by Ward Edwards. The two streams are clearly distinguishable on the basis of their methodological, epistemological and philosophical aspects. Despite sharp contrasts in their approaches to understand (rational) human behaviour, a clear distinction between them was not made until recently (Velupillai, 2010b). Behavioural economics, *in general*, challenges orthodox economic theory and its foundational assumptions regarding human behaviour, its institutional underpinnings, its poor prediction power and its intrinsic non-falsifiability.

The distinctions between *Modern* Behavioural Economics (henceforth, MBE) and *Classical* Behavioural Economics (henceforth, CBE) can be classified into three aspects. First, MBE assumes economic agents maximizing utility with respect to an underlying preference order – to which 'an increasingly realistic psychological underpinning' is attributed (Camerer et al., 2004, p. 3); CBE assumes no underlying preference order and an economic agent's decision-making behaviour, at any level and against the backdrop of every kind of institutional setting, is subject to bounded rationality and exhibits satisficing behaviour. Put another way, *MBE remains within the orthodox Neoclassical framework of optimization under constraints*; CBE is best understood in terms of decision problems (in the *metamathematical* sense, cf. Velupillai, 2010b).

Intuitively, the former is a static equilibrium; the latter is a dynamic one. This is similar to the distinction between a static equilibrium in a moneyless economy (with the validity of Say's Law paramount) and the dynamic (dis)equilibrium path of a monetary production economy.

Second, MBE concerns the behaviour of agents and institutions in or 'near' equilibrium;[10] CBE investigates disequilibrium or non-equilibrium phenomena. Third, MBE accepts mathematical analysis of (uncountably) infinite events (hence, almost routinely, the axiom of choice and Zorn's lemma are assumed, but to the best of my knowledge, without any implicit or explicit acknowledgement) or iterations, infinite horizon optimization problems and probabilities defined over σ-algebras and arbitrary measure spaces;[11] CBE only exemplifies cases which contain finitely large search spaces and constrained by finite-time horizons.

### §1.1  Modern behavioural economics

#### §1.1.1  Origins

> The combination of subjective value or utility and objective probability charac-terizes the expected utility maximization model; Von Neumann & Morgenstern defended this model and, thus, made it important, but in 1954 it was already clear that it too does not fit the facts. Work since then has focussed on the model which asserts that people maximize the product of utility and subjective probability. I have named this the subjective expected utility maximization model (SEU model).
> —Edwards (1961, p. 474)

The origins of *Modern* Behavioural Economics are often claimed to have ema-nated from the early works by Richard Thaler, along with Kahneman and Tversky, for example, in the following quote:

> Kahneman and Tversky provided the raw materials for much of behavioral economics – a new line of psychology, called behavioral decision research, that draws explicit contrasts between descriptively realistic accounts of judgement and choice and the assumptions and predictions of economics.[12] Richard Thaler was the first economist to recognize the potential applications of this research to economics. His 1980 article "Toward a theory of consumer choice," published in the first issue of the remarkably open-minded (for its time) Journal of Economic Behavior and Organization, is considered by many to be the *first genuine article in modern behavioral economics*.
> (Camerer et al., 2004, pp. xxi–xxii)

Contrary to these claims, the real origins of Modern Behavioural Economics can be traced back to Ward Edwards, particularly to Edwards (1954) and Edwards (1961), which provided the methodological framework for so-called *Modern* Behavioural Economics. Edwards, in turn, drew inspiration from the famous sub-jective probability theorist and statistician Leonard Savage. The two papers sum-marize the emergence of core notions that characterize what may, with hindsight, be called a *Neoclassical Theory of Behavioural Economics* and offer detailed philosophical and methodological discussions related to them. More important, Edwards posed challenges to orthodox Neoclassical notions, focusing on psy-chological and experimental foundations, constraints and predictions. He also introduces and provides a remarkable and detailed survey of the classic works in the field of behavioural economics till then.[13]

The most remarkable aspect of Edwards's paper is the formalization of weighted values and the introduction of *Subjective Expected Utility* (Ramsey, 1931; Savage,

1954). He also sheds light on the early studies on subjective probability before and after Savage's book in 1954. The standard formulation on the objective function faced by a decision maker in an economic model under risk/uncertainty is presented as a *linear combination* of the values of outcomes and probabilities attached to each of these outcomes. The values of outcomes and probabilities, both, can be *objective* or *subjective*. The formulation of expected utility can be stated as

$$E(U) = \sum_{i=1}^{n} p_i U_i$$

where $p_i$ is the probability of the $i_{th}$ outcome of $n$ possible ones and $U_i$ is the value of the $i_{th}$ outcome. Based on this we can have the following classification: when subjective values are weighted with objective probabilities, it results in Expected Utility. Instead, when subjective values are weighted with subjective probabilities, it becomes *Subjective Expected Utility*. The other two alternatives were considered to be unimportant or proved to be unrealistic in the literature.

The 'classic' Expected Utility formulation was first devised by von Neumann and Morgenstern (vN-M), who explicitly invoked formal, 'objective' probability theory and were even prepared to use the frequency theory of probability[14] – explicitly and forcefully rejected by Savage, whose work was deeply influenced by de Finetti's foundational work on subjective probability theory.

Thus, the probability with which they axiomatized expected utility maximization is actually objective. Since then, it became clear that Expected Utility fails to explain and predict individual behaviour under risk – let alone uncertainty (a distinction not carefully maintained by the practitioners of MBE). vN-M attempted to make the qualitative notion of utility and preference measurable just like, say force in physics. The main argument was that, for economics to be a rigorous science, formalized mathematically, preferences should be *measurable*.[15] Furthermore, for preferences to be measurable, they should be numerically definable and mutually comparable. Individuals are supposed to seek and be able to choose the outcome which will give them the highest satisfaction among all the possibilities. But neither the process that underpinned 'seeking' nor the process of 'choosing' was given any *procedural* content, unlike the way Simon, who from the outset sought to emphasize the search processes at the foundations of choice over a complex space of alternatives.

There was a great deal of effort that was dedicated to measuring utilities and probabilities under the framework of subjective (personal) probability around the time of the early work of Ward Edwards. This empirical work went hand in hand with the simultaneous formalization by Savage, who built his *foundations of statistics* on the basis of de Finetti's theory of subjective probability. In Savage's scheme, the assumptions of complete preference ordering and the *sure-thing* principle play a crucial role, and the individuals learn and adjust their prior beliefs with the occurrence of events according to the Bayes theorem. These properties for subjective probabilities proposed by Savage, in turn, implies that individuals with a different set of subjective probabilities, over the course of their experience, will end up having subjective probabilities which coincide with each other.

The critical point of rapid development of MBE can be attributed to the proposal of Prospect Theory by Kahneman and Tversky (in Kahneman & Tversky, 1979), which was considered as a satisfactory replacement of expected utility theory. The theory encapsulates the idea of subjective probability[16] (not directly) and loss aversion. Even today, loss aversion remains one of the most notable behavioural postulates used to interpret and model decision making in different contexts.

A series of 'anomalies' – resulting from the violation of transitivity and other axioms, inconsistency with some principles of Neoclassical economics – have been systematically collected and investigated by contemporary behavioural economists, notably, Richard Thaler, Colin Camerer, George Lowenstein and Matthew Rabin, among many others, since the late 1980s in the *Journal of Economics Perspectives* (for example). The inconsistency in behaviour is mainly observed in experimental environments, and thus, the neglect of psychological and social factors is proposed as a possible cause for this, according to MBE. The Neoclassical agents are now like physically weakened patients unable to predict even reasonably well, who are being examined with the benchmark idealized case of orthodox theory and its strict rational, constrained optimization, behaviour and the modern behavioural economists are assuming the role of seeking and proposing the remedies for them. The themes and fields challenged from which *anomalies*[17] are found cover Microeconomics, Macroeconomics, Finance Theory, Industrial Organization, Game Theory and even Development Economics. This has led to an encompassing field of behavioural economics, broadly divided into (at least) Behavioural micro, Behavioural macro, Behavioural finance and Behavioural game theory.

### 1.1.2 Subfields of Modern Behavioural Economics

BEHAVIOURAL MICROECONOMICS

Some anomalies concerning preference and utility in decision making are studied. Preference reversal is believed to be a robust anomaly. This field of research attempts to challenge the commonly agreed notions in Neoclassical theory – that the values of goods or outcomes do exist and that people know these values directly – by highlighting the presence of framing effects, reference-based effects and so on (Tversky & Thaler, 1990). It is also suggested that the assumption of a stable preference ordering should be discarded. The preference changes can be due to a variety of factors such as status quo bias, loss aversion, ambiguity aversion and endowment effects. Their thesis is that a consideration of these factors can make the analysis of preference more manageable and tractable.[18] The general worry is that importing psychological inspiration into existing economic models may create new complexities and reduce their predictive power (Kahneman et al., 1991). Furthermore, the difficulty and infeasibility of utility maximization were pointed out, and economists sought for possible psychological and social causes as explanations for the 'mistakes'[19] in decision making (Kahneman & Thaler, 2006).

In MBE, the majority of research seems to focus on suggesting so-called more 'realistic' utility functions in the context of modelling decisions. A whole taxonomy of varieties of MBEs could be catalogued on the basis of the criterion of 'realistic utility functions', but this will be a detour from our more basic aims. There is also a rich menu of research questioning the fundamental framework of preference maximization and the modelling of satisficing, even within one or another variety of MBE, where, in general, for formalizing the notion satisficing in a pseudo-procedural context, heuristic searches[20] are applied. Heuristics serve as guides helping decision makers to find shortcuts for relevant information. Together with satisficing, decision makers are supposed to stop searching – that is, an exogenously determined stopping rule for the search process is activated – whenever some (exogenously determined) criteria are reached (e.g., aspiration level). However, they are not necessarily aware of computability or undecidability which is inherent in many such procedures. If the heuristic search is programmed as a finite automaton, it will naturally terminate at some point. However, if it is programmed as a Turing Machine, then the decision maker is confronted with the famous result of the halting problem for Turing Machine. This means that the agent who is searching is not able to determine whether the heuristic reached the exogenously determined aspiration level or – even worse – whether it will ever do so within any reasonable, or even unreasonable, exogenously given time span.

## BEHAVIOURAL MACROECONOMICS

Similar psychological and social reasons are also applied to interpret some Macro-economic phenomena,[21] such as, money illusion, rigidity of (nominal) wages (loss aversion and fairness) and involuntary unemployment (gift-changing equilibrium of reciprocal preference). The most far-reaching challenge might be to address the questionable idea of the traditional notion of Discounted Utility. The presence of non-exponential discounting of utility was observed (Loewenstein & Thaler, 1989), and subsequently[22] more complex ways (hyperbolic, quasi-hyperbolic discounting, etc.) of discounting were devised, which are believed to be more realistic and better able to provide predictive models in the context of intertemporal choices. Other than time discounting, there is also research on behavioural life-cycle theories (e.g., mental accounting; Thaler, 1990) on saving and marginal propensity to consume and on regret theory, such as using counterfactual, introspective thinking and self-control of future misbehaviour on consumption and saving. But in no such case have non-traditional logics been utilized to derive counterfactual predictions based on introspective thinking.

## BEHAVIOURAL FINANCE

Behavioural finance appears to provide an alternative to the *Efficient Market Hypothesis* and it is probably one of the most developed subfields in Modern Behavioural Economics. In other words, it is commonly believed that the efficient market hypothesis has virtually died out. The well-known anomalies in finance include the *equity premium puzzle* (high risk aversion), *calendar effects, status quo effect, limits to arbitrage,* social preference and other stylized facts (De Bondt & Thaler, 1989; Froot & Thaler, 1990; Lamont & Thaler, 2003; Lee et al., 1990; Siegel & Thaler, 1997; Thaler, 1987a, 1987b). Because of the nature and functioning of financial markets, a huge amount of data points, at high frequencies, are available. Therefore, it is also a rich ground for behavioural and (so-called) computational economists to investigate and validate their models.

BEHAVIOURAL GAME THEORY

Similar to the other fields, behavioural game theory investigates how the results regarding *strategic interaction* deviate from the orthodox game theoretic predictions in the light of some behavioural assumptions regarding decision making in strategic situations. The psychological and social explanations such as *guilt aversion* and *fairness criteria* are incorporated into the traditional models. Behavioural game theory benefits from the fact that most of these models can be tested in laboratory environments by collecting a sufficient number of subjects. Therefore, it coexists with experimental economics and neuroeconomics. A reasonably up-to-date survey of behavioural game theory can be found in Camerer (2003).

### 1.1.3 Concluding remarks

Although Neoclassical economic theories have been critically questioned by economists and psychologists for many decades, it is still explicitly specified that *optimization, equilibrium* and *efficiency,* and on which Neoclassical economics – and its variants, such as Newclassical and New Keynesian – theories are based, are not completely rejected by behavioural economists (see, e.g., the opening, programmatic, pages of Camerer & Loewenstein, 2004). The ultimate goal of so-called modern behavioural economists seems to be to act as 'a bicycle repair shop', in the sense of finding ways to accommodate Neoclassical theories in a suitable emended sense.

Modern behavioural economists have, over the years, discovered and categorized different forms of deviations from the consistent behaviour postulated by the canons of Neoclassical precepts. A valid question here would be, 'Why do these anomalies arise and what are the anomalies with respect to?' Discoveries such as reference dependence, loss aversion, preference over risky and *uncertain* outcomes and time discounting came mostly from observations in experimental environments. The anomalies and puzzles that were discovered and discussed are departures with respect to the Neoclassical normative benchmark for judging rational behaviour, which is expected utility maximization. This evidence, or anomalies, is, in turn, used to formulate more realistic utility functions, and furthermore, these modified utility functions are incorporated into the existing models. In some sense, Modern behavioural economists modified fractured pieces in the foundations of Neoclassical theories, but still they worked within its basic premises (preferences, endowments, technology, with equilibria and optimization to make them implementable – thus choosing a non-constructive, uncomputable framework for its formalization).

Thus, MBE preserves the doctrine of utility maximization and does not go beyond it or discard it. Though the behavioural models do consider more realistic psychological or social effects, economic agents are still assumed to be optimizing agents whatever the objective functions may be. In other words, MBE is, still within the ambit of the Neoclassical theories, or it is in some sense only an extension of traditional theory by replacing and repairing the aspects which proved to be contradictory. These adjustments, in turn, are expected to enhance the predictive power of the original theories. On the contrary, CBE does not try to endow the economic agent with a preference order which can be represented by utility functions, nor, of course, do equilibria or optimization play any role in the activation of behavioural decision making by CBE agents.

### §1.2 Classical behavioural economics

It is interesting to note that even before the advent of behavioural economics, economics was richly based on (cognitive) behavioural principles and psychology. Keynes, of course, is the paradigmatic example of one who explicitly considered psychological factors in his macroeconomic theories.

One of the most essential and concrete lines separating MBE and CBE is that rational behaviour is adaptive or *procedural* in CBE; this makes rational behaviour naturally heuristic or algorithmic, and the need to underpin it with a model of computation enters right on the ground floor of theory and its empirical counterparts. Given the nature of adaptive behaviour and the complex environment in which it takes place, optimization principles and equilibrium analysis become meaningless and nearly infeasible (see, in particular, the Richard Day precept of Chapter 1). The resolving of these difficulties should not be to find approximations of sophisticated mathematical models using thoroughly *ad hoc* numerical techniques underpinned by any theory of probability that a particular modern behavioural economist is comfortable with (or competent in), like what we see in all parts of MBE. This is at considerable variance with the determined efforts by Ward Efforts to found his theories of behaviour on subjective probability-based expected utility theory. Not even von Neumann and Morgenstern can match Ward Edwards for his sustained efforts to base his kind of behavioural economics in the theories of probability of de Finetti and Savage.

As far as *dynamical rational behaviour* is concerned, where *procedure* is central, Simon, Richard Day, Richard Nelson and Sidney Winter are considered as the pillars of CBE (Velupillai, 2010b). This research was motivated by the questions, 'How does the mind work?'; 'What kind of Mechanisms should we postulate for the Mind, based on current knowledge and research in Cognitive Science, to make sense of observed behaviour?'; 'What postulates are useful to understand and predict behaviour?'; 'What metaphors are useful to formalize intelligent procedural behaviour?'; and 'How do operational institutions *emerge* and survive?' Research surrounding these questions is intrinsically underpinned by cognitive psychology, the theory of computation and a theory of evolution driven by aspects of nearly decomposable structures and systems. They lead also to what became the natural Simon framework of *Human Problem Solving*, of agents faced with complex and intractable search spaces, constrained by computationally underpinned cognitive processes facing time and resource constraints. A notable precursor for Simon, on these aspects, was Polya.

Simon is best known for the felicitous phrase he coined, "bounded rationality", which appeared in Simon (1957) for the very first time (although it had appeared in other forms already from his classic book on **Administrative Behaviour**, 1947). Bounded rationality generally refers to the internal cognitive limitations and the constraints of the external environment which confront human minds in decision-making contexts (Simon, 1959, especially §VI). The latter is more specifically contextualized by the institutional backdrop for individual behaviour. Therefore, in order to incorporate the notion of bounded rationality into the behavioural model more rigorously, one ought to investigate how human *thinking* is limited internally and how human beings adapt and interact with the environment, especially as members of an institution.

Simon's insight about modelling adaptive individuals in complex economic environments can be better understood in the fragment:

Suppose we are pouring some viscous liquid molasses into a bowl of very irregular shape. . . . How much would we have to know about the properties of molasses to predict its behavior under the circumstances? If the bowl were held motionless, and if we wanted only to *predict behavior in equilibrium*, we would have to know little, indeed, about molasses. The single essential assumption would be that the molasses, under the force of gravity, would minimize the height of its center of gravity. With this assumption, which would apply as well to any other liquid, and a complete knowledge of the environment, in this case the shape of the bowl, the equilibrium is completely determined. Just so, the equilibrium behavior of a perfectly adapting organism depends only on its goal and its environment; it is otherwise completely independent of the internal properties of the organism.

If the bowl into which we are pouring the molasses were jiggled rapidly, or if we wanted to know about the *behavior before equilibrium was reached*, prediction would require much more information. It would require, in particular, more *information* about the properties of molasses: its viscosity, the rapidity with which it "adapted" itself to the containing vessel and moved towards its "goal" of lowering its center of gravity. Likewise, to predict the short run behavior of an *adaptive organism*, or its behavior in a complex and rapidly changing environment, it is not enough to know its goals. We must know also a great deal about its *internal structure* and particularly its *mechanisms of adaptation*.

(Simon, 1959, p. 255; italics added)

Simon criticized orthodox normative economics for ignoring how human beings actually behave and questioned the result that only rational agents survive the forces of competition – with orthodoxy's Olympian assumptions (Simon, 1983) on how to formalize rational behaviour, which was – at least as far as Simon was concerned – remote from any cognitive realism. Besides, the study of equilibrium requires little understanding of the characteristics of individuals in *out-of-equilibrium* situations, simply because normative economics has nothing to say about *process* and *procedure*. In the real world, Simon saw that around him, there existed a great deal of turbulence, not only generated by external shocks, that kept the system *out of equilibrium* and agents needing to relocate their bearings almost ceaselessly.

Furthermore, Simon stated 'decision making under uncertainty' instead of 'decision making under risk' in Simon (1959). That is, an economic agent might respond to the changing environment in a personal way rather than knowing the objective probability of what outcomes might occur in the future. This property brings more difficulties on the prediction of rational individual behaviour by using so-called objective characteristics of the environment.

Simon's behavioural economics is almost comprehensively demonstrated by his encapsulation of *Human Problem Solving* and of agents and institutions as *Information Processing Systems*. Although the problems which Simon dealt with are well-structured problems, such as chess playing, the combinatorial complexity of the problem is massive enough to prevent human players using *minimax* strategies which are suggested in traditional game theory. In this chapter, only a few of Simon's massive and wide-ranging contributions are tackled.

## §2   Underpinnings of behavioural economics

In this section, different underpinnings and analytical tools of MBE and CBE are briefly mentioned. The purpose of this section is not to provide detailed theoretical and technical details but to try to make clear distinctions on how the two lines differ fundamentally. It is slightly puzzling that this distinction has never been made earlier. As one may realize from the following underpinnings and the sub-branches of MBE introduced in previous sections, MBE can be characterized as a massive magnet which attracts different resources, new tools and ways of explanations. We can almost claim that MBE has already become a new mainstream economics, as a consequence of it playing the role of a revised approach of orthodox economics rather than an alternative approach. On the other hand, CBE is developed on completely different grounds from MBE. From our point of view, MBE is fostered by Orthodox Economic Theory, Game Theory, Mathematical Finance Theory and Recursive[23] Methods, Experimental Economics and Neuroeconomics, Computational Economics[24] and Subjective Probability Theory.

CBE, in our reconstruction of it, on the other hand, is based fundamentally on a model of computation – hence, Computable Economics – computational complexity theory, non-linear dynamics and algorithmic probability theory.

## §2.1 Underpinnings of Modern Behavioural Economics

### §2.1.1 Orthodox economic theory

It is in human nature to aspire to predict, at least so the sages say, and the traditional wisdom of many cultures concur. Microeconomics, in general, is the study of individual choices and actions.

Gradually, economics has developed normative axioms and theories on how the individual entities (including organizations) *should* make choices and how they *seem* to make choices. There are, classically (but not necessarily exhaustively) the normative and positive approaches to behaviour, respectively. In Neoclassical theory, economic agents are assumed to be fully rational and completely[25] informed. It is not that they know everything but that they *can know* everything and that there are means to learn – epistemology – and they know how to make the best choices for themselves (even if only probabilistically). Second, in order for their choices to be tractable, axioms of rational preference were devised, within classical mathematical formalisms – which simply means the mathematics of (Zermelo-Fraenkel) set theory plus some variant of the *axiom of choice*. Individuals are assumed to have underlying preference orderings for *all* the alternatives (in a continuum) which are knowable, although the *means of getting to know them* is never specified. These rational preferences are, often, represented by a utility *function*, which is assumed to be well behaved. Third, the non-satiation assumption promises that the satiation point will never be reached, at least in the economic domain. Thus, the individuals are always in the state of the world where 'more is better'.

In passing, it should be mentioned that there have been serious and contentious discussions in the history of the development of economic theory as to whether utility should be cardinal or ordinal, since there might consequently result in differences in the way in which economists try to measure utility. Eventually, ordinal utility seems to have reached dominance, although not very 'consistently'; subsequently, the theory of individual decision making based on preference and choice-based approaches were developed.

In passing, in lieu of discussing game theory and its place in MBE, I would like to make two points: First, I disagree that game theory, even in its strategic form, originates with either von Neumann-Morgenstern or with von Neumann's 1928 paper. Our alternative history is outlined in several of my recent papers on computable economics. Second, it may be pertinent to add that no game theoretically defined Nash equilibrium is computable and no algorithm which has been claimed to determine it can be implemented without appealing to *undecidable disjunctions*.

### §2.1.2 Mathematical finance theory and recursive methods

A huge amount of mathematical theories and tools have been borrowed to develop finance theories and time series analysis. In these exercises, different stochastic or random processes are imported to represent the data generating process of finance or economic time series, for example, Brownian motion and Markov chains. The random processes applied here are based on measure theoretic concepts.

Recursive methods in macroeconomic are built on dynamic programming, Markov decision processes and Kalman filtering and again, measure theory, underpinning orthodox theories of stochastic processes and probability, plays a central role – all within one or another form of nonconstructive and non-recursion theoretic real analysis (e.g., for dynamic programming the notion of one or another form of contraction mapping in a suitable metric space).

Although the mathematical tools used are much more sophisticated than in non-dynamic methods – but only up to a point – economic entities are still modelled as optimizers (e.g., maximizing present values in intertemporal contexts, *Value func*tions and *Euler equations* in the context of dynamic programming and optimal control formulations) where it is little realized that the analysis is around uncomputable equilibria (cf. Ljungqvist & Sargent, 2004, Stokey & Lucas, 1989, with the collaboration of Edward C. Prescott).

### §2.1.3   Experimental economics and neuroeconomics

At the very outset I want to 'confess' to what may seem to be a 'prejudice': I am convinced that neuroeconomics is shallow and reactionary; the shallowness verdict is based on a serious study of at least three fields, in depth: neurophilosophy, neuropsychology and Simon's kind of cognitive economics with its clear stances on neural structures and the mechanisms that make these structures evolutionary and dynamic.

In addition, I am one of those who has been persuaded by the serious methodological critique of Gould, Lewontin, Noble and Jerry Fodor and Piatelli-Palmarini (cf. Gould & Lewontin, 1979; Bennett & Hacker, 2003; Noble, 2006, especially chapter 5; and Fodor & Piatelli-Palmarini, 2010).

Experimental Economics appears as a tool for examining economic theories in computational, numerical and other obviously implementable ways in which idealized subjects are placed in artificial settings that purport to mimic the theoretical environment. Narrowly speaking, it is not categorized as a branch in economics; instead, it is a methodology for researchers to support or refute specific economic theories. While, broadly, it can be considered to be cohabiting with behavioural economics. This is because – or claimed to be because – what people actually do can be observed in experimental environments, and almost all the anomalies are found and induced from laboratory environments or field studies. The methodology of experimental economics is heavily based on so-called induced value theory (Smith, 1976). Induced value theory suggests that in the controlled laboratory environment, if subjects are suitable motivated, experimenters can expect to obtain desirable induced values from choices of subjects on certain economic problems they are given to 'solve'.[26] This theory is obtained from non-satiation assumptions, and monetary payment is the most commonly used reward for inducing real values from subjects. However, if economic agents are actually applying satisficing principles to the experiments they attend; that is, they are satisfied by performing decently rather than trying their best or thinking hard in order to get the most reward, then the results of experimental economic could be very misleading.

Neuroeconomics is the new extension of experimental economics incorporating neuroscience to obtain the data of brain activity, simultaneously, when the subject is in a laboratory environment. It is also viewed as a young subfield of behavioural economics which is believed will be the main focus in the future. A popular claim is the dual system in our brain supervising our judgemental and intuitive thinking, corresponding to rational and emotional behaviours. It provides the technique to collect data in the brain for examining how and when the behaviour of decision makers could deviate from rational and consistent behaviour. A recent survey can be found in Camerer (2007); Glimcher et al. (2005); and Rustichini (2005); a critical view of the claims of Neuroeconomics can be founding Rubinstein (2008).

The linkage of neuroscience and human behaviour is seriously debatable, but we will reserve our discussion and contribution to this critique for a later exercise.

### §2.1.4  Computational economics

Computational Economics is also an extension of experimental economics from another perspective; that is, the subjects are not human subjects, but they are *software* entities. So far, there are at least two well-developed lines, which are heterogeneous agent models and agent-based modelling, and the survey for these respective lines can be found in Hommes (2006) and LeBaron (2006). A thorough critique of the excessive claims of both these lines – and of other strands of computational economics – is given in Velupillai and Zambelli (2011); a more technical critique, from the point of view of constructive mathematics and computability theory, is provided in Velupillai (2016).

Heterogeneous agent models seem to have been inspired by related results on cellular automata modelling in the physical sciences, resulting in unpredictable and complex phenomena generated by simple interaction rules. The claims in this line of research are as vacuous as those made by agent-based modelers in finance and economics. They both suffer from a serious lack of scholarship and a complete unhinging of their foundations in either serious computability theory or even a familiarity with the fruitful and frontier research in the interface among dynamical system theory, numerical analysis and computability. These interactions were the fulcrum around which von Neumann and Ulam, Conway and Wolfram and Turing (1952) pioneered their studies of emergent complex dynamics in interacting systems with simple rules of interaction.

### §2.1.5  Subjective probability theory

Subjective expected utility theory was proposed by Savage in 1954, between the period in which Edwards wrote his first and second survey papers on behavioural economics (Edwards, 1954, 1961). Savage followed the axiomatizations along the lines proposed by Ramsey (Ramsey, 1931) and de Finetti (de Finetti, 1937) and applied Bayes's rule for updating the prior probabilities over time.

The idea of subjective expected utility 'first' appeared in *Modern Behavioral Economics*[27] through the work of Kahneman & Tversky (1979), when building descriptive theory of decision making by individuals under risk. Their theory, in turn, borrowed heavily from Edwards (1962), who in turn built on Savage (1954). Both Edwards and later Kahneman and Tversky, however, do not refer to Bruno de Finetti, whose contributions are not mentioned in these two papers. There seems to be some ambiguity while they talk about probabilities in their model and this gets particularly unclear when they refer to decision weights:[28]

> In prospect theory, the value of each outcome is multiplied by a decision weight. Decision weights are inferred from choices between prospects much as subjective probabilities are inferred from preferences in the Ramsey-Savage approach. However, decision weights are not probabilities: they do not obey the probabilities axioms and they should not be interpreted as measures of degree of belief.
>
> (Kahneman & Tversky, 1979, p. 280)

In this framework, decision weight measures over stated probabilities do not obey the property of additivity.[29] In the Savage–de Finetti framework, the sum of the probabilities over exclusive and exhaustive events adds up to unity. In prospect theory, the sum of decision weights is considered less than one in most of the cases. However, while they invoke Ramsey's approach of inferring these decision weights from choices, it naturally raises the question as to what these decision weights are. Although the propositions of decision weights are derived in the paper, it is unclear how they are different from degrees of belief – although different they must be!

In Edwards (1962), two categories of subjective probability models are introduced: additive and nonadditive ones.[30] In Edward's elaboration, first of all, subjective probability is a number ranging from zero to one and describing a person's assessment of the likeliness of an event. Furthermore, it is assumed that objective probabilities exist and that they are related to subjective probabilities. Edwards argues that it is meaningless to debate whether objective probabilities can be defined, in contrast to de Finetti's and Savage's firm belief that there are no objective probabilities. He goes on to make a distinction between risk and uncertainty. He argues that there are some cases, such as die tosses, which have 'conventional' probabilities over their outcomes. Consequently, these events, which can be given objective probabilities, are defined as risky; otherwise, they are uncertain. However, both Edwards (1962) and Kahneman and Tversky (1979) considered only risky cases. Tversky and Kahneman (1992) is a revision of prospect theory including (allegedly) uncertain outcomes.

The concept of subjective probability is used ambiguously – to put it mildly – in MBE. On the other hand, MBE introduced the idea of personal probability, defining it and mapping it over the objective probabilities in risky choices. *This is quite different from the kind of subjective probabilities proposed by de Finetti and does not necessarily follow his axioms of subjective probabilities.*

Subjective probabilities of outcomes, for de Finetti, are the different degrees of belief regarding the occurrences of events that people possess. These degrees of belief, however, need not be the same for all the people. In an attempt to find admissible ways of assigning numbers to different degrees of belief, de Finetti constructed axioms over events and their probabilities, especially, through the logical relations of events. By standardizing a *random quantity* into 1 and 0 representing the truth and falsity of an event and by introducing the *coherence criterion*, de Finetti derives some basic consequences. The most important one amongst them is the concept of *finite additivity*, where the sum of assignments over finite events (logical sums), adds to unity. More specifically, for de Finetti, the qualitative criteria regarding coherence appears first, and then, the individuals are allowed to freely attach numbers to their degrees of belief over a complete set of *incompatible events* (i.e. exhaustive and exclusive events), however, within the coherence constraint. This way, a qualitative idea of coherence is linked to the mathematical expressions of (subjective) probability. The coherence principle demands consistency in assignments, based on the idea that no arbitrary gains should be available for either player by accepting certain books of bets (the *Dutch Book* argument). In order to satisfy the coherence principle, the sum of probabilities of the event has to be unity (the necessary and sufficient condition of coherence). Besides, it should be noted that Bayes's conditional probability formula is derived in turn form coherence, and it is not taken as a definition in de Finetti's theory of probability.

Before de Finetti, Frank Ramsey gave a talk in 1926, and the lecture was published in Ramsey (1931), of which de Finetti was not aware until 1937. Both of them, almost simultaneously but independently, formulated subjective probability as a *degree of belief* held by an individual and devoted his or her efforts to axiomatize it. In particular, de Finetti assumed and insisted only the use of finite additivity, because *the requirement of coherence implies finite additivity*. On the other hand, Ramsey simply and intuitively addressed this issue, saying that is meaningless to discuss infinite events, because he doubted a human being's capability of handling infinite events:

> [N]othing has been said about degrees of belief when the number of alternative[s] is *infinite*. About this I have nothing useful to say, except that I doubt if the mind is capable of contemplating more than a finite number of alternatives. It can consider questions to which an infinite number of answers are possible, but in order to consider the answers it must lump them into a *finite* number of groups.
>
> Ramsey (1931, p. 183)[31]

In contrast to finite additivity, frequentists and measure theorists advocate and justify the use of countable additivity (or denumerable additivity, infinite additivity and σ-additivity) by invoking the strong law of large numbers (Borel) and relative frequency in limits. Howson (2009) discusses these issues in detail and supports de Finetti's idea of finite additivity but not, in our opinion, in a convincing way.

In particular, we fundamentally disagree with Howson that 'de Finetti himself would have recommended' doing 'probabilistic reasoning . . . in an informal metatheory consisting the *usual mathematics of analysis and set theory*' so that

> Deductive consistency and probabilistic consistency are subspecies of the same fundamental notion of the *solvability of equations* subject to constraints: those of a classical truth-valuation in the deductive case, and the rules of *finitely additive formal probability in the probabilistic case.*
>
> Howson (*op. cit.*, pp. 55–6; italics added)

Let the obvious circularity pass! This is a fundamental violation of every tenet of epistemology and methodology advocated by de Finetti. Moreover, Howson does not seem to realize that it is *provably hard* to devise procedures to validate 'classical truth-valuation'.

Edwards (1962, p. 117), inexplicably, considers the *infinite* case to be more interesting as compared to the *finite case.*[32] More recently, Bayesian approaches, together with Savage's notion of subjective probability, are challenged by empirical evidence that suggests that agents are incapable of applying the Bayesian rule to revise their prior probabilities. Case-based theory, which is considered as one of the new foundations for behavioural decision theory, bases the probabilities assigned to different events on previous histories regarding similar cases and, consequently, adopts a (non-algorithmic) frequentist approach for the probabilities. (cf. Barberis & Thaler, 2005, Camerer & Loewenstein, 2004).

### §2.2  Underpinnings of classical – or cognitive – behavioural economics

> If we hurry, we can catch up to Turing on the path he pointed out to us so many years ago.
>
> —Simon (1996, p. 101)

Classical Behavioural Economics was underpinned, always and at any and every level of theoretical and applied analysis, by a *model of computation*. Invariably, although not always explicitly, it was *Turing's model of computation*.

The fundamental focus in Classical Behavioural Economics is on *decision problems* faced by *human problem solvers*, the latter viewed as *information processing systems*, as we emphasize in this chapter. All these terms are given computational content, *ab initio*. But given the scope of this chapter we shall not have the possibility of a full characterization. The ensuing 'bird's-eye' view must suffice for now.

First, a *decision problem* asks whether *there exists*[33] *an algorithm to decide* whether a mathematical assertion does or does not have a proof or a formal problem does or does not have an *algorithmic solution*. Thus, the characterization makes clear the crucial role of an underpinning model of computation; second, the answer is in the form of a yes/no response. Of course, there is the third alternative of 'undecidable' (algorithmic), too. It is in this sense of decision problems that we interpret the word decisions here.

As for 'problem solving', we shall assume that this is to be interpreted in the sense in which it is defined and used in the monumental classic by Newell and Simon (1972), which is, in our opinion, an application of the theory underlying Turing (1954).[34]

Finally, the model of computation is the Turing model, subject to the Church–Turing Thesis. To give a rigorous mathematical foundation for bounded rationality and satisficing, as decision problems,[35] it is necessary to underpin them in a dynamic model of choice in a computable framework. However, these are not two separate problems. Any formalization underpinned by a model of computation in the sense of computability theory is, dually, intrinsically dynamic. Moreover, *Decidable–Undecidable, Solvable–Unsolvable, Computable–Uncomputable* and so on are concepts that are given content *algorithmically*, within a model of computation.

Now consider the Boolean formula:

$$(x_1 \lor x_2 \lor x_3) \land (x_1 \lor \{\neg x_2\}) \land (x_2 \lor \{\neg x_3\}) \land (x_3 \lor \{\neg x_1\}) \land (\{\neg x_1\}\{\neg x_2\}\{\neg x_3\})$$

*Remark:* Each subformula within parenthesis is called a clause; The variables and their negations that constitute clauses are called literals; It is 'easy' to 'see' that for the truth value of the above Boolean formula to be $t(xi) = 1$, all the subformulas within each of the parenthesis will have to be true. It is equally 'easy' to see that no truth assignments whatsoever can satisfy the formula such that its global value is true. This Boolean formula is *unsatisfiable*. This is the kind of 'satisfiability' we ascribe to Simon's notion of 'satisficing'.

*Problem:* SAT – The *Satisfiability* Problem

Given $m$ clauses, $C_i$ ($i = 1, \ldots, m$), containing the literals (of) $x_j$ ($j = 1, \ldots, n$), determine if the formula $C_1 \land C_2 \land \ldots \land C_m$ is *satisfiable*.

Determine means 'find an (efficient) algorithm'. To date it is not known whether there is an efficient algorithm to solve the satisfiability problem – that is, to determine the truth value of a Boolean formula. In other words, it is *not known* whether **SAT** $\in$ **P**. But

*Theorem:* **SAT** $\in$ **NP**

*Definition:* A Boolean formula consisting of many clauses connected by conjunctions (i.e. $\land$) is said to be in Conjunctive Normal Form (CNF).

Finally, we have *Cook's famous theorem*:

*Theorem: Cook's Theorem* (Cook, 1971)

*SAT is NP – complete*

It is in the preceding kind of context and framework within which we are interpreting Simon's vision of behavioural economics.[36] In this framework, optimization is a very special case of the more general decision problem approach. The real mathematical content of satisficing[37] is best interpreted in terms of the satisfiability problem of computational complexity theory, the framework used by Simon consistently and persistently – and a framework to which he himself made pioneering contributions.

We have only scratched a tiny part of the surface of the vast canvass on which Simon sketched his vision of a computably underpinned behavioural economics. Nothing in Simon's behavioural economics – that is, in Classical Behavioural Economics – was devoid of computable content. There was – is – never any epistemological deficit in any computational sense in Classical Behavioural Economics (unlike in Modern Behavioural Economics, which is copiously endowed with epistemological deficits, from the ground up).

## §3    Classical behavioural economics – notes on the special role of Herbert Simon

A basic tenet of Simon's approach to behavioural economics is that the limitations of cognitive processing should be linked, in some formal way, with the definable limitations of computation, subject to the Church–Turing Thesis (without say space or time constraints). The limits of computational complexity, on the other hand, are naturally bounded by the time and space. Behavioural models, in which agents are supposed to exercise rational behaviour, whether psychologically more realistically constrained or not, hypothesizing capabilities transcending these theoretical and practical limitations are, for Simon, empirically meaningless. Simon has taken the limits of human cognition into account, transformed into computational complexity measure, for describing agents who make decisions. This is why we are convinced that computable foundations and nonlinear dynamics can be found in *Information Processing Systems*,[38] the paradigmatic formalization of agents and institutions in the kind of behavioural economics Simon advocated.

### §3.1    Bounded rationality

The idea of bounded rationality was first proposed by Herbert Simon in the paper titled *A Behavioural Model of Rational Choice*, which was published in 1953. It was further polished and republished with a same title as the much more famous Simon (1955) and was phrased also as 'limited rationality'. In this paper, an example was constructed where agents tend to be satisfied by using certain information they have and avoid information they do not really have any means of obtaining in algorithmically meaningful ways. They anticipate something acceptable in the near future without calculating any probabilities or assigning probabilities to prospective future events. Simon further described human behaviour as 'intendedly rational' in Simon (1957, p. 196).

The book **Models of Man** collected the papers which he published in early to mid-1950s. It is where the phrase *Bounded Rationality* appeared for the first time, in the introduction of Part IV (p. 196). The phrase was, then, much maligned in its uses and misuses, compared to the original definition and formalizations by Simon. Subsequently, bounded rationality became one of the frequently used terminologies of MBE. On the contrary in Simon's advocacy, human beings can solve their problems relying on heuristics and intuition without a given model in mind.[39] Therefore, there seems to be a mismatch between the contemporary interpretation of bounded rationality and its original definitions. In Simon's point of view, human beings have no capability and willingness to always find procedures to reach the best alternative, even if such a thing is meaningfully definable, or to make the 'Olympian choice'. Reasoning capabilities, formally defined as algorithmic procedures, are constrained by the limits of computability theory and, at an empirical level, by measures of computational complexity.

Simon's definition of bounded (limited, procedural) rationality encapsulates different notions, such as limited attention, limited cognitive capacity of computation, satisficing, and sequential decision making (naturally dynamic; Simon, 1955, 1956). That is to say, it is not evident and admissible to assume that human beings are able to exhaust all the information and make the 'best' choice out of it. Indeed, the notion of 'best' is given content via the formulation of problem solving by information processing systems in what is known in metamathematics as a decision problem. In such a framework one seeks algorithms to solve problems and classifies them as 'easy' or 'hard' using measures of computational complexity. There is no such thing as 'best' algorithm or a 'best' *heuristic*.

Therefore, the dynamics of *non-maximizing agents* can be described adequately in the following way. The *knowledge* we have, and *interpretation* of the world where we are living in, are associated with our *experience* and *memories*. Gradually, our tastes and understanding are *constructed*. The process of construction is the central pre-analytic, Schumpeterian visionary (Schumpeter, 1954, p. 51, ff.) stage in the decision problem. Therefore, the pursuit for stable gain in taste and knowledge also relies on what has been constructed. This is one part of requiring a programme to modify itself. The unhappiness and satisfaction which are associated with our aspirations depends on whether the desires are satisfied in terms of our anticipation. The aspiration level expends with satisfaction and shrinks with disappointment. Nonetheless, the memory that is stored in our mind prevents our aspiration level from becoming null. Thus, we are in the loop of unhappiness and satisfaction, a loop given formal content via the structure of a programme for a Turing Machine or a heuristic implemented on one of them (Simon, 1991).

### §3.2 Human problem solving

The notion of bounded rationality has been encoded implicitly and explicitly into the *information processing system* (IPS) which was proposed in Simon et al. (1958) and analysed thoroughly with detailed recording and interviews with human subjects in Newell and Simon (1972). IPSs have shown their capability of solving problems, such as cryptarithmetic, logic, and chess games, algorithmically, In the conclusion, it is suggested that task environments of greater complexity and openness ought to be studied. Thus, we can see that they are on the track of pursuing Turing' suggested programme of research on *Solvable and Unsolvable Problems* (Turing, 1954).

Simon's notion of bounded rationality, encapsulated within the formalization of an IPS is, in turn, used in simulating (representing) human problem solving. Simulation, even if not precisely theorized in Simon's monumental work on **Human Problem Solving**, nevertheless, is defined in an analogy with the dynamics intrinsic to partial differential functions or their machine embodiment in the definition of the processing of information by a Turing Machine or its specialized variants. Problem solving is the implementation, via *heuristics*, themselves algorithms, of *search processes for paths* from initial states to the target states. The complexity of a problem-solving process – the complexity, therefore, of the algorithm that is implemented in the search processes from initial conditions to 'halting' states – defines its hardness on a well-defined computational complexity measure. This also means that there could be problems that will be subject to the famous theorem of the *halting problem for Turing Machines*.

The methods that a problem solver uses are strongly associated with his or her memory and experience. The accumulated knowledge in the memory will form the heuristics – the current state of the programme and its structure – to guide the problem solving him- or herself. Intuition is copiously invoked, and defined computationally and cognitively, in seamlessly leading the problem solver to one or another path at a node, when he or she faces a huge number of possible choices, in the *Nondeterministic Turing Machine* formulation of a problem.

### §3.2.1    *Theory of human problem solving*

Literally, we need a problem and the problem solver to achieve problem solving, and the problems should be presented, recognized and understood. A problem is faced when one wants to do something about a particular task but does not know what series of actions can be done to implement it immediately. The three main factors that characterize problems are *the huge size of possible solutions, the dispersion of actual solutions* and *the high cost of searching*. The problem space contains a set of elements which represent knowledge, a set of operators which generate new knowledge from existing knowledge, an initial state of knowledge, a problem which is specified by a set of desired states and the total knowledge available to problem solvers. The problem can be further formulated (represented by) *set-predicate* formulations and *search* formulation.

REPRESENTATION

In the former representation, the set of elements includes symbolic objects which are all possible solutions, not necessarily formally definable. Precisely, the set can be generated by a certain enumerative procedure. Thus, the problem solver will not be given the entire set, rather, is given a process to generate elements out of the set. This is exactly analogous to Brouwerian *constructive spreads*, arising out of *free choice sequences*. In a search representation, solutions as elements of a set, have the format of sequences. For instance, a proof of a theory contains a sequence of steps and chess representations contain continuations for some players.

TASK ENVIRONMENT

A *Task Environment* describes the attributes that are associated with the problem that problem solvers encounter. It consists of external and internal representations, where the former is the format in which the problem is exactly presented and the latter stands for the subjective representation the player applies. Accordingly, not only the presentation of the current problem but also the *ability* and *intelligence* of the problem solver, should be considered. This is because players with diverse abilities may perceive the problem differently. It should be made very clear that in Simon's framework of *human problem solving*, as well as in Turing's consideration of *Solvable and Unsolvable Problems*, concepts like *ability* and *intelligence* are precisely defined, even if *pro tempore*, in terms of computability theory.

INFORMATION PROCESSING SYSTEM

The information processing system which is capable of problem solving can be characterized as follows. An Information Processing System (IPS) is a serial, adaptive (dynamic) and deterministic system which receives input and generates output. It is composed of internal building blocks such as long-term memory (LTM), short term memory (STM) and external memory (EM). LTM and STM share identical patterns but are distinguished by their size. LTM can contain all the symbolic objects without limitation, while STM contains only five to seven symbols. The fact of sequential decision making is inherent in IPS; moreover, how a problem solver retrieves objects from LTM to STM relies on heuristic search. This is exactly equivalent to the partial recursive function formalization of computability or a Turing Machine definition of computable process (cf. Davis, 1958, chap. 1, in particular, and part 1, in general; indeed, reading and mastering the foundational mathematics of computability theory simultaneously with an approach to problem solving in the Simon or Turing sense is the best way to understand all the equivalences inherent in all these formalizations).

### §3.2.2 Heuristics[40]

Heuristic is a *method* of "rule of thumb" that serves as a guide in searching. Intuitively, it is an ability and process to refer to one's own memory and experience and lead oneself to focus on appropriate subsets of knowledge. Without external help, one can learn and discover new knowledge by him- or herself. Essentially, it is the ability of the machine to reconstruct its internal structure by itself.

When an IPS receives information from the task environment, it generates the goals and the methods for the achievement by heuristic search. If heuristics cannot achieve a satisfactory solution, then either the heuristic method will be reprogrammed or the representation, namely, the internal representation in the task environment, will be reformulated. It will be clear that 'satisfactory' here is precisely defined by means of time and space computational complexity measures. In short, IPS and task environment are interdependent, and the process of change is *learning*. This is one way the human problem solver as a learner encounters him- or herself as a learning machine.

In addition to bounded rationality and satisficing, Simon uncovered an interesting property, which became a recurring theme in his works observed in many entities. In the very early 1950s Simon became familiar with Goodwin (1947) and the concept of *near decomposability*, culled from Goodwin's notion of unilateral (weak) coupling, began to be used in his papers and he applied it to diverse problems, such as identifying causality, counterfactuals, aggregation, organizational behaviour, the evolution of organisms and human and machine thinking. Near decomposability has its rigorous mathematical characterization, while conceptually the idea can also be connected to heuristics. Especially, in Simon (2002), near decomposability is the basis for causing a greater speed of evolution in organisms with a hierarchical structure. When the hierarchical structure is applied to the problem and problem solver in human problem-solving circumstances, then evolution is analogous to learning and discovery.

Near decomposability in human problem solving can be interpreted as *decomposing* a problem into sub-problems when the sub-problems are not completely independent. In Polya's little book (1945), 'heuristic method' was demonstrated by an educator decomposing and reformulating a problem step by step for a student who is asked to solve the problem. Turing, at the same time, also proposed his idea of a *child's machine* and education process in Turing (1950, p. 456). The influence of Polya, Turing and Goodwin are unambiguously evident in Newell and Simon (1972) and in Simon et al. (1958) for their postulation of the internal structure of minds and the representation of task environments in human problem solving.

### §3.3 Classical behavioural economics and computable economics

#### §3.3.1 Satisficing, SAT and Diophantine problems

I advocated that the faithful encapsulation of Simon's bounded rationality and satisficing ought to be through models of computation in the context of decision problems. Particularly, I suggested posing problems of rational choices as SAT problems (satisfiability problem; Velupillai, 2010a). A SAT problem looks for the truth assignments of the arguments which can make the global statement true. If such assignments can be found, then the SAT problem is satisfiable.

Solving SAT problems can be formulated, equivalently, as linear Diophantine equations, linear systems with nonnegative integer variables, or integer linear programming problems. Theoretically, SAT is NP-Complete (Cook's theorem), that is, an SAT problem is *not solvable* in nondeterministic polynomial time in its inputs but can be *verified* in polynomial time. However, the 'senior' author has realized very recently that Simon's notions should be better formalized in terms of space computational complexity. In particular, SAT can be solved with a *linear* space algorithm. An intuitive explanation might be that in real human problem solving, subjects are never given sufficient amount of time to make decisions; rather, they are trained to restructure their short-term memory in order to process a problem in a given time. Subsequently, Velupillai has proved, via duality between computability and dynamic systems, that Simon's information processing system is capable of computation universality which is the relevant model of computation for rational choice. Furthermore. orthodox notions of rationality (through optimization) has been shown as a special (easy) case of the more general (difficult) case of an SAT problem, in terms of the models of computation in a decision problem context.

### §3.3.2  Chess and GO

Like many other *strategic game*, though the final target is to defeat the opponent in one's own way, chess players care about many other actions while the game is ongoing. For example, it is important to capture, block and otherwise threaten the opponent. There are the sub-goals that come to players' mind alternatively, simultaneously to playing the game with the global goal and in the pensive phases between moves. Being aware of the sub-goals, players can reduce their attention to relatively small groups of good moves and play accordingly.

GO and chess are very fundamentally different.[41] GO has no concrete configuration of terminal conditions, like "checkmate" in chess. Instead, a GO game is finished when both players pass, and the side which occupies greater territory wins. This is a most intricate 'stopping rule' for the programme to implement the process of playing GO by a Turing Machine. The best moves in the GO games are even more meaningless than the ones in chess. Similarly, though *it is difficult* to list out all the terminal positions in chess, it is very possible to decide whether each configuration belongs to the set of checkmate. It is only possible for some of the games of GO. Unlike chess, GO players rarely benefitted by playing forcefully or aggressively – assuming these concepts can be given formal definitions in the relevant mathematics – because by doing that they can create unforeseeable 'dangerous' configurations to their own group as well.

A GO game can be officially played on a $9 \times 9$, $13 \times 13$ and $19 \times 19$ board. Practically, GO games can be set from $2 \times 2$, $3 \times 3$, ..., $9 \times 9$, ..., $13 \times 13$, ..., $19 \times 19$, ... boards. The *combinatorial complexity* increases exponentially when the board size is enlarged. Thus, the complexity of GO games can be expanded theoretically to countable *infinites*, of a kind. This is the flexibility that the chess game may lack.

The main task in playing GO is to enclose some areas on the board so that the stones of the opponent which are in this area have no space to escape and are captured. On the other hand, when a group of stones are in danger of being captured, the task is to create holes (eyes) to save a region. No matter how big the board size is, the *warfare* will be localized into separate regions on the board. When the game is being played, the attribution of some regions can be determined, and it is known to both players that there is no need to fight on those regions anymore. That is to say, the players will *decompose* the board into several blocks to try to invade or defense those regions. We conjecture, therefore, that near decomposability will turn out to be a useful way of representing some configurations in a game of GO.

In formalizing the GO games, it is reasonable to start with smaller sizes and apply them to the bigger board with the idea of decomposing into smaller blocks. In spite of the fact that the complexity of a game of GO increases exponentially with the board size, human players can reduce the practical complexity drastically by decomposing the board configurations and attack them separately. However, the GO board can *never be partitioned unambiguously*, this is where a plausible application of near decomposability can be envisaged. Despite all the differences between the two games, there are important similarities, too. GO players need to come up with sub-goals, such as Joseki (ding shih in Chinese), creating Atari (da chi in Chinese), making eyes and escaping from being captured, among others, in order to resolve some situations.

## §4  A brief conclusion

Science, in most of the cases, is built on asking and answering – often unanswerable – questions. In order to proceed properly, it is critical in most of the cases, that appropriate questions be asked. Decision theory deals with the problems of human choices, and plenty of models have been constructed and examined through the formalizations of orthodox mathematical economics, econometrics or experiments. Nevertheless, behavioural economics emerged based on the failure of orthodox economic frameworks. Anomalies have been collected and discovered with respect to the normative human behaviours which are predicted by orthodox economics. The central doctrines of orthodox economics are optimization subject to constraints and equilibrium analysis. Modern behavioural economics emerged as a field of finding and explaining anomalies in human decision behaviour. The difficulties of solving these problems (optimization and equilibrium) have been noticed; however, their solvability has not yet been questioned and challenged in Modern Behavioural Economics.

Solvability of problems, by problem solvers, requires formal characterizations of both concepts, neither of which has ever been attempted by modern behavioural economists. They are almost defined and characterized in Classical Behavioural Economics and computable economics, as we have argued earlier.

Herbert Simon introduced the notion of 'bounded rationality' and 'satisficing' into economic fields along with their psychological and computational underpinnings. Intuitively, computability theory tackles the solvability of a problem, and computational complexity theory measures the difficulty of solving a problem.

Thus, if a programme is designed to mimic human thinking, naturally, the computability of programme has the counterpart in reasoning. Simon's ideal models of economic agents can be demonstrated by an *Information Processing System* and its nature of adaption can be captured in the theory of "human problem solving". Within this framework, "anomalies" are, possibly, those that result in uncomputabilities, undecidabilities and unsolvabilities of problems, forced into solvable modes by inappropriate models, precisely definable as, for example, the use of finite automata where a Turing Machine is required and so on.

If Simon's postulates are taken into account, then 'Olympian' rationality (coined in Simon, 1983, p. 19) is merely the special case of bounded rationality, and an optimization problem is, again, the special case of a satisfiability problem (satisficing), within the formal framework of metamathematical decision problems.

Apart from making, hopefully, clear distinctions between Modern and Classical Behavioural Economics, a more faithful encapsulation of Simon's notions – with clear computable underpinnings – was presented in this chapter. In continuing work, we are expanding the scope of Simon's notions of bounded rationality and satisfying, within a formal computable formulation, an exercise already begun in Velupillai (2010a) to the more general and complex cases of combinatorial game theory. Studying, for example, boundedly rational agents, choosing satisfying strategies in a game of GO will, we think, form a meaningful milestone in research along this line.

It is even possible to interpret some strands in Simon's thinking that human beings do try to *solve the formally unsolvable problems*, even while they somehow find 'only' the methods (heuristics) to satisfactorily solve them. This is to say, they try to make good decisions for only the near future but with long-term targets in mind. No actual agent in his or her right mind (sic!) would even dream of formulating infinite horizon optimization problems in the economic sphere, except of course those endowed with Olympian notions of rationality, solvability, computability and decidability.

## Notes

1 This chapter is a revised version of Velupillai and Kao (2015).
2 Subjective Expected Utility.
3 As it is in the university's Graduate School of Social Science, University of Trento, Trento, Italy. It was once given by me, till my responsibility for the course on Behavioural Economics was abruptly terminated by the director and academic director of the previous incarnation of the graduate school, then called CIFREM. His course emphasized the distinction between classical and Modern Behavioural Economics, emphasizing the underpinning of the former in a model of computation and the latter, at least in its origins, in subjective probability theory *á la* de Finetti–Savage. The current rendering of behavioural economics, as a graduate course, makes no such distinction between two kinds of behavioural economics.
4 Held in Berlin on 14–19 March 1999.
5 The two paradigmatic examples of this genre, representing old Neoclassical and Newclassical economics, are by Frank Hahn and Roy Radner, on one hand, and y Thomas Sargent, on the other (cf. Gigerenzer-Selten, p. 5, Radner, 1975; Hahn, 1985, pp. 15–16; Sargent, 1993, pp. 21–24).

6   van Winden et al. (2008) is also taken into consideration in this critique, but that I do not go into details here are the same reasons for which it was regrettably necessary to omit discussions of Fehr, Selten and Gigerenzer.

7   I no longer make this identification (see previous chapter), but even then my interpretation of Simon's notion of heuristics is very different from Gigerenzer's important notion(s).

8   I would like to substantiate the use of this word, in the context of the 'rise' of behavioural economics, from the point of view of the 'emergentist' philosophy of John Stuart Mill, G. H. Lewes and Lloyd Morgon and W. T. Stace. But such an exercise must wait for a different occasion.

9   *Pace* Machlup (1958).

10  The 'near' is defined, in all case we are aware of, by uncomputable approximation *processes* of uncomputable equilibria.

11  The most intuitive definition of this essentially measure theoretic concept would be to define it as a non-empty class of sets, closed under the formation of complements and countable unions. However, the kind of subjective probabilities defined by de Finetti and Ramsey avoided, for epistemological and methodological reasons, consideration of events as subsets in a σ-algebra.

12  These were, surely, also prime motivations for Simon when he launched his programme of research on behavioural economics. It is just that Simon's psychological and cognitive bases for modelling *realistic* economic behaviour were always underpinned by a *model of computation*.

13  So the claim that behavioural economics was not even a field till 1980 is highly questionable, even from the works by the precursors of Kahneman, Tversky and Thaler.

14  But not its modern re-founding and reformulation as *algorithmic probability*.

15  How to measure variables over the *real numbers* was never specified – except by vague references to varieties of approximations.

16  But neither consistently, nor meaningfully. In the whole literature on MBE, all the way from the early works of Kahneman and Tversky, there is a remarkable confusion and conflation of a variety of theories of probability, even within one and the same framework of modelling rational, psychologically underpinned, individual behaviour in economic contexts. (See, in particular, Amos Tversky, 1972)

17  Velupillai refers to this trait in MBE as anomaly mongering in his lectures on Behavioural Economics. His point is that both the Newclassicals, whose analogous notion is 'puzzle' – 'equity premium puzzle' being paradigmatic – and the Modern Behavioural Economists are consciously invoking Kuhn's terminology and, therefore, suggesting that their programme of research is leading to that much-maligned concept of a 'paradigm shift'.

18  Not formalized in terms of tractability in the formal hierarchy of degrees of computational complexity simply because these models are not underpinned by any formal model of computation.

19  In other words, 'Anomalies'!

20  Without, however, any recognition that 'heuristics' are, formally, 'algorithms' (a view I no longer hold, if 'algorithms' are predicated upon the validity of the Church–Turing Thesis; for example, proof procedures in Brouwerian and Bishop's constructive mathematics do not assume the validity of this thesis).

21  Akerlof and Shiller (2009), categorize five types of animal spirits (I do not agree with their characterization and nomenclature): they are confidence, fairness, corruption and antisocial behaviour, money illusion and stories.

22  Not quite 'subsequently', because the notion of hyperbolic discounting has been 'around' in intertemporal macroeconomic policy models at least since the early 1960s. But it is to the credit of the MBE's practice and insistence that traditional and almost routine recourse to exponential discounting in intertemporal optimization models is being challenged.

23  **Not** Recursion Theory.

24 **Not** Computable Economics.

25 Often this 'completeness' is probabilistic of a naïve variety.

26 But this is not the search for 'solutions' in any kind of 'problem-solving' context, as in CBE.

27 Ignoring, for the moment, the much earlier work of Edwards, who was more than a mentor to Kahneman and Tversky.

28 Decision weights, in Kahneman and Tversky (1979), are a measure associated with each probability, reflecting the impact of probability of the overall value of the prospect.

29 Additivity of probability is defined as follows: If *n* numbers of events form a complete set of incompatible evens (meaning exactly one of the events has to be true), then the probability of the logical sum (the logical sum of a group of events is true, *if and only if*, one of the events is true) is equal to the sum of their respective probabilities. Since *n* is a *finite natural number*, the preceding definition is more precisely *finite additivity*. On the other hand, when *n* approaches infinity, it becomes *countable additivity*.

30 The distinction of additive and non-additive probability made in Edwards (1962) is that additive probabilities sum up to specific (*real*) numbers, nonadditive ones are not supposed to do so – then, *what are they* and *if they do not do so*?

31 It may be apposite to point out that Ramsey's equally distinguished fellow Kingsman, a few years later, in his classic on computability theory, appealed to the same kind of 'finiteness' for the same kind of reason (cf. Turing, 1936, p. 249). A discerning reader, with a comprehensive knowledge of Ramsey's *oeuvre*, would wonder at the way *infinite* and *finite* were interpreted and used in the main two theorems of what has come to be known as Ramsey Theory (chapter III, in Ramsey, 1931; see also, the Introduction)!

32 Edwards (1962), p. 117 (italics added):

> As will become clear later, finite event sets immensely complicate the mathematics, and at the same time reduce the value of the model by making it inapplicable to situations in which *the set of possible events is infinite*. Although this paper discusses finite models below, I consider such models far less interesting then the infinite models.

This is definitely not the case in the *finite* and *infinite* contrasts of the theorems of Ramsey Theory (cf., e.g., Graham et al. (2013).

33 Not in the *Brouwerian intuitionistic* sense, or in the sense of *Bishop's constructive mathematics* – or even in the sense of *Smooth Infinitesimal Analysis* (Bell, 2008), or, of course, in many of the other varieties of constructive mathematics (Bridges & Richman, 1987).

34 Except in the sense that I no longer subscribe to the view that heuristics are algorithms predicated on the Church–Turing Thesis.

35 The three most important classes of decision problems that almost characterize the subject of computational complexity theory, underpinned by a model of computation – in general, the model of computation in this context is the Nondeterministic Turing Machine – are the P, NP, and NP-Complete classes. Concisely, but not quite precisely, they can be described as follows:

1 **P** defines the class of computable problems that are solvable in time bounded by *a polynomial function* of the size of the input;

2 **NP** is the class of computable problems for which a solution can be *verified in polynomial time*;

3 A computable problem lies in the class called **NP-Complete** if every problem that is in NP can be *reduced to it in polynomial time*.

36 Subject to the caveat now expressed in note 34, above!

37  In Simon (1997), p. 295, Simon clarified the semantic sense of the word *satisfice*:

> The term 'satisfice', which appears in the Oxford English Dictionary as a Nor-
> thumbrian synonym for 'satisfy', was borrowed for this new use by H. A. Simon
> (1956) in 'Rational Choice and Structure of the Environment'.

38  Agents and institutions and all other kinds of decision making entities, in CBE, are
    information processing systems which, in their ideal form, are Turing Machines.
39  This may well be one way for agents in CBE to transcend the limits of Turing Comput-
    ability subject to the Church–Turing Thesis. However, I do not subscribe to the view
    that Simon assumed that the limits of Turing Computability are violable; I believe
    Simon could have resorted to *oracle* computations, when necessary, and formalize
    via nondeterministic and alternating Turing Machines to encapsulate *procedures –
    heuristics* and other algorithms – that give an impression to the uninitiated that there
    are formal means to transcend Turing Computability.
40  Recall my current stance, stated, for example, in note 41 and in the previous chapter,
    which is elaborated in my more recent writings.
41  The claim of *effectively computable counterstrategies* in Weiqi (GO), made in note 6,
    p. 210 of Boorman (1969), is incorrect.

# References

Akerlof, George A. & Robert J. Shiller (2009), *Animal Spirits: How Human Psychology
Drives the Economy and Why It Matters for Global Capitalism*, Princeton University
Press, Princeton, NJ.

Appiah, Kwame Anthony (2008), *Experiments in Ethics*, Harvard University Press, Cambridge, MA.

Barberis, Nicholas and Richard Thaler (2005), A Survey of Behavioral Finance, chapter 1,
pp. 1–75, in: *Advances in Behavioral Economics*, Vol. 2, edited by Richard H. Thaler,
Princeton University Press, Princeton, NJ.

Bell, John L. (2008), *A Primer of Infinitesimal Analysis* (Second Edition). Cambridge
University Press, Cambridge.

Bennett, M. R. and P. M. S. Hacker (2003), *Philosophical Foundations of Neuroscience*,
Blackwell Publishing, Oxford.

Boorman, Scott A. (1969), *The Protracted Game: A Wei-Ch'i Interpretation of Maoist
Revolutionary Strategy*, Oxford University Press, Oxford.

Bridges, Douglas & Fred Richman (1987), *Varieties of Constructive Mathematics*, Cambridge University Press, Cambridge.

Camerer, C. F. (2003), *Behavioral Game Theory: Experiments in Strategic Interaction*,
Princeton University Press, Princeton, NJ.

Camerer, C. F. (2007), Neuroeconomics: Using Neuroscience to Make Economic Predictions, *The Economic Journal*, Vol. 117, pp. C26–C42.

Camerer, C. F. & Ernst Fehr (2006), When Does 'Economic Man' Dominate Social Behaviour?, *Science*, Vol. 311, No. 47, pp. 47–52.

Camerer, C. F. & G. Loewenstein (2004), Behavioral Economics: Past, Present, Future,
chapter 1, pp. 3–51, in: *Advances in Behavioral Economics*, edited by Camerer, et al.,
Princeton University Press, Princeton, NJ.

Camerer, C. F., G. Loewenstein & M. Rabin (eds.) (2004), *Advances in Behavioral Economics*, Princeton University Press, Princeton, NJ.

Cook, S. A. (1971), The Complexity of Theorem Proving Procedures, *Proceedings of the
Third Annual ACM Symposium on the Theory of Computing*, pp. 151–158.

Davis, Martin (1958), *Computability and Unsolvability*, McGraw-Hill Book Company, New York.

De Bondt, Werner F. M. and Richard H. Thaler (1989), Anomalies: A Mean-Reverting Walk Down Wall Street, *The Journal of Economic Perspectives*, Vol. 3, No. 1, pp. 189–202.

de Finetti, Bruno (1937), Foresight: Its Logical Laws, Its Subjective Sources, Annales de l'Institut Henri Pioncaré, 7, translated by Henry E. Kybrug, Jr, pp. 93–158; reprinted in; *Studies in Subjective Probability*, edited by Henry E. Kyburg, Jr. & Howard E. Smokler, John Wiley & Sons, Inc., New York, 1964.

Edwards, Ward (1954), The Theory of Decision Marking, *Psychological Bulletin*, Vol. 51, pp. 380–417.

Edwards, Ward (1961), Behavioral Decision Theory, *Annual Review of Psychology*, Vol. 12, pp. 473–498.

Edwards, Ward (1962), Subjective Probabilities Inferred From Decisions, *Psychological Review*, Vol. 69, No. 2, pp. 100–135.

Fehr, Ernst & Ian Krajbich (2009), Social Preferences and the Brain, pp. 193–218, in: *Neuroeconomics – Decision Making and the Brain*, edited by Paul W. Glimcher, Colin F. Camerer, Ernst Fehr & Russell A. Poldrack, Academic Press, London.

Fehr, Ernst and Antonio Rangel (2011), Neuroeconomic Foundations of Economic Choice – Recent Advances, *Journal of Economic Perspectives*, Vol. 25, No. 4, Fall, pp. 3–30.

Fodor, Jerry & Massimo Piatelli-Palmarini (2010), *What Darwin Got Wrong*, Farrar, Straus and Giroux, New York.

Froot, Keneth A. & Richard H. Thaler (1990), Anomalies: Foreign Exchange, *The Journal of Economic Perspective*, Vol. 4, No. 3, pp. 179–192.

Gigerenzer, Gerd & Reinhard Selten (eds.) (2001), *Bounded Rationality: The Adaptive Toolbox*, The MIT Press, Cambridge, MA.

Glimcher, P. W., M. C. Dorris & H. M. Bayer (2005), Physiological Utility Theory and the Neuroeconomics of Choice, *Games and Economic Behavior*, Vol. 52, No. 2, August, pp. 213–256.

Goodwin, R. M. (1947), Dynamical Coupling with Especial Reference to Markets Having Production Lags, *Econometrica*, Vol. 15, No. 3, July, pp. 181–203.

Gould, S. J. & R. C. Lewontin (1979), The Spandrels of San Marco and the Panglossian Paradigm: A Critique of the Adaptationist Programme, *Proceedings of the Royal Society of London: Series B, Biological Sciences*, Vol. 205, No. 1161, September. 21, pp. 581–598.

Graham, Ronald L., Bruce L. Rothschild & Joel H. Spencer (2013), *Ramsey Theory*, (Second (Paperback) Edition), John Wiley & Sons, Inc., New Jersey.

Hahn, Frank H. (1985), *Money, Growth and Stability*, Basil Blackwell, Oxford.

Hommes, Cars H. (2006), Heterogeneous Agent Models in Economics and Finance, chapter 23, pp. 1109–1186, in: *Volume 2 of Handbook of Computational Economics*, Elsevier B.V., New York.

Howson, Colin (2009), Logic and Finite Additivity: Mutual Supporters in Bruno de Finetti's Probability Theory, pp. 41–56, in: *Bruno de Finetti: Radical Probabilitist*, edited by Maria C. Galavotti, King's College, London, UK.

Kahneman, Daniel and Richard H. Thaler (2006), Anomalies: Utility Maximization and Experienced Utility, *Journal of Economic Perspectives*, Vol. 20, No. 1, Winter, pp. 221–234.

Kahneman, Daniel, Jack L. Knetsch & Richard H. Thaler (1991), Anomalies: The Endowment Effect, Loss Aversion and Status Quo Bias, *The Journal of Economic Perspective*, Vol. 5, No. 1, pp. 193–206.

Kahneman, Daniel and Amos Tversky (1979), Prospect Theory: An Analysis of Decisions Under Risk, *Econometrica*, Vol. 47, pp. 313–327.

Kolmogorov, A. N. (1932; 1988), On the Interpretation of Intuitionistic Logic, chapter 25, pp. 328–334, in: *From Brouwer to Hilbert: The Debate on the Foundations of Mathematics in the 1920s*, Oxford University Press, Oxford.

Lamont, Owen A. and Richard H. Thaler (2003), Anomalies: The Law of One Price in Financial Markets, *The Journal of Economic Perspectives*, Vol. 17, No. 4, pp. 191–202.

LeBaron, Blake (2006), Agent-Based Computational Finance, chapter 24, pp. 1187–1233, in: *Volume 2 of Handbook of Computational Economics*, edited by Leigh Testfatsion & Kenneth Judd, Elsevier B.V., New York.

Lee, Charles M. C., Andrei Shleifer and Richard H. Thaler (1990), Anomalies: Closed-End Mutual Funds, *The Journal of Economic Perspectives*, Vol. 4, No. 4, pp. 153–164.

Ljungqvist, Lars & Thomas J. Sargent (2004), *Recursive Macroeconomic Theory*, MIT Press, Cambridge, MA.

Loewenstein, George & Richard H. Thaler (1989), Anomalies: Intertemporal Choice, *The Journal of Economic Perspective*, Vol. 3, No. 4, pp. 181–193.

Machlup, Fritz (1958), Structure and Structural Change: Weaselwords and Jargon, *Zeitschrift für Nationalökonomie*, Vol. 18, No. 3, pp. 280–298.

Newell, Allen and Herbert A. Simon (1972), *Human Problem Solving*, Prentice-Hall, Inc., Englewood Cliffs, NJ.

Noble, Denis (2006), *The Music of Life: Biology Beyond Genes*, Oxford University Press, Oxford.

Polya, George (1945), *How to Solve It: A New Aspect of Mathematical Method*, Princeton University Press, Princeton, New Jersey.

Ramsey, Frank P. (1931), Truth and Probability, pp. 156–198, in: *The Foundations of Mathematics and other Logical Essays*, edited by R. B. Braithwaite, Routledge, London.

Rubinstein, Ariel (2008), Comments on Neuroeconomics, *Economics and Philosophy*, Vol. 24, pp. 485–494.

Rustichini, Aldo (2005), Neuroeconomics: Present and Future, *Games and Economic Behavior*, Vol. 52, pp. 201–212.

Sadrieh, Abdolkarim & Axel Ockenfels (eds.) (2010), *The Selten School of Behavioral Economics: A Collection of Essays in Honor of Reinhard Selten*, Springer-Verlag, Berlin Heidelberg.

Sargent, Thomas J. (1993), *Bounded Rationality in Macroeconomics*, Clarendon Press, Oxford.

Savage, Leonard J. (1954), *The Foundations of Statistics*, John Wiley & Sons, New York.

Schumpeter, Joseph A. (1954), *History of Economic Analysis*, Edited from Manuscript by Elizabeth Boody Schumpeter, George Allen & Unwin Ltd., London.

Siegel, Jeremy J. and Richard H. Thaler (1997), Anomalies: The Equity Premium Puzzle, *The Journal of Economic Perspectives*, Vol. 1, No. 1, pp. 191–200.

Simon, Herbert A. (1947; 1997), *Administrative Behavior: A Study of Decision-Making in Administrative Organizations* (Fourth Edition), The Free Press, New York.

Simon, Herbert A. (1953), *A Behavioral Model of Rational Choice*, The Rand Corporation, P-365, Santa Monica, CA.

Simon, Herbert A. (1955), A Behavioral Model of Rational Choice, *Quarterly Journal of Economics*, Vol. 69, No. 1, pp. 99–118.

Simon, Herbert A. (1956), Rational Choice and the Structure of the Environment, *Psychological Review*, Vol. 63, No. 2, pp. 129–138.

Simon, Herbert A. (1957), *Models of Man*, John Wiley & Sons, Inc., New York.

Simon, Herbert A. (1959), Theories of Decision-Making in Economics and Behavioral Science, *The American Economic Review*, Vol. 49, No. 3, pp. 253–283.

Simon, Herbert A. (1983), *Reason in Human Affairs*, Basil Blackwell, Oxford.

Simon, Herbert A. (1991), *Models of My Life*, The MIT Press, Cambridge, MA.

Simon, Herbert A. (1996), Machine as Mind, chapter 5, pp. 81–101, in: *Machines and Thought – the Legacy of Alan Turing*, Vol. 1, edited by Peter Macmillan & Andy Clark, Oxford University Press, Oxford.

Simon, Herbert A. (1997), Satisficing, chapter 4.4, pp. 295–298, in: *Models of Bounded Rationality, Vol. 3 – Empirically Grounded Economic Reason*, The MIT Press, Cambridge, MA.

Simon, Herbert A. (2002), near decomposability and the Speed of Evolution, *Industrial and Cooperate Change*, Vol. 11, No. 3, pp. 587–599.

Simon, Herbert A. (2002), Science Seeks Parsimony, Not Simplicity: Searching for Pattern in Phenomena, chapter 3, pp. 32–72, in: *Simplicity, Inference and Modelling: Keeping it Sophisticatedly Simple*, edited by Arnold Zellner, Hugo A. Keuzenkamp & Michael McAleer, Cambridge University Press, Cambridge.

Simon, Herbert A., A. Newell & J. C. Shaw (1958), Elements of the Theory of Problem Solving, *Psychological Review*, Vol. 65, pp. 151–66.

Smith, Vernon (1976), Experimental Economics: Induced Value Theory, *The American Economic Review*, Vol. 66, No. 2, pp. 274–279.

Stokey, Nancy L. & Robert E. Lucas, Jr., (with Edward C. Prescott) (1989), *Recursive Methods in Economic Dynamics*, Harvard University Press, Cambridge, MA.

Sweezy, Paul (1953), *The Present as History: Essays and Reviews on Capitalism and Socialism*, Monthly Review Press, New York.

Thaler, Richard H. (1987a), Anomalies: Seasonal Movements in Security Prices II: Weekend, Holiday, Turn of the Month, and Intraday Effects, *The Journal of Economic Perspectives*, Vol. 1, No. 2, pp. 169–177.

Thaler, Richard H. (1987b), Anomalies: The January Effect, *The Journal of Economic Perspectives*, Vol. 1, No. 1, pp. 197–201.

Thaler, Richard H. (1990), Anomalies: Saving, Fungibility, and Mental Accounts, *The Journal of Economic Perspectives*, Vol. 4, No. 1, pp. 193–205.

Turing, A. M. (1936; 1937), On Computable Numbers, with an Application to the Entscheidungs Problem, *Proceedings of the London Mathematical Society*, Series 2, Vol. 42, pp. 230–265.

Turing, A. M. (1950), Computing Machinery and Intelligence, *Mind*, Vol. 59, No. 236, pp. 433–460.

Turing, A. M. (1952), The Chemical Basis of Morphogenesis, *Philosophical Transactions of the Royal Society, Series B, Biological Sciences*, Vol. 237, No. 641, August, 14, pp. 37–72.

Turing, A. M. (1954), Solvable and Unsolvable Problems, pp. 7–23, in: *Science News*, Vol. 31, edited by A. W. Haslett, Penguin Books, London.

Tversky, Amos (1972), Elimination by Aspects: A Theory of Choice, *Psychological Review*, Vol. 79, No. 4, pp. 281–299.

Tversky, Amos & Daniel Kahneman (1992), Advances in Prospect Theory: Cumulative Representation of Uncertainty, *Journal of Risk and Uncertainty*, Vol. 5, pp. 297–323.

Tversky, Amos & Richard H. Thaler (1990), Anomalies: Preference Reversals, *The Journal of Economic Perspectives*, Vol. 4, No. 2, pp. 201–211.

van Winden, Frans, Mirre Stallen & K. Richard Ridderinkhof (2008), On the Nature, Modeling and Neural Bases of Social Ties, pp. 125–160, in: *Neuroeconomics, Vol. 20, Advances in Health Economics and Health Services Research*, edited by Daniel E. Houser & Kevin A. McCabe, Emerald Group Publishing Limited, Bingley, UK.

Velupillai, Kumaraswamy (2000), *Computable Economics*, Oxford University Press, Oxford.

Velupillai, K. Vela (2010a), Foundations of Boundedly Rational Choice and Satisficing Decisions, *Advances in Decision Science*, April, p. 16.

Velupillai, K. Vela (2010b), *Computable Foundations for Economics*, Routledge, London.

Velupillai, K. Vela (2016), Seven Kinds of Computable and Consturctive Infelicities in Economics, *New Mathematics and Natural Computation*, Vol. 12, No. 3, pp. 219–239.

Velupillai, K. Vela & Ying-Fang Kao (2015), Behavioural Economics: Classical and Modern, *The European Journal of the History of Economic Thought*, Vol. 22, No, 2, pp. 236–271.

Velupillai, K. Vela & Stefano Zambelli (2011), Computing in Economics, chapter 12, pp. 259–295, in: *The Elgar Companion to Recent Economic Methodology*, edited by John Davis & Wade Hands, Edward Elgar Publishing, Cheltenham.

# Appendix to Chapter 3
## De Finetti's theory of probability and its Jaynesian critique

Five remarks are in order here, before the main subject matter of this Appendix can be presented. First, this appendix should, ideally, be part of the main chapter, as an exposition of the subjective probability that substantiates Savage and Edwards on subjective expected utility theory – as well as a clarification of Frank Ramsey's pioneering work on the Dutch Book Method and the fact that he confined his analysis to finite alternatives – not very different from de Finetti's views on finite countability.

Second, I have been deeply influenced by the comprehensive 'de Finetti scholarship' of Professor Eugenio Regazzini (just three of his relevant contributions are Berti et al., 2007; Regazzini & Bassetti, 2008; Regazzini, 2012) of the University of Pavia and the abiding interest in de Finetti's many-splendoured technical and expository writing shown by my friend, Professor Maria Carla Galavotti of the University of Bologna. Moreover, the important way in which Professor Daniele Mundici has harnessed de Finetti's notion of coherence, especially to elucidate the variety of metamathematical ways of explicating the richness of the *Dutch Book Method*, has been a rich source of inspiration for me (cf. especially, Mundici, 2008). None of them are responsible for the remaining infelicities.

Third, I refer, of course, to E. T. Jaynes and his critique of de Finetti (and others, as well ahistorical and, largely, unsophisticated – the word vulgar also comes to mind, especially since it is unfairly used in referring to the great Italian probabilist's classic invoking of the Dutch Book Method – remarks on a variety of fundamental mathematical concepts). Being an economist, with a Cambridge background, I am not uninfluenced by being a sort of Keynesian, to coin the word Jaynesian!

Fourth, it may not be inappropriate to mention that the initial impetus for my reflections on de Finetti – expressed in the more comprehensive companion paper (Velupillai, 2014) – was a stillborn 'invitation' by Professor Enrico Zaninotto, in April 2011, to give the 'Inaugural Lecture' at the aborted de Finetti Graduate School of Social Science, at the University of Trento. Needless to say, the 'school' was as stillborn as the 'invitation', about which I never heard anything after the personal communication of 11 April 2011. *This was not the first time Professor Zaninotto was instrumental in aborted promises to me.* He is, indeed, a master of false promises.

Finally, an earlier version of this appendix appeared in **Economia Politica**, Vol. XXXI, No. 4, 2014.

## §1  Introduction

> Hayek has not read my book with that measure of 'good will' which an author is entitled to expect of a reader. Until he can do so, he will not see what I mean or know whether I am right. He evidently has a passion which leads him to pick on me, but I am left wondering what his passion is.
>
> —J. M. Keynes[1]

Reading the preceding characteristically elegant, yet melancholy – although also probably (*sic!*) tinged with anger – reflection by Keynes, substituting Jaynes for Hayek and de Finetti for Keynes, one is led to wonder 'what' Jaynes's 'passion is'? But, then, Jaynes does not reserve his critique exclusively to de Finetti; no less hallowed mathematicians and probabilists of the caliber of Kolmogorov and Feller are equally chastised, albeit for obviously different reasons.[2] Moreover, the butt of Jaynes' sharp views are also directed at metamathematical – that is, foundations and philosophy of mathematics – issues, of course, as they pertain to the mathematical foundations of probability theory.

In this brief contribution I set out to 'defend' de Finetti – not that a defense by a minor student of the great Italian probabilist is going to deflect the imprint of a critical Jaynes – but misrepresentations of a legendary scholar of one of the most renowned representation theorems in any form of probability theory should, surely, not go unremarked?

The overall impression in reading the magnum opus by Jaynes, Probability Theory: The Logic of Science (nothing less!), is that he displays the lack of 'good will' Keynes thought 'an author is entitled to expect of a reader'. It is this aspect, negative though it may well be,[3] that is highlighted in this paper. In emphasizing this negative aspect, I hope I am myself not guilty of a lack of the 'good will' 'which an author is entitled to expect of a reader'.

Accordingly, the next section summarizes the three-plus-one-point critique of de Finetti in Jaynes (*op. cit.*). In §3 an attempt is made to deflect the critique from a de Finetti point of view, textually and historically substantiated.[4] A brief §4 concludes the paper.

## §2  Jaynes's 'critique' of de Finetti

Jaynes opens his critical appendix on *The de Finetti System of Probability* (Jaynes, 2003, p. 655; italics added), with a claim that is more reminiscent of Hamlet's famous injunction to Horatio,[5] than what is appropriate in an avowedly 'scientific' treatise:

> [F]ollowers of Bruno de Finetti are concerned with matters that *Bayes never dreamt of.*

A generous interpretation would be to ignore it as a 'figure of speech' and pass on[6] to the more substantially founded criticisms – but the latter are as fantastically dream-like that one is forced to pay attention to every critical assertion that attempts to undermine the efforts of de Finetti and his followers[7] to develop a rigorous, subjectively grounded *Theory of Probability*. I am not sure how Jaynes had access to the world of *Bayes's dreams*, unless there were 'unpublished diaries' by the good Reverend, found in the wreckage of a plane crash[8] in the imaginary universe of maximum entropy followers! However, this fantastic assertion sets the tone for the three-pronged, loose and unjustified critique, by Jaynes, of the foundations of de Finetti's *Theory of Probability*. The *historical scholarship* is scanty and self-serving; the *conceptual analysis* is weak and misleading, and the *technical basis* of the critique is seriously faulty.

Jaynes claims (*loc. cit*) that de Finetti 'sought to establish the foundations of probability theory itself on the notion of 'coherence' . . . [and] appears to derive the rules of probability theory very easily from this premise'. It is not clear to me why Jaynes uses the adverb 'appears' here; is it because he believes de Finetti's derivations are un-rigorous? If so, there is no evidence of such a demonstration in the 727 plus xxiv pages of **Probability Theory: The Logic of Science**.

Jaynes, then, goes on to assert that 'coherence is an unsatisfactory basis [for deriving the Rules of Probability Theory] in three respects' (ibid., p. 655; italics added).

The first reason is 'admittedly only aesthetic', he states, and goes on (p. 655; italics added): 'it seems to us inelegant to base the principles of logic on such a *vulgar* thing as expectation of profit.'

The second reason for coherence being an 'unsatisfactory basis', is supposed to be 'strategic'. Jaynes's claim (loc. cit) is that the assigning of 'betting preferences' properly 'belongs to the field of psychology rather than probability.'

The third reason is 'thoroughly pragmatic', claims Jaynes. Here he adumbrates as follows (ibid., p. 656; italics added):

> [I]f any rules were found to possess the property of *coherence* in the sense of de Finetti, but not the property of *consistency* in the sense of Cox, they would be clearly unacceptable – indeed, functionally unusable – as rules for logical inference. There would be no 'right way' to do any *calculation*, and no 'right answer' to any question. Then there would be small comfort in the thought that all those different answers were at least 'coherent'.

To these reasons, tagged on to the concept of *coherence*, as used in the de Finetti scheme, Jaynes adds a *fourth* criticism (ibid., p. 656; italics added): that de Finetti defines his probabilities on '*arbitrary uncountable sets*, but he views *additivity* differently'.

In passing, it is necessary to point out, in the interests of historical scholarship and its accuracy, that Jaynes refers to the de Finetti classic of 1937 – itself presented at a lecture in Paris, in May, 1935 (cf. Foreword to de Finetti, 1937) – as the fountainhead of the Italian probabilist's fundamental contributions to the development of an original subjective theory of probability. There is no evidence whatsoever that Jaynes is aware of any of the previous decade of work and publications, entirely in Italian, except for one in French, by de Finetti, that culminated in the unified presentation in the classic of 1937.

In the next section I discuss and dissect the three plus one Jaynesian critiques of the de Finetti framework, ultimately founded on a rigorously measurable[9] notion of *coherence*. In doing this I shall also take the opportunity to outline and expose the aesthetic gaps, strategic lapses and pragmatic holes in Jaynes's own reliance on the notion of a *Robot* to found his version of *a Theory of Probability*, as a basis for a *Logic of Induction*.

## §3  In praise of de Finetti

> The old-established way of measuring a person's belief is to propose *a bet*, and see what are the lowest odds which he will accept. This method I regard as fundamentally sound; . . .
>
> —Frank Ramsey (1926; italics added)

*Balancing books* is a hallowed principle of any kind of economics, but most particularly in the tradition that has its origins in the pre-medieval Italian city states adopting the principle of *double-entry bookkeeping*, itself an Italian invention, following close on the heels of Fibonacci's introduction of the Hindu-Arabic following close on the heels of Fibonacci's introduction of the Hindu-Arabic numerals to replace the cumbersome Roman system of numbers, in tabulating profit-loss accounts of firms, banks, city states and also individuals of means (the Fuggers, the Medicis and, much later, the Rothschilds).

In Macroeconomics, as the system of national accounting took centre stage in the inter-war years, bookkeeping, the profit–loss accounts of the state and its balance sheet, often mediated by what came to be known as the *ex ante/ex post* dichotomy, became common practice in the evaluation of policy alternatives. This trend culminated in the *System of National Accounts* (**SNA**), constructed by Sir Richard Stone, for the United Nations, and now adopted by almost all the nations of the world.

It is easy to narrate a history that links Fibonacci and Luca Pacioli with Sir Richard Stone and Lance Taylor and to tell a *coherent* (*sic!*) story of the perversity of book-balancing in every kind of *dynamic* economic decision-making exercise.

As soon as the time dimension was non-trivially introduced into decision making, expectations or anticipations – whether underpinned by a formal calculus of probability, or not – came to dominate evaluations of alternative prospects in circumstances under risk and uncertainty.

The notion of the **Dutch Book Method** is only one version of double-entry bookkeeping, within the ambit of an individual decision-making entity – not necessarily confined to agents, whether rational or not, but also applicable to firms and other decision-making units.

De Finetti did not 'base the principles of logic on such a *vulgar* thing as expectation of profit'; he – and the intellectually saintly Frank Ramsey, just before him – *used* (one kind of) principles of logic, constrained by a rigorous notion of *coherence* (cf. de Finetti, 1974, ch. 3, in particular, pp. 88–90), to *derive rules for rational* (defined in one particular way, culled from a millennium of years of experience in 'everyday life') *choice*, in the face of risky futures.

Jaynes's condemnation, as *vulgar*, the notion of an 'expectation of profit', is reminiscent of the ethical objections to *profit* – usury, by another name – by the medieval Christian Church. Suppose de Finetti, and Ramsey before him, had referred to the expectation of growth, would it become non-vulgar in the eyes of Jaynes? The medieval Christian Church proscribed *usury* – that is, profit – on *ethical* grounds; Jaynes would like to banish the notion of profit, in the operational implementation of coherent expectations, on *aesthetic* grounds. What's the difference? The ethics of the church did not prevent the calculation of gains and losses and, thereby, the balancing of books, based on reasonable expectations of an uncertain (in the form of risky) future, by means of coherent rules.

It is to the credit of de Finetti – and Ramsey, just before him – to have used 'the old established way' of reconciling diverse expectations, by means of formalizing the notion of *calculating* odds and devising the notion of *coherence* in this process of balancing books. I can do no better than refer a Jaynesian, who is tempted to indulge in *ethical* or *aesthetic* strictures against the normal, 'age-old established way of measuring a person's belief' by proposing a bet, and see what are the lowest odds which he will accept', to Bernard Shaw's classic study of the *The Vice of Gambling and the Virtue of Insurance* (Shaw, 1960).

Finally, that Jaynes has misconstrued de Finetti's (and Ramsey's) method of imposing *coherent beliefs* in the expectation of gains – or the avoidance of losses – is exactly equivalent to the notion of a Fair Game – in the simplest case of two persons dividing a cake, 'You Cut, I Choose' – underpinning one way of formalizing Algorithmic Probability (cf. Shafer & Vovk, 2001, especially pp. 14 and 59–60). In the companion is exactly equivalent to the notion of a Fair Game – in the simplest case of two equivalent to the notion of a Fair Game in the simplest case of two persons equivalent to the notion of a *Fair Game* – in the simplest case of two persons dividing a cake, 'You Cut, I Choose' – underpinning one way of formalizing *Algorithmic Probability* (cf. Shafer & Vovk, 2001, especially pp. 14 and 59–60).

As for the second, 'strategic' reason for coherence being an 'unsatisfactory basis' for assigning 'betting preferences' to (rational) individuals, it is claimed that this is an activity that properly 'belongs to the field of psychology rather than probability'.

The problem here is, first, that Jaynes does not specify to what kind of *psychology* this assigning of 'betting preferences' belongs. This is a crucial issue since both, *classical* and *Modern Behavioural Economics* (cf. Velupillai & Kao, 2014 for the formal descriptions of the two fields) claim foundations in one or another kind of psychology. For example, the foundations of Classical Behavioural Economics, as a basis for a decision theoretic framework, lies in *cognitive psychology* which, in turn, is underpinned by *computability theory* (this is *my* framework for interpreting of Simon's Classical Behavioural Economics; I no longer think it is also Simon's framework). The strict dichotomy that Jaynes tries to emphasize, between psychology and (mathematically founded) probability theory, is a vestige of logical positivistic false enthusiasm, long since discarded by most philosophers of science.

Second, the notion of 'common sense' (Jaynes, op. cit., pp. 29 & 86–7) that is harnessed for the activities of his *Robot*, is – at best – an intuitive concept that can only be formalized by assuming something analogous to a Church–Turing *Thesis* to determine the equivalence between a formal notion and its intuitive counterpart. Such an equivalence, via the invoking of a thesis, is 'psychology' by any other name, especially in the 'assignment' of a formal notion of 'common sense' to a *Robot*, whose computing activities are implemented with a formal program.

Thirdly, assigning 'betting preferences' to a *Nondeterministic Turing Machine*, a generalized *Jaynesian Robot*, is a perfectly normal task – so long as it can be shown that the computing activities of such a machine are equivalent to the choice behaviour of a rational agent, as defined in economic and game theories (cf. Putnam, 1967, 1975; Velupillai, 2000, especially ch. 3).

The third, pragmatic, reason for the Jaynesian claim that *coherence* is an unsatisfactory basis (for assigning preferences), is supposed to be the superiority of '*consistency* in the sense of Cox' (ibid., p. 656; italics added), from a variety of points of view of 'calculation',[10] Jaynes goes on, in addition, to make what I can only refer to as a 'preposterous' claim, by stating that (*loc. cit.*):

> To the best of [Jaynes'] knowledge, de Finetti does not mention consistency as a desideratum, or test for it.

Has not Jaynes read even the classic by de Finetti (1937), which he quotes as the fountainhead of the research programme of the Italian probabilist? Just for clarification and elucidation, I quote here the relevant parts from the *Translator's Note* (Henry Kyburg, Jr.,) to de Finetti (*ibid.*; bold and italics added):

> 'Cohérence' has been translated 'coherent' following the usage of Shimony, Kemeny, and others. 'Consistency' is used by some English and American authors, and *is perfectly acceptable to de Finetti*, but it is ambiguous (from the logician's point of view) because, applied to beliefs, it has another very precise and explicit meaning in *formal logic*. As the words are used in this translation, to say that a body of beliefs is 'consistent' is to say (as in logic) that it contains no two beliefs that are contradictory. To say that in addition the body of beliefs is 'coherent' is to say that the *degrees* of belief satisfy certain **further conditions**.

But more important, even 'damagingly' (to the Jaynesian claims), there are three statements in §2.6.2 (pp. 45–47, Jaynes, 2003), where in his attempts to deflect the impact of *Gödel's Second Incompleteness theorem* (itself stated inaccurately and *incompletely* (*sic!*)), that are fundamentally incorrect or inappropriate.

First, he claims (*ibid.*, p. 46) that

> [i]f the computer program [that is implemented in the Jaynesian Robot] does not crash, but prints out valid numbers, then we know that the conditioning propositions are mutually consistent, and we have accomplished what one might have thought to be impossible in view of Gödel's theorem.

'We have accomplished' NOTHING of the sort! This is a mathematically false claim, due to a basic lack of knowledge of the fundamentals of computability theory. The alternatives are not just the two: a computer programme that 'crashes' (the exact meaning of which is unclear); one that prints our 'valid numbers (valid according to the interpretation of what kind of *mind* – that of the *Robot*?). There is the third alternative: the computing can go on 'forever', especially if the data that are 'fed' for processing by the computer programme of the Robot, is *recursively enumerable but not* recursive (empirically the most prevalent kind of data set).

Second, Jaynes claims (*ibid.*, p. 47; italics added),

> There are situations in which one can *prove* that a certain property must *exist* in a finite set, even though it is *impossible to exhibit* any member of the set that has that property.

Clearly, Jaynes is not referring to a *proof of existence* in a *constructive* sense. But even more importantly he is not even referring to the mathematics that underpins the activity of the Robot! In the kind of computability theory that characterizes a Robot, *even in a finite set* with a complex *recursive structure*, it is not possible to 'exhibit any member of the set that has' the desired property – but only by making precise the process-oriented notion of 'exhibit' (cf. Harrop, 1961); i.e. as an *effective procedure*.

Third, the domain of applicability of Cox's Theorem(s) is *not* the domain of relevance for implementing the computer programme for the activation of the *digital* Robot, which is the tacit assumption in the Jaynesian 'construction' and assumption for it. Therefore, the claim that the Robot 'can manipulate plausibilities, granted that it must associate them with real numbers', *consistently* (ibid., p. 37) can only be taken with the proverbial 'pinch of salt'.

Finally, as for the 'fourth criticism', that de Finetti defines his probabilities on '*arbitrary uncountable sets*, but he views *additivity* differently', all I have to do is to ask the Jaynesians to reread – or, as appears to be case, read *carefully*, for the first time – at least §3.3.3, p. 84, of de Finetti (1974). de Finetti's assumption (ibid., p. 84), 'that in principle P could be evaluated . . . for every event E', but 'under the restriction of a certain criterion'. Moreover, de Finetti goes on (p. 84; italics in the original),

> On the other hand, however, we certainly do not pretend that P could actually be imagined as determined, by any individual, for *all* events. . . .

## §4  Concluding notes

> A program has common sense if it automatically deduces for itself a sufficiently wide
> class of immediate consequences of anything it is told and what it already knows.
> —McCarthy (1959, p. 78; italics in the original)

Quite apart from a series of misguided interpretations of de Finetti's foundations –
conceptually, mathematically and philosophically – there are also a plethora
of infelicities of a deep and serious nature, on topics in the foundations of
mathematics and metamathematics. These range from thoroughly ahistorical and
'throw-away' remarks on the history and genesis of Generalized Functions, the
way the Dirac-delta function was developed by Dirac,[11] the rigorous proof of
Weierstrass's[12] famous 'continuous everywhere differentiable nowhere' function,
the altercation between Weierstrass and Kronecker, all the way to inane statements
about the personal dietary proclivities of Ramanujan and Gödel (ibid., p. 422).

Jaynes, for example, claims (ibid., p. 668), that 'Laurent Schwartz . . . persisted
in defining the term 'function' in a way inappropriate to analysis' and made the
'notion of a delta-function rigorous, but awkwardly'. He, then, goes on to state
that 'G. Temple (1955) and M. J. Lighthill (1957)[13] showed how to remove the
awkwardness . . . '. These kinds of statements, inaccurate technically and incorrect textually, are the ways in which Jaynes tries to cast doubts on de Finetti's
valiant efforts to provide rigorous, yet intuitive (even, at times, in the formal sense
of invoking principles of Intuitive Logic) foundations for the construction of a
subjective theory of probability.

For example, Schwartz – and Sobolev, almost simultaneously – generalized the
classic Dirichlet–Kuratowski notion of the set-theoretically underpinned definition of a function, by developing the theory of distributions. It was not that they
'persisted in defining the term "function" in a way inappropriate to analysis'; it
was that (classical) analysis was inappropriate for the new challenges of physics
and, dare I say, also economics. This was the way – or, at least, one of the ways –
de Finetti tried to 'justify' his completely original construction of the coherence
constrained, exchangeability based, subjective theory of probability.

Neither Temple (1955) nor Lighthill (1958) even hint at anything 'awkward'
about the Schwartzian development of the theory of distributions. In fact, Temple
is candid enough to 'confess' that he is 'vulgarising' the rigorous definition by
Schwartz (without, however, compromising on 'rigour').

Even the (in)famous Weierstrass function, on p. 669, is stated incorrectly[14] –
and the analytic statements accompanying it are seriously misconstrued.

The views expressed by Jaynes, in §B.4, on 'Kronecker vs. Weierstrasz', on
finite sets, on the 'certitude of arithmetic', on the characterization of algorithmic
methods and on 'our computer mentalities' are loose, even mathematically and
conceptually dangerous.

Above all, given the Jaynesian alternative of a *common-sense-driven Robot*,
to de Finetti's elicitation of preferences via the Dutch Book Method, it is

surprising that there is no evidence of any knowledge of the vast and rich literature on formalizing the intuitive notion of common sense, for the purposes of automatic, digital computer-aided, programming. This is a venerable tradition, an offshoot of the official origins of the Artificial Intelligence movement with the Dartmouth Conference of 1956, etched for posterity in the proceedings of the National Physical Laboratory conference held in 1958. At this conference, John McCarty, one of the pioneers of the Dartmouth Conference, began the noble line of research on formalizing the *intuitive notion of common sense computably*. I find it incredible that the Jaynesian notion of a formalized, common-sense-driven Robot stands completely outside this tradition – and to that extent it remains a limping, meaningless device for any kind of foundation for probability, definitely not for a subjective alternative to de Finetti's rich and rigorous constructions.

However, the positive task ahead now, from the point of view of developing de Finetti's rich framework, as I see it, is to emphasize its combinatorial, computable and constructive possibilities. If this task can be accomplished successfully, then it will be immediate, I conjecture, that the links between algorithmic and de Finetti's kind of subjective probability can be shown to be obvious.

## Notes

1 Keynes's 'penciled marks or comments' (Keynes, 1973, p. 243) at the end of his personal copy of Hayek's review of the **Treatise on Money**, which appeared in the August, 1931 issue of the **Economica**.

2 The unscholarly remarks on *generalized functions*, Dirac's introduction of the *delta function*, the role of Laurent Schwartz, George Temple and James Lighthill (whose book, Lighthill, 1958, by the way, is dedicated to *Dirac, Schwartz* and *Temple*), seem to be symptomatic of Jaynes's deficient historical scholarship (cf. Jaynes, 2003, Appendix A & B).

3 Negative aspects have a curious way of having positive effects on clarifying the issues in discussion. This is amply demonstrated by both Sraffa's brilliantly devastating review of Hayek's book (Sraffa, 1932) and the development of *algorithmic probability* as a result of unsympathetic mathematical attitudes towards von Mises' noble attempts to found the *frequency theory of probability* on a rigorous definition of *place selection functions*, taken by 'orthodox' probability theorists like Fréchet (see Van Lambalgen, 1987, especially §2.6). A concluding theme in this essay is that there is, after all, a strong affinity between the mathematics of de Finetti's *subjective theory of probability* and the algorithmically founded frequency theory of probability of von Mises.

4 In this effort I am also greatly indebted to the fine 'de Finetti scholarship' exhibited in von Plato (1974, chapter 8).

5 '*There are more things in heaven and earth, Horatio, than are dreamt of in your philosophy*', **Hamlet**, act. 1, sc. 5. Hamlet seems to be pointing out to Horatio that what can be explained is *limited*.

6 **Dante**'s advice, in **Inferno** (III, 51) comes to mind: *Non ragioniam di lor, ma guarda e passa!*

7 Among whom I am one, albeit a very minor, member of a noble set! However, it gives me unreserved pleasure to note that many of de Finetti's early and fundamental contributions (e.g., de Finetti, 1928, 1930a, 1930b, 1930c) were published in the **Rendiconti del Reale Istituto Lombardo di Scienze e Lettere**.

8   I am referring to the scandal surrounding the authentication of the so-called *Hitler Diaries*, allegedly found in the *Börnersdorf* crash.

9   I do not refer to *measurable* in its formal, mathematical, senses – but in its normal, engineering, geometric and craftsman's ways of usage. de Finetti, like most Italian mathematicians of the time, was a maestro of geometry (cf. Guerraggio & Nastasi, 2000).

10   This should be read as '*computability*', in the various contexts in which 'calculation' and 'consistency' are explicated in Jaynes (op. cit.).

11   Remarkably, the genesis of Dirac's innovative idea of the delta-function in his early engineering education, where Oliver Heaviside's operational calculus was crucial, is not mentioned (cf. Farmelo, 2009, p. 113; Kragh, 1990, pp. 206–207). In my own engineering education I was introduced, first, to the operational calculus of Heaviside and only much later, in fourth year undergraduate classes on quantum mechanics, to the Dirac δ-function. On the other hand, Richard Goodwin's lectures on advanced economic theory, at Cambridge in the early 1970s, routinely invoked the Duhamel 'folding'.

12   Strangely, the spelling of this great German analyst is consistently (sic!) given as Weierstrasz (Jaynes, ibid., p. 665, ff.)!

13   To the best of my knowledge this should be 1958.

14   It should be

$$f(x) = \sum_{n=0}^{\infty} a^n \cos(m^n \pi x)$$

# References

Berti, Patrizia, Eugenio Regazzini & Pietro Rigo (2007), Modes of Convergence in the Coherent Framework, *Sankhyā*, Vol. 69, Pt. 2, pp. 314–329.

de Finetti, Bruno (1928), Sulle probabilità numerabili e geometriche, *Rendiconti del Reale Istituto Lombardo di Scienze e Lettere*, Vol. 61, pp. 817–824.

de Finetti, Bruno (1930a), Sui passaggi al limite nel calcolo delle probabilità, *Rendiconti del Reale Istituto Lombardo di Scienze e Lettere*, Vol. 63, pp. 155–166.

de Finetti, Bruno (1930b), Ancora sull'estensione alle classinumerabili del teorema delle probabilità totali, *Rendiconti del Reale Istituto Lombardo di Scienze e Lettere*, Vol. 63, pp. 1063–1069.

de Finetti, Bruno (1930c), Sulla proprietà congolomerativa delle probabilità subordinate, *Rendiconti del Reale Istituto Lombardo di Scienze e Lettere*, Vol. 63, pp. 414–418.

de Finetti, Bruno (1937; 1974), Foresight: Its Logical Laws, Its Subjective Sources, translated by Henry E. Kyburg, Jr., pp. 94–158, in: *Studies in Subjective Probability*, edited by Henry E. Kyburg & Howard E. Smokler, John Wiley & Sons, Inc., New York.

de Finetti, Bruno (1974), *Theory of Probability – A Critical Introductory Treatment*, Vol. 1, translated by Antonio Machi and Adrian Smith, John Wiley & Sons, Chichester, UK.

Farmelo, Graham (2009), *The Strangest Man: The Hidden Life of Paul Dirac, Quantum Genius*, Faber & Faber, Ltd., London.

Guerraggio, Angelo & Pietro Nastasi (2000), *Italian Mathematics between the Two World Wars*, Birkhäuser Verlag, Basel.

Harrop, Ronald (1961), On the Recursivity of Finite Sets, *Zeitschrift für Mathematische Logik und Grundlagen der Mathematik*, Vol. 7, No. 2, pp. 136–140.

Jaynes, Edwin Thompson (2003), *Probability: The Logic of Science*, Cambridge University Press, Cambridge, UK.Keynes, John Maynard (1973), *The Collected Writings of John*

*Maynard Keynes, XIII: The General Theory and after – Part I: Preparation*, Published for the Royal Economic Society, St. Martin's Press, Macmillan, London.

Kragh, Helge S. (1990), *Dirac: A Scientific Biography*, Cambridge University Press, Cambridge.

Lighthill, Michael James (1958), *An Introduction to Fourier Analysis and Generalised Functions*, Cambridge University Press, Cambridge, UK.

McCarthy, John (1959), Programs with Common Sense, Session 1, Paper 3, pp. 75–91 (with Discussion), in: *Mechanisation of Thought Processes, Vol. 1 – Proceedings of a Symposium Held at the National Physical Laboratory on 24th, 25th, 26th and 27th November, 1958*, HMSO, London.

Mundici, Daniele (2008), Łukasiewicz Logic and De Finetti Coherence Criterion: Recent Developments, *Studies in Logic*, Vol. 1, No. 2, pp. 1–16.

Putnam, Hilary (1967; 1975), The Mental Life of Some Machines, chapter 20, pp. 408–428, in: *Mind, Language and Reality: Philosophical Papers*, Vol. 2, Cambridge University Press, Cambridge, UK.

Ramsey, Frank Plumpton (1926), Truth and Probability, chapter 3, pp. 58–100, in: *Foundations: Essays in Philosophy, Logic, Mathematics and Economics* (1931; 1978), edited by D. H. Mellor, Routledge & Kegan Paul, London.

Regazzini, Eugenio (2012), The Origins of de Finetti's Critique of Countable Additivity, *IMS Collections*, accessed via: arXiv:1206.4769v1[math.ST] 21 Jun 2012.

Regazzini, Eugenio & Federico Bassetti (2008), The Centenary of Bruno de Finetti (1906–1985), *Scientifica Acta*, Vol. 2, No. 1, pp. 56–76.

Shafer, Glenn & Vladimir Vovk (2001), *Probability and Finance: It's Only a Game!*, John Wiley & Sons, Inc., New York.

Shaw, Bernard (1960; 1944), The Vice of Gambling and the Virtue of Insurance, chapter 7, pp. 1524–1531, in: *The World of Mathematics*, Vol. 3, edited by James R. Newman, George Allen and Unwin, Ltd., London.

Sraffa, Piero (1932), Dr Hayek on Money and Capital, *Economic Journal*, Vol. 42, No. 165, March, pp. 42–53.

Temple, George (1955), The Theory of Generalized Functions, *Proceedings of the Royal Society of London, Series A, Mathematical and Physical Sciences*, Vol. 228, No. 1173, February 22, pp. 175–190.

Van Lambalgan, Michiel (1987), *Random Sequences*, Academisch Proefschrift, Universiteit Van, Amsterdam.

Velupillai, Kumaraswamy (2000), *Computable Economics*, Oxford University Press, Oxford, UK.

Velupillai, K. Vela & Ying-Fang Kao (2014), Computable and Computational Complexity Theoretic Bases for Herbert Simon's Cognitive Behavioural Economics, *Cognitive Systems Research*, Vol. 29–30, pp. 40–52.

von Plato, Jan (1974), *Creating Modern Probability – In Mathematics, Physics and Philosophy in Historical Perspective*, Cambridge University Press, Cambridge, UK.

# 4   The *zeitgeist*[1]

## Cybernetics, servomechanisms, information, communication and computation

In this [*chapter 12 on the Roots of Artificial Intelligence*] and the following chapters [of Models of My Life] I will give a blow-by-blow account of our research during 1955 and 1956, and place it in *the intellectual atmosphere*, the *zeitgeist*, within which it took place.

—Simon (1991, p. 190; italics added)[2]

## A brief formative backdrop

A period or a generation is not defined by, or circumscribed by, a single thought, feeling, idea or movement. Music, Art, Mathematics, Physics, Chemistry, Biology – and the other human and social sciences – and Politics, even History and Economics, have been dominated by sequential *and* parallel forces, at least in the 20th century.

The atonal music of Schönberg and Hindemith, even if sequential in their *individual* lives, did not displace the symphonic tendencies of the previous romantic and classical music.

In mathematics, for example, there were *parallel* developments, not only in the foundations of mathematics but also in the philosophy and techniques of the subject. Examples galore – especially if framed and studied in terms of the famous set of 23 'problems' for the mathematics and mathematicians of the 20th century, given by David Hilbert in his celebrated address to the first International Congress of Mathematicians, on 8 August 1900, in Paris (Hilbert, 1902).

In Art, Music and (pure analytic) Philosophy, often in close association with the developments in the foundations of mathematics, logic and phenomenology, and in Literature, there were parallel but distinctly different processes at work in Western and Eastern (and other) societies. For example, the notion of proof in Japan and India, as used in mathematics, had different philosophical underpinnings than those that were conventional in the 'West'. In Art, the notion of perspective had rich and diverse evolutions in Japan compared to the traditions in European painting. The so-called synthesis of the 'new biology' was based on the strictly individually motivated work of Darwin and Mendel. A similar case in Physics can be developed, by taking the examples of Einstein and Planck; in the foundations of mathematics by contrasting intuitionism versus formalism, Brouwer and Hilbert.

But in almost all cases, without exception, it is possible to identify an individual and – for want of a better word – a collective force in the evolutionary emergence of new forms of expressions and interpretations. This was, of course, most clearly evident in Art, due to the nature of the medium of expression – Dadaism versus *Die Blaue Reiter*, for example, as well as futurism and its connections with the political ideology of fascism – in the works of D'Annunzio, for instance. But it was also pervasive in Music, Architecture, Mathematics, Physics, Biology and Literature. Even in 'popular culture', the background of the dystopian forces of the Machine Age, as depicted in Chaplin's *Modern Times*.

The music of Stravinsky offers a good example of the dichotomy, between the individual and the collective, as clearly shown in the figure below. In it, trying to describe the 'evolution' of modern music, Robert Croft and Igor Stravinsky 'doodle' on the changing, kaleidoscopic nature of modern music – and the emergence of his vision and stance on musical composition, his way of writing music (see Figure 4.1).

I am convinced that Stravinsky's music emerged from a musical *zeitgeist* – a musical *intellectual atmosphere* – in its collective sense, but I have no doubts whatsoever that it was the product of an *interaction* of the individualistic and collective *zeitgeist*, and not as one based on the other, that is, one as a foundation or a building block of the other.

One striking feature of the above attempt at a pictorial characterization of his music, on the basis of a particular kind of inference – a causal mechanism, perhaps – is its two-dimensional nature: lines, curves and combinations thereof (even if it is a 'free-hand' drawing) on a plane. However, there is no easy or direct way of inferring – deriving – his music in terms of a 'law' that can be applied to

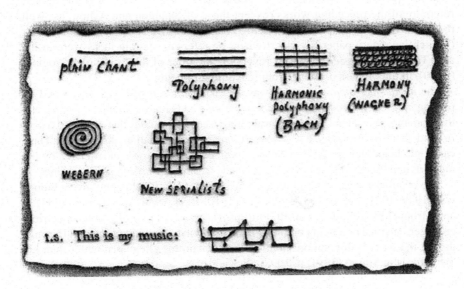

*Figure 4.1* (From) Stravinsky in Conversation with Robert Croft
Source: Faber and Faber (1960).

the other types. This is, for example, the case with the first three – plain chant, polyphony and harmonic polyphony; thus, the standard narrative that there was a culmination of a strand of thought with Bach but not a new beginning with his – Bach's – musical compositions.

It seems to be otherwise with Stravinsky's music – it is a new beginning, but of what?

It is this kind of evolution from an intellectual atmosphere – from a *zeitgeist* – that I wish to outline for the case of Simon's vision of human problem solving, on the basis of information, communication and computation, the trio that acts as the fulcrum upon which Wiener built his world of *Cybernetics*.

## Simon and the cybernetic *zeitgeist*

> All such [servomechanism] systems would be included in Wiener's[3] general program for *cybernetics*.
>
> —Simon (1952, pp. 247–248; italics added)

The *cybernetic zeitgeist* was formed in the seven-year period between 1936 and 1943 by Turing (1936), Shannon (1938), Ashby (1940), Piaget (1941), McCulloch and Pitts (1943), Craik (1943) and Bigelow, Rosenblueth and Wiener (1943). The story that unified the novel and audacious frameworks they introduced was summarized under the 'new' encompassing name of *Cybernetics* and was elegantly and effectively presented in Wiener (1948, 1961).[4]

In his interesting introduction to McCulloch (1965, p. XV), Seymour Papert refers to all the preceding works (except those of Shannon and Ashby) as 'well rooted in that period', and Cordeschi (2002, p. 153) also quotes from a later (French-language) paper by Papert where he refers to 'certain ideas were in the air'. The *cybernetic zeitgeist* was, reversing the order of the words of Prigogine[5] (1980), in the process of going from 'becoming to being'.

The *intellectual atmosphere* that was the *cybernetic zeitgeist* was determined by placing *information, communication, computation* and *control*,[6] in man, machine and the man–machine interaction, by constructing *feedback systems* that exhibited *learning* and, thereby, displaying a repertoire of *intelligent* explanation of *behaviour.* Thus, came into being that which was called servomechanism theory, underpinned by the methods and framework that cybernetics made feasible to implement in machines.

The *economic cybernetic* pioneers, and their foundational papers, were Goodwin (1949, 1951, 1951a, 1955),[7] Phillips (1950, 1954, 1958)[8] and Tustin (1953)[9] – apart from Herbert Simon himself. Phillips was trained as a professional electrical engineer, Tustin a practicing engineer and Goodwin had taught physics at Harvard during the war. As for Simon, nothing can explain his allegiance better than his own words in Simon (1991, p. 109; italics added):

[I]n the 1980s, when I was elected an honorary member of the Institute of Electrical and Electronic Engineers, and subsequently received the Harold

Pender Award from the Moore School of Electrical Engineering at the University of Pennsylvania, *I decided that I had been a closet engineer since the beginning of my career.*

The three economic 'closet engineers' – Goodwin, Phillips and Simon – constructed and implemented servomechanistic models, emphasizing feedback in a way that the full force of the *cybernetic quadruple* was called forth in macroeconomic and microeconomic stabilization exercises and microeconomic decision processes.

## Servomechanisms – Simon's *interim* framework for behavioural decisions

> Two dynamic macrosystems that have been represented by *analogue circuits* (and in one case experimentally investigated)[10] may also be regarded as *servomechanisms*.
> —Simon (1952, pp. 247–248; italics added)

Simon's interim – for simplicity, between his *Wiener and Turing periods* – framework for behavioural decision making, emphasizing information, computation and communication, together with 'error control feedback', was the broad umbrella that was servomechanism theory. They are represented in Simon (1951, 1952, 1955, 1956), Holt et al. (1955) and Holt et al. (1960).[11] The important additional element of his Wiener period was the dominance of analogue computation, using varieties of servomechanistic formalizations in the preceding works.

Right at the outset it may well be useful, at least for doctrine-historical reasons, that Goodwin (1950)[12] was, perhaps the first to refer to Wiener (1948) and develop error-correcting feedback versions of the Neoclassical models of Walras and Marshall (and, later, Keynes):[13]

> A modern automatic control device (*servomechanism*) uses the *error* between actual result and desired result as a basis for further *adaptation* in such a way as *to reduce the error and thus attain the desired value.* Human beings may be regarded as complicated *servomechanisms* (cf. *N. Wiener, Cybernetics*) and the direct applicability to a wide variety of economic response mechanisms is evident.
>
> (Goodwin, *ibid.*, p. 196; italics added)

Another prescient element in Simon's essentially servomechanism, 'error control feedback', models are that they were alternatives to the frontier definition of Newclassical macroeconomics in terms of the three recursive tools: (optimum) stopping rules, (Kalman) filtering and dynamic programming. These three elements were part of Simon's repertoire of concepts and tools fashioned under his *Wiener period* of servomechanism theories. Thus, in Simon (1951), the role of *optimum stopping rules* is emphasized – but not uncritically.[14] In Simon (1955) the *optimal filter* problem is developed again within the framework of servomechanism theory (see also the lead quote of the next section). Finally, Simon (1956) is an elegant precursor to the most pervasive tool at the frontiers of Newclassical economics: *dynamic programming*.

Why, then, did Simon not pursue a path that may have led to being a pioneer of Newclassical economics – especially since the latter 'claim' that they, too, are working within a scheme that attempts to formalize recursive decision rules? There are many possible conjectural answers to this query and, of course, I have my own story – which is (apart from ideology) based on Simon's sustained use of a model of computation, the relative importance given to computational complexity, the utterly different interpretation and definition of information and communication by agents and institutions that are *not Olympian*. Of course, there are other finesses that delineate the different frameworks of Simon and the Newclassicals (even though there was an early period when even the latter extolled the virtues of an approach to economic modelling in terms of the theory of servomechanisms). In addition, I am convinced that the Newclassicals do not understand the differences between analogue, digital and hybrid computing, nor do they have any mastery of so-called scientific computing.

Above all, the Newclassical theory of macroeconomic oscillations could not have been more *ad hoc*, more underpinned by the kind of expected utility maximizing agents and less disciplined by a theory of computation than Simon's lifelong research interests.

The three circuit diagrams[15] (pp. 248, 251 and 258 of Simon, 1952) are not linked to the kind of economic modelling exercises in the works of the economic cyberneticists, Goodwin (1949, 1951, 1951a) or Phillips (1950). But Figure 4.1, page 266, in Simon (*op. cit.*), is a step towards oscillation theory underpinned by circuits built for analysis in terms of 'feedback error controls', in the sense of servomechanism theory.

The *cybernetic quadruple*, in particular *information* and *computation*, were realized, in the models of Goodwin and Phillips, via analogue circuits, block and stock–flow circuit diagrams and dynamical oscillatory systems, incorporating intrinsic 'error-control feedback' mechanisms. This latter feature enabled Goodwin and Phillips to obviate monotone dynamics that were patently unobservable in operating systems. Moreover, the opening quote of this section shows Simon's characteristic and perceptive perspicacity, especially with respect to the fertile power of modelling with the principles of servomechanism theory.

There are, however, three important aspects of oscillation theory, based on circuit constructions and their fluctuating dynamics operating with 'error-correcting feedback' elements defining the analogue computation of experimental paths, for alternative parameter configurations, with given initial conditions.

First of all, it was an important component of Wiener's path towards *Cybernetics* (Wiener, 1961, p. x, ff.), which was facilitated by the writing of *Nonlinear Problems in Random Theory* (Wiener, 1958) and showing the limitations of linear theory in general and the superposition principle, in particular.

Second, the work of Mary Cartwright (singly and jointly with J. E. Littlewood) on non-linear oscillations was initiated with (Cartwright, 1964, p. 193; italics added):

> [A] memorandum from the Department of Scientific and Industrial Research dated 11 January, 1938 which was sent to the London Mathematical Society. . . . It appealed to pure mathematicians for 'really expert guidance' if only to prevent the waste of time and energy spent in pursuit of a will-o'-the-wisp' of *explicit analytical solutions* having something of 'the same comparative simplicity and utility as those available for the *linear differential equations*' with which the *engineer* was familiar.

Third, the extremely perspicacious invoking of typically cybernetic, error-control feedback, mechanisms of (implicit) nonlinear oscillators, in the observations of Walter Grey and Ross Ashby, by Stanly-Jones[16] (1960), is a strengthening of the themes, detailed earlier, by Wiener and Cartwright. The Walter Grey observation was (Stanley-Jones, *i*, pp. xi–xii;[17] italics added) that

> [a] system with *positive feed-back* which is responsive to steady states tends to run away to an extreme position and stay there. The introduction of a differentiating network *makes it respond only to changes* and instead of the runaway, *oscillations will build up* . . . It would be well worth analyzing any *cyclic phenomenon* in these terms, whether it is *boom-and-bust economics* or manic-depressive psychosis.

Ross Ashby's equally pertinent observation[18] was (*ibid.*, p. xii; italics added) that

> [t]he difference between *machines that are goal-seeking* and machines which are not is identical with the difference between machines which do, and which do not, possess properly arranged *feed-back* . . . *Feed-back enables the machine to correct its own errors*.

Goal-seeking agents and institutions were the perennial themes in Simon's research program, right through the *Wiener and Turing periods*. Modelling oscillations in boom–bust economies, by incorporating error-correcting feedback mechanisms, in a classic non-linear oscillatory system, equivalent to a nonlinear circuit's dynamics, was what was attempted – successfully – by Goodwin (1949, 1951) and with only slightly less success by Phillips[19] (1950).

This particular fact, with respect to Goodwin (1951), is best exemplified by an extremely interesting observation by McAnulty et al. (1953, pp. 391–392). They observe, and implement, the non-linear circuit model implicit in Goodwin (*op. cit.*), by means of an experimental analogue computation of the non-approximated final equation:

$$\in \dot{y}(t) + (1-\alpha)y(t) = \phi[\dot{y}(t-\theta)] + \beta(t) + l(t) \tag{1}$$

An analogous electric circuit equation to (1) is

$$RC\dot{q}(\tau)+(1-\alpha)q(\tau)-\phi[\dot{q}(\tau-\theta)]=q_0(\tau) \tag{2}$$

**Notation**

$y(t)$: income, and its rate of change is denoted by, $y$;
$\epsilon$: constant with the dimension of years;
$\alpha$: dimensionless coefficient (constant);
$\beta(t)$: autonomous component of consumption expenditure;
$\phi$: a nonlinear (S-shaped) induced investment function;
$\theta$: time-lag, in years;
$t$: time, in years;
$R$: resistance in *Ohms*;
$C$: capacitance in *Farads*;
$RC$: a time constant, in seconds;
$q(\tau)$: charge in Coulombs, $q(\tau)$, is the rate of change of charge per second – that is, *Amperes*;
$\phi[dq/dt(\tau-\theta)]$: time-lagged charge-function, in Coulombs, analogous to the 'S-curve' in (1);
$\tau=t/k_1$; $\Theta=\theta/k_1$;
$t$: time, in years;
$k_1$: time-scaling factor of 62.9 yr/sec.

Figure 2, in McAnulty et al. (*ibid.*, p. 393) is the *electric circuit* corresponding to (2), which, in turn, is an analogue of (1). This kind of construction of an electric circuit, corresponding to a dynamic oscillatory model of the (macro)economy, and using results similar to Smale (1972) and Hirsch and Smale (1974, chapter 10) and Cartwright (*op. cit.*), it is possible to derive the following type of theorem:[20]

*Theorem 1*

Corresponding to every nonlinear oscillatory dynamical system model of the (macro)economy, a nonlinear electric circuit can be constructed.

*Remark 1*

Such an electric circuit can be used in a way as to build an analogue computer.

*Remark 2*

Goodwin (1951) was based on the dynamical system derived from a van der Pol electric circuit by Le Corbeiller (1936).[21]

*Remark 3*

Phillips (1950), on the basis of which the Phillips Machine[22] was constructed, is an instance of such an analogue computing implementation, entirely based on the principles of error-correcting feedback mechanism of a servomechanism type.

### Remark 4

The analogy, or analogical model building, of electrical circuits and the dynamics of nonlinear oscillatory systems, requires careful minding of *stocks, flows*,[23] definitions of equilibrium or balance relations and *laws*[24] (Ohm's, Kirchoff's, Boyle's, Newton's and so on) in formulating correspondences.

As always, Simon was in the 'eye of the storm', in the sense that *servomechanism* theory was an important defining component of *Cybernetics*; that, in turn, meant (analogue) computation, control, communication and information was at placed at the centre of research focus. It is most appropriate, therefore, to end this section with Simon's own thoughts on his servomechanism theoretic work of this *Cybernetic Zeitgeist*:

It is probable that the results set forth here are well known, at least intuitively, to *designers of servomechanisms*, but I have not seen them set forth.

(Simon, 1955, p. 438; italics added)

## Concluding notes

Work that too far anticipates its appropriate *zeitgeist* tends to be ignored, while work that fits the contemporary *zeitgeist* is recognized promptly.

—Simon (1991, p. 194; italics added)

In many senses, Simon's work in the *post-Wiener period* 'anticipates its appropriate zeitgeist', particularly in economics. Thus, it has been 'ignored', misunderstood and misrepresented, again particularly in economics – to this day. But his work, interest and writings during the heat of the *cybernetic zeitgeist* were very much of the *contemporary* 'intellectual atmosphere' – but not in economics. Still, for reasons I do not understand, they have not been accorded the importance that, for example, Goodwin's and Phillips's macroeconomic oscillatory and stabilization policy frameworks were given. Allen's exceptionally well-written textbooks (Allen, 1956; 1959; Allen, 1967) may have been the cause of the latter case. He – Allen – presented the various Goodwin and Phillips macroeconomic models of oscillation, growth and stabilization policy in terms of crystal-clear feedback, block (or elementary) circuit diagrams.

But analogue computing, despite its honourable pedigree, was on the wane; the digital computer and the extraordinary works of Turing heralded a new *zeitgeist* – one that saw Simon at the frontiers of research which emphasized agents as information-processing systems, experimenting and solving problems, using heuristics and applying the notions of the new intellectual atmosphere fruitfully. Learning by man and machine, not only in error-correcting feedback systems, simulating non-numeric models, experimenting with logical, cryptarithmetic and ostensible 'parlour' games (chess being the prime example) became defining approaches in the *Turing era*, which came after the fertile and promising *Wiener zeitgeist*.

Yet, there has not been the hollowing out of the analogue computing approach, especially from a theoretical point of view. I have attempted to tell an updated story in Velupillai (2004) and the continuing work of Graça and his collaborators in Portugal (e.g., Graça & Costa, 2003). This is an attempt to explore new possibilities with analogue computing and, at the same time, to understand to what extent and how such a method differs from the power and methods of digital computing and the Turing Machine. There may still be some 'life' left in the theory of servomechanism.

## Notes

1 *Zeitgeist: The thought or feeling peculiar to a generation or period* (p. 2594, **The Shorter Oxford English Dictionary on Historical Principles**, Third Edition, Clarendon Press, Oxford, 1973).

2 To the best of my knowledge of Simon's voluminous writings, this and the mention on pages 194 and 196 in the same chapter are the only occasion when the word *zeitgeist* is used is by him – but he qualifies its meaning as describing, or being, 'the intellectual atmosphere' of a period.

3 Wiener (1948).

4 All these classical works that characterized the *cybernetic zeitgeist* – and more – were very well known to Simon (see Simon, 1991, pp. 194–197, in particular).

5 A later enthusiastic adherent of the *Cybernetic* outlook in the life and natural sciences and philosophy.

6 The *cybernetic quadruple*, as I shall refer to them.

7 In addition to Goodwin (1951b), mentioned in Simon (1952).

8 At the Zurich meeting where Phillips presented this paper, he met Dennis Gabor, who is felicitously mentioned in Wiener (*op. cit.*, p. xi).

9 Both Goodwin (1955) and Phillips (1954) wrote extensive and felicitous reviews of Tustin (*op. cit.*) in leading economic journals.

10 Morehouse et al. (1950) and Enke (1951).

11 Particularly chapter 19, pages 363 to 371, of this book, which is, essentially, a summary of Simon (1952). The latter is a particularly good introduction to the Laplace transform analysis as used in the servomechanism theories of the late 1940s and early 1950s.

12 Which is an abstract of Goodwin (1951a). The quoted passage does *not* appear Goodwin (*ibid.*).

13 In personal conversations with me, during my happy period as his research student, at Cambridge (UK), in the early 1970s, Goodwin told me that he had attended the interdisciplinary meetings arranged by McCulloch and Wiener, at the 'other' Cambridge! He was, then (till the end of 1951), a member of Harvard University's economics faculty.

14 Most illuminatingly stated in the final sentence of the paper (p. 305):

> The most serious limitations of the model lie in the assumptions of rational utility-maximizing behavior incorporated in it.

15 However, that in Simon (1977), chapter 6.5, an extremely interesting background discussion of using Ohm's *Law* to derive the triptych of *experiment, abduction* and *inference* in enriching *the axiomatization of physical theories* (the title of ch. 6.5) appears, is not within the formal scheme of servomechanism theory.

16 A book to which Winer wrote an important preface.

17 Presumably from Walter (1950).

18 Most likely from Ashby (1950).

19 This was because – I conjecture – Phillips was trained in traditional, linear circuit theoretical, electrical engineering and the analogue machine he built, although capable of nonlinear analysis, was used only for linear stabilization purposes.

20 A word of caution to the (possibly) unwary reader: this does not mean any circuit representation of an economic theory has a dynamical system equivalent; this is so, especially, because the circuit representation is fundamentally and technically *incorrect* (such as in Leijonhufvud, 1970).

21 Serendipitously, Richard Goodwin gave me his reprint copy of this classic by Le Corbeiller!

22 'Christened' the **MONIAC** – **MO**netary National Income Analog Computer – by Abba Lerner, invoking an analogy with **ENIAC**, among others.

23 Joan Robinson (1982, p. 295; italics added), with characteristic perspicacity, observed, through the use of an observation by her friend, Kalecki,

> We [Kahn and I] arrived first, and as Michal [Kalecki] came over to the table where we were sitting he announced '*I have found out what economics is; it is the science of confusing stocks with flows*'.

24 One should remember that Emil Post referred to *Church's Thesis*, what I have called the *Church–Turing Thesis*, as a *Natural Law*. I'll return to this issue later in this manuscript, particularly in the next chapter. A thesis is *not* a theorem; a proof is not unambiguous, unless one constrains the logic or the mathematics to severely constrained varieties.

# References

Allen, R. G. D. (1956; 1959), *Mathematical Economics* (First & Second Editions), Macmillan, St. Martin's Press, London.

Allen, R. G. D. (1967), *Macro-Economic Theory: A Mathematical Treatment*, Macmillan, St. Martin's Press, London.

Ashby, W. Ross (1940), Adaptiveness and Equilibrium, *Journal of Mental Science (now The British Journal of Psychiatry)*, Vol. 86, No. 362, May, pp. 478–483.

Ashby, W. Ross (1950), Cerebral Mechanisms of Intelligent Action, in: *Perspectives in Neuropsychiatry: Essays Presented to Frederick Lucien*, edited by Derek Richter, H. K. Lewis & Co. Ltd, London.

Cartwright, Mary (1964), From Non-Linear Oscillations to Topological Dynamics, *Journal of the London Mathematical Society*, Vol. 39, No. 1, pp. 193–201.

Cordeschi, Roberto (2002), *The Discovery of the Artificial: Behavior, Mind and Machines Before and Beyond Cybernetics*, Springer Science+Business Media, Dordrecht.

Craik, Kenneth (1943), *The Nature of Explanation*, Cambridge University Press, Cambridge.

Enke, Stephen (1951), Equilibrium among Spatially Separated Markets: Solution by Electric Analogue, *Econometrica*, Vol. 19, January, pp. 40–47.

Goodwin, Richard M. (1949), The Business Cycle as a Self-Sustaining Oscillation, Presented at the Cleveland Meeting of the Econometric Society, December, 1948, *Econometrica*, Vol. 17, No. 2, April, pp. 184–185.

Goodwin, Richard M. (1950), Abstract of Iteration, Automatic Computers, and Economic Dynamics [Goodwin, 1951a], Report of the Varese Meeting, September 6–8, 1950, *Econometrica*, Vol. 19, No. 2, April, 1951, pp. 196–198.

Goodwin, Richard M. (1951), The Nonlinear Accelerator and the Persistence of Business Cycles, *Econometrica*, Vol. 19, No. 1, January, pp. 1–17.

Goodwin, Richard M. (1951a), Iteration, Automatic Computers, and Economic Dynamics, *Metroeconomica*, Vol. 3, Fasc. 1, April, pp. 1–7.

Goodwin, Richard M. (1951b), Econometrics in Business-Cycle Analysis, chapter 22, pp. 417–468, in: *Business Cycles and National Income*, edited by Alvin H. Hansen, W. W. Norton and Co., New York.

Goodwin, Richard M. (1955), *Review* of Tustin (1953), *The Review of Economics and Statistics*, Vol. 37, No. 2, May, pp. 209–210.

Graça, Daniel Silva & José Félix Costa (2003), Analog Computers and Recursive Functions Over the Reals, *Journal of Complexity*, Vol. 19, No. 5, October, pp. 644–664.

Hilbert, David (1902), Mathematical Problems, *Bulletin of the American Mathematical Society*, Vol. 8, No. 10, pp. 437–479.

Hirsch, Morris W. & Stephen Smale (1974), *Differential Equations, Dynamical Systems, and Linear Algebra*, Academic Press, New York.

Holt, Charles C., Franco Modigliani, John F. Muth & Herbert A. Simon (1960), *Planning Production, Inventories and Work Force*, Prentice-Hall, Inc., Englewood Cliffs, NJ.

Holt, Charles C., Franco Modigliani & Herbert A. Simon (1955), A Linear Decision Rule for Production and Employment Scheduling, *Management Science*, Vol. 2, No. 1, October, pp. 1–30.

Le Corbeiller, Ph. (1936), The Non-Linear Theory of the Maintenance of Oscillations, *Proceedings of the institution of Electrical Engineers*, Vol. 11, pp. 292–309.

Leijonhufvud, Axel (1970; 1981), Notes on the Theory of Markets, *Intermountain Economic Review*, Fall; reprinted as chapter 12, pp. 221–237, in: *Information and Coordination – Essays in Macroeconomic Theory*, Oxford University Press, Oxford.

McAnulty, J. C., J. B. Naines, Jr. & R. H. Strotz (1953), Goodwin's Nonlinear Theory of the Business Cycle: An Electro-Analog Solution, *Econometrica*, Vol. 21, No. 3, July, pp. 390–411.

McCulloch, Walter & Walter Pitts (1943), A Logical Calculus of the Ideas Immanent in Nervous Activity, *Bulletin of Mathematical Biology*, Vol. 52, Nos. 1–2, pp. 99–115.

McCulloch, Warren (1965), *Embodiments of Mind*, The MIT Press, Cambridge, MA.

Morehouse, N. F., R. H. Strotz & S. J. Horwitz (1950), An Electro-Analog Method for Investigating Problems in Econometric Dynamics: Inventory Oscillations, *Econometrica*, Vol. 18, October, pp. 313–328.

Phillips, A. W. (1950), Mechanical Models in Economic Dynamics, *Economica*, N.S., Vol. 17, No. 67, August, pp. 283–305.

Phillips, A. W. (1954), *Review* (of, The Mechanism of Economic Systems – An Approach to the Problems of Economic Stabilisation from the point of view of Control-System Engineering by Arnold Tustin), *The Economic Journal*, Vol. 64, No. 256, December, pp. 805–807.

Phillips, A. W. (1958), La Cybernetique et le Controle des Systemes Economiques, Etudes Cahiers de l'ISEA, *Etudes sur la cybernétique et l'économie*, Série N, Vol. 2, November, pp. 41–48.

Piaget, Jean (1941), *The Child's Conception of Number*, Routledge & Kegan Paul, London.

Prigogine, Ilya (1980), *From Being to Becoming: Time and Complexity in the Physical Sciences*, W. H. Freeman & Company, San Francisco.

Robinson, Joan (1982), Shedding Darkness, *Cambridge Journal of Economics*, Vol. 6, No. 3, pp. 295–296.

Rosenblueth, Arturo, Norbert Wiener & Julian Bigelo (1943), Behavior, Purpose and Teleology, *Philosophy of Science*, Vol. 10, No. 1, January, pp. 18–24.

Shannon, Claude E. (1938), A Symbolic Analysis of Relay and Switching Circuits, *Transactions American Institute of Electrical Engineers*, Vol. 57, No. 12, pp. 713–723.

Simon, Herbert A. (1951), A Formal Theory of the Employment Relationship, *Econometrica*, Vol. 19, No. 3, July, pp. 293–305.

Simon, Herbert A. (1952), On the Application of Servomechanism Theory in the Study of Production Control, *Econometrica*, Vol. 20, No. 2, April, pp. 247–268.

Simon, Herbert A. (1955), Some Properties of Optimal Linear Filters, *Quarterly of Applied Mathematics*, Vol. 12, No. 4, January, pp. 438–440.

Simon, Herbert A. (1956), Dynamic Programming Under Uncertainty with a Quadratic Criterion Function, *Econometrica*, Vol. 24, No. 1, January, pp. 74–81.

Simon, Herbert A. (1977), *Models of Discovery – and Other Topics in the Methods of Science*, D. Reidel Publishing Company, Dodrecht-Holland.

Simon, Herbert A. (1991), *Models of My Life*, Basic Books, New York.

Smale, Stephen (1972), On the Mathematical Foundations of Electrical Circuit Theory, *Journal of Differential Geometry*, Vol. 7, Nos. 1–2, pp. 193–210.

Stanley-Jones, D and K. Stanley-Jones (1960), *The Kybernetics of Natural Systems: A Study in Patterns of Control*, Pergamon Press, New York.

Turing, Alan (1936), On Computable Numbers, with an Application to the Entscheidungs Problem, *Proceedings of the London Mathematical Society*, Series 2, Vol. 42, pp. 230–265.

Tustin, Arnold (1953), *The Mechanism of Economic Systems, an Approach to the Problem of Economic Stabilisation from the Point of View of Control-System Engineering*, William Heinemann, London.

Velupillai, K. Vela (2004), Economic Dynamics and Computation – Resurrecting the Icarus Tradition, *Metroeconomica*, Vol. 55, Nos. 2–3, May–September, pp. 239–264.

Walter, W. Grey (1950), Features in the Electrophysiology of Mental Mechanisms, in: *Perspectives in Neuropsychiatry: Essays Presented to Frederick Lucien*, edited by Derek Richter, H. K. Lewis & Co. Ltd., London.

Wiener, Norbert (1948), *Cybernetics*, John Wiley & Sons, New York.

Wiener, Norbert (1958), *Nonlinear Problems in Random Theory*, The Technology Press of Massachusetts Institute of Technology, Cambridge, MA.

Wiener, Norbert (1961), *Cybernetics* (Second Edition), The MIT Press, Cambridge, MA.

# 5   Heuristics[1] versus algorithms

> In general, the machine's problem solving is much more elegant when it works
> with a selected list of strategic theorems than when it tries to remember and use *all*
> the previous theorems in [*Principia Mathematica*].
>
> —Simon (1991, p. 209; italics added)

Let me begin with a version of the implication for the *existence* of *algorithms* as
a 'theorem' (Aiserman et al., p. 349):

*Theorem 1*

> An *algorithm* can exist *only if* a corresponding general recursive function
> can be constructed.

An analogous 'theorem' for the possible construction of *heuristics* is

*Theorem 2*

> *Heuristics* can exist *even if* it is *not* the case that corresponding general
> recursive functions *cannot* be constructed.

*Remark 1*

> The difference between the connectives, *only if* and *even if* is crucial in
> characterizing the distinctive ways of using *algorithms*, in contrast to
> *heuristics*, especially in problem solving contexts.

*Remark 2*

> The use of the word constructed, earlier, is *not* in the sense of Brouwer's,
> Bishop's or Martin-Löf's constructivism. The notion of *existence* used
> in the above two theorems are *not* necessarily constructive, in the sense
> of rejecting the *tertium non datur* in their *proofs*.

I agree with the great Knuth that there are modes of thinking that are *mathematical*, and other ways of thought that are *algorithmic* (Knuth, 1985). But I would

like to fine texture his characterization of thought processes, in human problem solving, of which mathematical problems are a (small) subset, with the further subdivision into *heuristics*, in addition to mathematical and algorithmic ways of thinking.

Polya (1945, 1962, 1954a, 1954b),[2] I *now* think, used *heuristics*, predominantly, to discuss analogical and plausible reasoning in discovering solutions to mathematical problems, combining algorithmic and mathematical modes of problem solving. Heuristics, in the rich and many-splendoured world of discovering solutions to mathematical problems, in Polya, was different from the way Simon (and Turing) approached problem solving by humans with reasoning powers, underpinned by *common sense*. This was why Turing (1954, p. 23; italics added) was able to conclude his perceptive essay by pointing out the crucial role played by *common sense* in buttressing mathematical and algorithmic ways of thinking problem solving by purely formal means:

> The results which have been described . . . [set] certain bounds to what we can hope to achieve *purely by reasoning*. These, and some other results of mathematical logic may be regarded as going some way towards a demonstration, within mathematics itself, of the *inadequacy of 'reason' unsupported by common sense.*

It is in this particular sense that I have revised my views on Turing's approach to problem solving; my belief now is that Turing tempered his views on algorithmic thinking and argued for infusing it with Simon's kind of *heuristics*.

*Heuristics* was set in its noble Simonian paces – taking into account '*reason supported by common sense*' – in the monumental *Human Problem Solving* (Newell & Simon, 1972), which – I surmise – had its origins twenty years earlier, in the 'planning document' that Harold Guetzkov[3] and [Simon] wrote on February, 28, 1952 (Simon, 1991, p. 161). Simon went on (ibid., p. 163; italics added):

> When Harold [Guetzkov] brought to these [working sessions in which Guetzkov, Jim March, Simon and others participated] his earlier research on *problem solving*, we began more and more to see *decision-making processes as essentially the same as problem-solving processes.* . . .
> Our growing interest in *problem solving* led us to *restudy* the writings of psychologists . . . especially Gestaltists such as . . . *Karl Duncker* . . . This was a first tentative step on the road that led soon afterward to my collaboration with Al Newell and Cliff Shaw[4] in building *a computer simulation of heuristic problem solving.*

Thus it was that the term *heuristic*, and its implementation, owed more to its human, psychological – cognitive – definition, particularly by Duncker (1945, pp. 20–21, and chapter IV, for example), than its mathematical encapsulation in Polya's influential work (particularly, in Polya, 1945). The definition of heuristic by Duncker, within the context of *human* thought processes, fit well into Simon's preoccupation with *Human* Problem Solving. Thus, Duncker (ibid.) defined heuristics, in the context of *human thought processes* being directed towards problem solving as (pp. 20–21; bold italics added):

> We find that a solution always consists in a variation of some crucial element of the ***situation*** . . .
> *We can therefore say that "insistent" analyses of the situation, especially the endeavor to vary appropriate elements meaningfully sub specie of the goal, must belong to the essential nature of a solution through thinking. We may call such relatively general procedures, "heuristic methods of thinking."*

It was this that made Simon react to Kleene and Wang in a way that can only be described as incomprehension at their lack of finesse in understanding the difference between 'learning and wisdom'. In particular, his reaction to Wang's uncharacteristically severe criticism of NSS using heuristics rather than algorithmic processes (Wang, 1960, p. 227; Cordeschi, 1996, pp. 2–3), was easily understandable (Simon, 1991, pp. 209–210; bold italics added):

> [F]rom the beginning we [*NSS*] were interested in simulating *human problem solving*, and ***not simply*** in demonstrating how computers could solve hard problems. . . . Later, the logician Hao Wang and others, taking ***computational efficiency*** as their *only* criterion, designed faster computer proof procedures and denigrated the Logic Theorist as primitive. ***They simply misunderstood*** the objectives of the research on L[ogic]T[heorist].

These are the reasons I now think the characterization of proof procedures should be finer than just in terms of a *mathematical* way of thinking and an *algorithmic* mode; there should also be the *heuristic* procedural approach – whereby one dies not explore *all* possible or feasible alternatives in a search space. Crudely, but not unrealistically, the mathematical way of thinking can be identified with the classical, non-constructive mode of proof procedure, where – for example – the *tertium non datur* is unrestrictedly utilized. On the other hand, equally crudely, the algorithmic mode of proof procedures can be referred to as constructive proofs, especially with the privilege of hindsight offered by the vast developments in automatic theorem-proving applications in graph theory – especially in map colouring and Ramsey Theoretic problems – group theory and even in dynamical system theory.[5]

I have tried to outline the origins of the way Simon considered heuristics as a basis for human problem-solving procedures. Simon, however, was not averse to thinking in terms of proof procedures where computational efficiency was of paramount concern, nor did he refrain from using the mathematical way of thinking in proof procedures – particularly when it came to proving the propositions in chapter 2 of Whitehead and Russel (1927). However, in both cases his method was – at least the way I see it – to infuse them with heuristic elements at appropriate junctures.

In Simon (1991, p. 205; italics in the original), Simon states,

> The first note I have in writing, dated November 15, 1955, consists of an analysis of the proof of theorem 2.15 of *Principia [Mathematica]*.[6]

Assuming familiarity with the (archaic, no doubt!) notation of the *Principia*, theorem 2.15 is (*PM*, p. 102):

$$\vdash: \sim p \supset q \supset \sim q \supset p \tag{1}$$

The second step in the proof appeals to the *law of the excluded middle* (implicitly – cf. *PM*, p. 101). This entails an undecidable disjunction which means the Logic Theorist cannot infer the proof by an unrestricted search procedure of the space of alternatives of given axioms, definitions and previously derived theorems. This is where Simon would have used *heuristics* to constrain the space of search alternatives.

On the other hand, in Knuth (*op. cit.*, p. 174), the example on page 100 of Kelley (1955), is the following:

> Problem A: The image under a continuous map of a continuous space is connected

Knuth *constructs* a proof, using the axioms, definitions and so on, he imagines Kelley the mathematician would have in mind – hence, the 'mathematical way of thinking' – and concludes (*ibid.*; italics added):

> The mathematical thinking involved here is somewhat different from what we have seen before; it consists primarily of constructing *chains of implications from the hypotheses to the desired conclusions*, using a repertoire of facts like "$f^{-1}$ ($A \cap B) = f^{-1}$ ($A) \cap f^{-1}$ ($B$)". This is *analogous to constructing chains of computer instructions that transform some input into some desired output, using a repertoire of subroutines*, although the topological facts have a more abstract character.

This is precisely the way the propositions of *PM* were proved (and so reported) in Newell and Simon (*op. cit.*, Part 3) – but where *heuristics* entered the proof procedure, to supplement the *mathematical way of thinking* and make it viable on the LT (or, later, in the *General Problem Solver*, *GPS*) was in using, implicitly, constructive definitions of *continuous* and *connected*, or, as clearly explained by Knuth (*ibid.*),

> Somebody had to define the concepts of *continuity* and *connectedness* in some way that would lead to a rich theory having lots of applications, thereby generalizing many special cases that had been *proved before the abstract pattern was perceived*.

On the other hand, in dissecting the proof[7] of corollary 3 to the Stone-Weierstrass Theorem given on page 100 of Bishop (1967), Knuth (ibid., p. 181) is able to make explicit the notion of *computational efficiency* – that is, a measure of computational complexity – and its *absence* in this essentially constructive – in this case, therefore, algorithmic – procedure. The fundamentally algorithmic nature of all of Bishop's proofs are devoid of any consideration of their computational efficiencies, say, as measured by some notion of computational complexity.

This is exactly the same as in the heuristic procedures used by Simon and with which Wang found himself in disagreement. Thus, heuristics, derived from processes of thought, used in exploring the space of procedures to discover proofs of (logical) propositions, in human problem-solving exercises, do not consider the constraints of computational efficiency.

But I may have drawn too hasty a conclusion in limiting human thought processes to being a heuristic hybrid of a mathematical and an algorithmic way of thinking. Knuth, in fact, concludes (*ibid.*, p. 180; italics added),

> I also had other hats representing *various modes of thought* that I used . . .
>    Thus, it seems better to think of a model in which *people have a certain number of different modes of thought*, something like genes in DNA.

Surely, this was the point that Simon was trying to make to Hao Wang?

Finally, I wish to make one final point with regard to accepting an algorithmic way of thinking. The recursion theoretic algorithmic procedures are predicated on the validity of the Church–Turing Thesis. The following are two important observations by Post (1936; 1994, p. 105; bold italics in the original):

1   Church's identification of effective calculability [an informal notion] with [the formal] notion of effective calculability . . . hides the fact that a fundamental discovery in the **limitations of the mathematizing power of Homo Sapiens has been made and binds us to the need of its continual verification**.
2   The success of [the hypothesis of identifying an informal with a formal notion, in the form of the Church–Turing Thesis] change [it] to a **natural law**.

First, it is the process of 'continual verification' that has led to valid scepticism of the universal validity of the theorem of the Halting Problem for Turing Machines. Second, 'the limitations of the mathematicing poser of Homo Sapiens' put on at least an equal footing different 'procedural ways of thinking' in discovering proofs of solutions in the context of human thought processes. Third, and – at least from my point of view – the Church–Turing *Thesis* should be viewed as a Natural *Law*. Newtonian mechanics was underpinned by *Laws* of Motion; ideal dynamics in heat physics are constrained by the Second *Law* of Thermodynamics.

That these were laws, and *not theorems*, made it possible for human imagination to conceive of violations of Euclid's fifth postulate and work with, say, hyperbolic spaces; ditto for the life lived by Homo sapiens in regions which violate the Entropy *Law, itself derived from the Second Law* of Thermodynamics.

Theorems seem to have the air of eternal truths; laws appear to need 'continual verification', and – hence – 'updating'. The point I wish to make here is that Simon implicitly worked with *heuristic laws*.

## Notes

1 See, in particular, also §3.2.2, in Chapter 3 and §2.3 in Chapter 10.
2 One of the reasons I was forced to re-evaluate my stance on algorithms versus heuristics was the belated reaction to the fact that every one of these important books by Polys had the words mathematics or mathematical in their book titles. This, coupled with a careful reading of the Knuth (*op. cit.*, pp. 176–177) reference to page 100 of volume 1 of Polya and Szegö (1972), persuaded me to alter my previous interpretations of heuristics in Polya.
3 To whom Simon's first collection of essays was dedicated (Simon, 1957):

> To
> HAROLD GUETZKOW
> Friend and Companion in Adventure.

4 The monumental *Human Problem Solving* (Newell & Simon, *op. cit.*) was, appropriately, dedicated to Cliff Shaw:

> TO CLIFF
> . . . . . who helped us
> start all this.

Why was Cliff Shaw not a co-author of Newell and Simon (ibid.)? It is a rhetorical question (I have often wondered why Shapley was not a co-author of Shubik's two-volume treatise on *Game Theory in the Social Sciences*), the answer to which only Newell or Simon (or both) knew. It seems not insignificant to note that Cliff Shaw left RAND permanently in 1971 – one year before the Newell/Simon *magnum opus* was published. In the years of their fertile collaboration, the trio were referred to as **NSS** – Newell, Shaw, Simon!
5 I dare say, in addition, also in *circuit theory* – which can be viewed graph theoretically or from the point of view of abstract dynamical systems theory. I shall deal with these issues in later chapters, particularly on constructive proof procedures beginning with the Brouwer–Heyting–Kolmogorov contributions, all the way to Martin-Löf–type theory.
6 Referred to, henceforth, as *PM*.
7 Strangely, Knuth refers only to the first part of the proof of this corollary in Bishop (ibid.), which tackles *only* the 'one-dimensional' case! Corollary 3 is (Bishop, *ibid.*, p. 100; italics in the original):

> *Every continuous function f on a compact set $X \subset R^n$ can be arbitrarily closely approximated on X by polynomial functions p: $R^n \rightarrow R$.*

Bishop considers explicit – even if ultra-'compact' – proofs of *all three* cases – that is, of $n = 1$, $X = [a, b]^n$ and $X \subset [a, b]^n$ – separately and sequentially, in increasing degrees of generality.

## References

Aiserman, Mark A., Leonid A. Gusev, Lev I. Rozoner, Irina M. Smirnova & Aleksey A. Tal (1971), *Logic, Automata and Algorithms*, Academic Press, New York.

Bishop, Errett (1967), *Foundations of Constructive Analysis*, McGraw-Hill Book Company, New York.

Cordeschi, Roberto (1996), The Role of Heuristics in Automated Theorem Proving: J.A. Robinson's Resolution Principle, *Mathware & Soft Computing*, Vol. 3, Nos. 1–2, pp. 281–293.

Duncker, Karl (1945), On Problem Solving, translated by Lynne S. Lees, *Psychological Monographs*, Vol. 58, No. 5, pp. iii–ix, 1–113.

Kelley, John (1955), *General Topology*, D. Van Nostrand, Princeton, NJ.

Knuth, Donald (1985), Algorithmic Thinking and Mathematical Thinking, *The American Mathematical Monthly*, Vol. 92, No. 3, March, pp. 170–181.

Newell, Allen & Herbert A. Simon (1972), *Human Problem Solving*, Prentice-Hall, Inc., Englewood Cliffs, NJ.

Polya, George (1945), *How to Solve It: A New Aspect of Mathematical Method*, Princeton University Press, Princeton, NJ.

Polya, George (1954a), *Mathematics and Plausible Reasoning: Volume I – Induction and Analogy in Mathematics*, Princeton University Press, Princeton, NJ.

Polya, George (1954b), *Mathematics and Plausible Reasoning: Volume II – Patterns of Plausible Inference*, Princeton University Press, Princeton, NJ.

Polya, George (1962), *Mathematical Discovery: On Understanding, Learning, and Teaching Problem Solving*, John Wiley & Sons, Inc., New York.

Polya, George & Gabor Szegö (1972), *Problems and Theorems in Analysis*, Vol. 1, Springer-Verlag, Berlin.

Post, Emil L. (1936; 1994), Finite Combinatory Processes – Formulation I, reprinted, pp. 103–105, in: *Stability, Provability, Definability – the Collected Works of Emil L. Post*, edited by Martin Davis, Birkhäuser, Basel.

Simon, Herbert A. (1957), *Models of Man: Social and Rational*, John Wiley & Sons, Inc., New York.

Simon, Herbert A. (1991), *Models of My Life*, Basic Books, New York.

Turing, Alan M. (1954), Solvable and Unsolvable Problems, *Science News*, No. 31, February, pp. 7–23.

Wang, Hao (1960), Toward Mechanical Mathematics, *IBM Journal for Research and Development*, Vol. 4, No. 1, January, pp. 2–22.

Whitehead, Alfred North & Bertrand Russell (1927), *Principia Mathematica*, Vol. 1 (Second Edition), Cambridge University Press, Cambridge.

# 6 Computable and computational complexity theoretic bases for cognitive behavioural economics[1]

## Introduction

> [L]otka was read by a few biologists; a few logicians were aware of the rapid strides of logic and the esoteric discoveries of Kurth Gödel, Alan Turing, Alonzo Church, and Emil Post. All this changed in the early postwar years,
>
> . . .
>
> Through these teachers [i.e., Carnap, Rashevsky and Schulz] I learned of Lotka . . . of Gödel – but not immediately of Church or Turing.
>
> —Simon (1991, p. 195)

These were 'the early post-war years'; by the mid-1950s Simon had mastered the fundamental contributions of Gödel, Turing, Church and Post. A little later he was a pioneering contributor to computational complexity theory and algorithmic information theory.[2]

Herbert Simon's *Cognitive Behavioural Economics* is underpinned by *a model of computation*, highlighting the complexity of behavioural decision processes on the basis of *computational complexity theory*. Simon was aware, from the outset, of the theoretical possibilities of interpreting the emerging field of computer science, providing a foundational anchor to his conviction that the best way to study decision problems in the behavioural sciences – particularly in economics – was to view *the rational agent as an information processer faced with problem solving*.

It is in this context that *problem solving* was formalized, by Simon, as that which a *boundedly rational agent*, facing a *complex environment*, and invoking the powers of a *computationally constrained cognitive mind*, satisficed – in contrast to the mathematical economist's paradigmatic Olympian rational agent's (Simon, 1983b, p. 19) optimizing framework.

Problem solving, heuristics, computation and computational complexity, in the specific context of human decision processes, underpinned by a sustained vision of *rationality as a process*, was the main foundation of Simon's research programme in the refocusing of the social sciences as cognitive behavioural decision sciences. It began with Simon's early familiarity, through his lifelong collaborator, colleague and friend, Allan Newell, with Polya's classic *How to Solve It* (Polya, 1945),[3] and continued with a serious study of Turing's pioneering studies on the *triptych* of *computability* (1936), *mechanical intelligence* (1951) and formal *problem solving* (1954). It continued with the refinement of the notion of *complexity* that had been a recurring theme in Simon's work, even in organization theory, administrative behaviour and hierarchical systems – not only in formal human problem solving in a behavioural decision making context. The study of *causal structures*, initially inspired by his work in these fields, displayed possibilities for *simplification* – but a measure of complexity (and its 'dual', simplicity) had to wait till formal computational complexity theory, nascent in the mid-1950s, became central in the core research area of computability theory.[4]

Against the backdrop provided earlier, in a sense it can be said that the main aims of this chapter are twofold: first, to clarify, interpret and reformulate bounded rationality, remaining faithful to the definitions and vision of Herbert Simon, and, second, to emphasize that bounded rationality ought to be placed and studied within a well-structured *algorithmic* context, which Simon had been advocating all his life (even if, in the early years, still only implicit).

This chapter elaborates the *computability theoretic underpinnings* of the concept of bounded rationality and discusses the modelling philosophy involved in characterizing economic agents. The discussion proceeds along the lines of *Turing computability, computational complexity* and heuristics, in the belief that this hypothetical reconstruction of the intellectual path traversed by Simon is fruitful to explore – and see where it may lead. In other words, I aim to be able to reconstruct a coherent theoretical narrative for underpinning Simon's path from bounded rationality as a basis for consistent behaviour in decision contexts, to its finessing via satisficing, in human problem solving by agents as information-processing systems. For this I underpin the narrative in terms of computable and computational complexity theory. This theoretical underpinning allows me to put the pieces of the fascinating mosaic that are the intellectual vision and life of one of 20th century's most versatile thinkers.

For example, while viewing bounded rationality in the context of human problem solving, three aspects of *problem solving* become relevant: the *existence of a method*, the *construction of a method* and *the complexity of the constructed method*. A message that this chapter hopes to convey, then, is that the bounds to human rationality will also be dictated by the complexity of different problems that the problem solver encounters and the research programme on *Human Problem Solving* initiated by Herbert Simon becomes a natural path along this direction.

In section 2, therefore, an analysis of such a definition of *bounded rationality* and discussions on *satisficing, procedural rationality* and *heuristics* can be found. In section 3, the meeting ground between *Turing's computability* and *problem solving*, on one hand, and Simon's work on *Human Problem Solving* and *Information Processing Systems*, on the other, is explored. Section 4 contains a discussion and interpretation of Simon's empirical grounding of behaviourally rational behaviour via computational complexity theory. A brief concluding section summarizes the vision aimed at, in this *computable and computational complexity theoretic interpretation of Simon's research programme* – in addition to my own vision of how one may go 'beyond Simon', standing on his giant intellectual shoulders.

I would like to point out that Simon's cognitive behavioural economics, as characterized above, is to be distinguished sharply from what I have in other writings (Kao & Velupillai, 2012; Kao & Velupillai, 2015) called *Modern Behavioural Economics.*[5] The latter is simply a 'revisionistic' form of traditional Neoclassical, subjective expected utility maximization economics, with no anchoring whatsoever in a model of computation. This was strongly underlined by Simon himself, when he – presciently, as always – pointed out (Simon, 1958; 1982, p. 384, footnote 4) that

> [t]here is a great danger at the present moment that the economists and statisticians will carry the day even within the territories of psychology and sociology. As can be seen from the recent review article, 'The Theory of Decision Making,' by Ward Edwards, *Psychological Bulletin*, July, 1954, and *Decision Processes*, edited by Robert Thrall et al., John Wiley & Sons, 1954, the behavioral scientists are currently much entranced by the economic models of rationality, and inclined to accept the 'definition of the situation' proposed by the latter.

Alas, Modern Behavioural Economics seems to have confirmed Simon's prescience!

## A boundedly rational reconstruction of Simon's computable behavioural economics

> In my 1956 paper, 'Rational Choice and the Structure of the Environment,' I wove around the metaphor of the maze a formal model of how an organism (a person?) could meet a multiplicity of needs and wants at a satisfactory level and survive without drawing upon superhuman powers of intelligence and computation. The model provided a practicable design for a creature of *bounded rationality*, as all we creatures are.
>
> —Simon (1991, p. 175; italics added)

*Bounded rationality* – together with *satisficing* – is the central theme of the *Classical Behavioural Economics* of Herbert Simon. It appears, now, to be ubiquitously accepted as a replacement for the otherwise *computably infeasible* notion of *Olympian rationality*, which was strongly disapproved by Herbert Simon. Contrary to popular understanding, Simon perceived bounded rationality as *the more general notion* compared to Olympian rationality. Orthodox economics literature (e.g., Sargent, 1993) tends to promote the opposite view, that bounded rationality is a formally constrained version of Olympian rationality.

The theory of *Human Problem Solving* (Newell & Simon, 1972) incorporates these two essential notions in interpreting the decision making processes of the rational agent, now interpreted as an information processor. Although Simon almost never phrased his theories and concepts in terms of computability and computational complexity theories *explicitly*, he devoted himself to construct more realistic boundaries of human rationality, however, always *implicitly* within the framework of rationality as being procedural (algorithmic) and in turn, encapsulated by Turing computability and constrained by theories of computational complexity. This is amply evident in the two pioneering classics of Classical Behavioural Economics, Simon (1955, 1956), where, in fact, even the notion of *computability*, in its strict recursion theoretic senses, and *complexity*, in its computational complexity theoretic senses – although the theory was still in its very nascent stage – are copiously invoked and used.

## §2  Computable bounded rationality

> Theories that incorporate constraints on the information-processing capacity of the actor may be called *theories of bounded rationality.*
>
> —Simon (1972, p. 162; italics added)

The term bounded rationality was coined by Herbert Simon in his introduction to the fourth part of his collected works – **Models of Man**. He wrote,

> The alternative approach employed in these papers is based on what I shall call *the principle of bounded rationality*:
>
> > *The capacity of the human mind for formulating and solving complex problems is very small compared with the size of the problems whose solution is required for objectively rational behavior in the real world – or even for a reasonable approximation to such objective rationality.*
>
> If the principle is correct, then the goal of classical economic theory – to predict the behavior of rational man without making an empirical investigation of his psychological properties – is unattainable.
>
> (Simon, 1957, pp. 198–199; italics in the original)

Although the term appeared in 1957, the original idea of bounded rationality can be found in both Simon (1955) and Simon (1956) and can eventually be traced back to Simon (1947).

After Simon proposed his initial models of rational behaviour, successive models of bounded rationality that were developed had an early and reliable report in March (1978), showing the many different directions in which it was developed by Simon and others, its mild extension and reinterpretations. Often, any *inconsistent* behaviour with respect to orthodox, Olympian, rationality is perceived as a *mistake* on the part of the agent. Consequently, bounded rationality has been explained as the mistake or shortcoming of human beings that arises because of a variety of factors (largely non-cognitively psychological) for about 50 years. Modern behavioural economics is not the only field that considers bounded rationality as a compromised concept from normative rationality. As March – surely with Simon's endorsement – noted very early on,

> [a]lternatively, one can recall all of the deviations from normative specifications as stupidity, errors that should be corrected; and undertake to transform

the style of exciting humans into the styles anticipated by the theory. This has, for the most part, been the strategy of operations and management analysis for the past twenty years; and it has had its successes. But it has also had failures.

(March, 1978, p. 597)

On the surface, Simon's descriptions of bounded rationality might seem that the existence of a 'bound' is simply due to the limitations of a psychological – more precisely, a *cognitive*, computationally underpinned – nature in human decision making. When we consider *both* the decision maker *and* the associated, or 'coupled', environment, bounded rationality emerges naturally within such a setting. Given the characteristics of the environment and the decision maker, '*satisficing*' (first used in Simon, 1956, p. 129, contrasting it, explicitly, with optimize) is the reasonable action to be pursued in a procedurally rational decision-making setting, and *heuristics* are the means through which boundedly rational satisficing behaviour becomes algorithmically implementable.

Later, through the interpretation of the principle of bounded rationality, with computable foundations, it is made clear that bounded rationality is neither *irrationality* (Simon, 1957, p. 200) nor *approximate* optimality (Simon, 1972, p. 170).

The models of *rational* decision making suggested in Simon (1955, 1956) do not require utility functions to be defined over (even *countably finite*[6]) alternatives. They provide some important ideas regarding how a boundedly rational entity could be – indeed, should be – modelled. In, for example, Simon (1955), a simplified value function $V(\cdot)$ which takes only two values (1,0) was introduced.[7] The binary values can be associated with 'satisfactory and unsatisfactory', 'accept and reject' and so on. The domain of function $V$ is $S$, the set of all possible outcomes which is mapped to $A$, a set of all *behavioural alternatives*. This is in order to distinguish the means from the ends.

The ensuing rational decision-process is defined as follows:

1    Search for a set of possible outcomes $S' \subseteq S$ such that the pay-off function is satisfactory ($V(s) = 1$), $\forall s \in S'$.
2    Search for behavioural alternatives $a \in A'$, whose possible outcomes are all in $S'$ through the mapping.

This process does not guarantee the existence and uniqueness of a solution until the sequence in which the alternatives arrive and the dynamics of *aspiration levels* (a *psychological concept*) are *formally* incorporated into it.

In real life, the alternatives are often examined sequentially, and the first satisfactory alternative evaluated is the one that is selected. The difficulty of discovering a satisfactory choice depends on the cost of obtaining better information regarding the mapping of $A$ on $S$. Thus, *if* the aspiration level grows when the cost of search is low and declines when the cost of search is high, then this dynamic can lead to near uniqueness and existence of a solution in the long run.[8]

In Simon (1955), the focus is on suggesting a dynamic process for decision makers, without going into the details of the mapping between $A$ and $S$. However, in Simon (1956), the focus is more on the other important aspect – the environment. Here, the organism is assumed to have a single and a fixed aspiration level – it needs only food. But the food heaps are located in such a way that the organism has to walk in a maze, where there are branches at each node. Each node is a possible location for food. This is combined with the constraint that its vision is limited and therefore it cannot see as far as it would like. However, if it sees a food heap in the range of its vision, it knows the way to reach the food. It has to eat the food before it dies of starvation, and there is a maximal number of moves it can make after eating before its energy runs out. These are some of the parameters[9] regarding the environment that the organism faces and the 'physical constrains' that the organism have:

- $p$, $0 < p < 1$, is the percentage of branch points, randomly[10] distributed, at which food is found.
- $d$ is the average number of paths diverging from each branch point.
- $v$ is the number of moves ahead the organism can see.
- $H$ is the maximum number of moves the organism can make between meals without starving.

The first two parameters concern the environment (exogenously given *problem space*), on how the targets are distributed and (conjectures) on the size of the problem space is. The last two parameters are regarding the organism on how far it can search and its capacity for searching. This setting can be applied to a much broader class of problems. The parameters do not have to be limited only by physical needs and constraints. Especially, *probability* is *not* central in many realistic cases of decision making for Simon. For example, in chess, a game that was studied intensively by Simon, the goals (some particular patterns) that a player might seek are *not* randomly distributed in the problem space.

Integrating the models in the two papers mentioned earlier, we can summarize the situation of rational decision making postulated by Simon as the following: There are always two aspects of decision making – the environment and the mechanism of the decision maker. The two aspects are highly interrelated.

The characteristics of the environment or the problem space are the following:

- The alternatives are assumed to be formalizable as discrete values – that is, can be *effectively enumerated*.
- The alternatives or the offers arrive in a *sequence*, while the order is not necessarily known.

The characteristics of decision makers are as follows:

- Satisficing (influenced by aspiration levels – hence, eventually, coupled to the *SAT* problem of computational complexity theory)

- Limited computational capacities (such as time and memory – hence, eventually, underpinned by computational complexity theory)
- Use of *heuristics* to search (hence, in some cases, *algorithmic* search)
- Some knowledge or clue regarding the *stopping rule* for searching (starting from any node – the *halting state for a Turing Machine*)
- Adapting aspiration levels (the eventual notion of learning machines is built from the basics here)
- Knowledge of what to choose and what not to choose (depending on the 'state' of a Turing Machine)

The problem space, viewed formally, as a tree, is 'explored' by the decision maker, often initial conjectures are obtained by prior theoretical understanding and some elementary, preliminary, computer simulations. This problem step-up of 'searching in a tree' is, surely, inspired by the means–end schema proposed in chapter IV of Simon (1947). In Simon's view, the description of the environment depends on the needs, drive and goals of the decision maker. This seems to underpin the '*maze*' metaphor that Simon frequently and fruitfully invokes and suggests for many decision problems in real life. Therefore, human decision making, which is part of human thinking activity, can be associated in fertile ways to many deep areas, such as computer science, graph theory, formal logic and so on, as Savitch, whose important result will be referred to later, observed, in a similar context:

> Informally, a maze is a set of rooms connected by one way corridors. Certain rooms are designated goal rooms and one room is designated the start room. Thus, a maze is a directed graph with certain nodes or rooms distinguished. The maze is threadable if there is a path from the start room to some goal room.
>
> (Savitch, 1970, p. 187)

It is important to note that the probabilities that are used to calculate the likelihood of failing to survive or finding a solution in the model discussed earlier are *trivial or meaningless* in many real-life problems:

> From still a third standpoint, the chess player's difficulty in behaving rationally has nothing to do with *uncertainty* – whether of consequences or alternatives – but is a matter of *complexity*. For there is no risk or uncertainty, in the sense in which those terms are used in economics or statistical decision theory, in the game of chess. As von Neumann and Morgenstern observe, it is a game of perfect information. No probabilities of future events need enter the calculations, and no contingencies, in a statistical sense, arise.
>
> From a game-theoretical standpoint, the presence of the opponent does not introduce contingencies. The opponent can always be counted on to do his worst. The point becomes clear if we replace the task of playing chess with the task of proving theorems. In the latter task, there is no opponent. Nor are there contingencies: the true and the derivable theorems reside eternally in

Plato's heaven. *Rationality in theorem proving is a problem only because the maze of possible proof paths is vast and complex.*

(Simon, 1972, pp. 169–170; italics added)

However, it is debatable whether the opponent can be counted on to do the worst in games like chess. The search spaces of games like chess or GO are *certain*, known to both players, but only waiting to be *discovered* (as in 'Plato's heaven'). We can also imagine the opponent as using *heuristics* in her own mind, in order to decide what the possible reacting moves of his opponent will be, where outguessing as infinite regress indeterminacy has plenty of scope for indeterminacies, but can be tamed by constructive or computable formalisms with convincing simplicity. Facing such indeterminacies, and interpreting them as complexity, the decision maker has to incorporate *some mechanisms to terminate the searching process.* This leads to *satisficing.*[11]

Many problems have relatively closed and a pre-defined problem spaces, though the problem space (tree) may be – in fact, *are* – massive. There are many other problems which are far more complex, for example, finding a particular quotation amongst the books in a library. However, most of the time, the material that one is looking for is in the formalizable neighbourhood of an initially conjectured structure of the complex problem space, but it is hard to find a good *heuristic* – a *practicable* algorithm – to reach it.

### §2.1 Algorithmic satisficing and Olympian optimizing

A decision maker who chooses the best available alternative according to some criterion is said to *optimize*; one who chooses an alternative that meets or exceeds specified criteria, but that is not guaranteed to be either unique or in any sense the best, is said to *satisfice*. The term 'satisfice' which appears in the *Oxford English Dictionary* as a Northumbrian synonym for 'satisfy', was borrowed for this new use [in Simon, 1956].

—Simon (1997, p. 295; first two italicized words added)

Satisficing is the other pillar, the first being bounded rationality, on which Simon's behavioural economics is underpinned. Here, the decision maker does not look for an optimal choice, the search 'procedure' will itself, if constructed adaptively, lead the decision maker and problem solver to choose a satisfactory outcome as and when one encounters it.[12] This would mean that even though there might be an outcome that could yield a higher level of satisfaction, the choice process stops once a 'good enough' alternative that matches the aspiration level is met. Simon also comments on the relation between satisficing and optimizing and that the latter is a special case of the former:

A satisficing decision procedure can often be turned into a procedure for optimizing by introducing a rule for optimal amount of search, or, what amounts to the same thing, a rule for fixing the aspiration level optimally. . . .

Although such a translation is formally possible, to carry it out in practice requires additional information and assumptions beyond those needed for satisficing.

(Simon, 1972, p. 170)

For a decision maker, the act of optimization would require *a priori* knowledge of *all* the available options and the associated outcomes. Moreover, the decision maker also requires *a method* (i.e., an algorithm) for listing all the options and to compare each of them. When the decision maker is confronted with multiple goals, then the association between choice and outcomes becomes even more complex. As Simon remarks, this is both unrealistic and excessively demanding (Simon, 1956, p. 136). Simon further emphasizes that the optimizing approach facing real-life complexity is, indeed, approximate optimization. The statisficing approach, on the other hand, is linked to the dynamics of aspiration levels and tackles the problem very differently. I have developed two formal results, in Velupillai (2000, chapter 3) that conceptualize, as theorems, the preceding considerations by Simon:

*Theorem 1*
There is no *effective procedure* to generate preference orderings.
*Theorem 2*
Given a class of choice functions that do generate preference orderings (pick out the set of maximal alternatives) for any agent, there is no *effective procedure* to *decide* (algorithmically) whether or not any arbitrary choice function is a member of the given class.

In Velupillai (*op. cit.*, 2010), I have recursion theoretically formalized decision making as an act of algorithmically choosing a subset from a finite, non-empty, countable set, as opposed to uncountable infinite sets, by using a computable choice function. *Solving* optimally an instance of the latter class can be shown to be equivalent to *solving* linear integer programming problems. I, then, transformed the linear integer programming problem into the optimization problem of a combinatorial system, and then constructed abstract Turing machines to study the characteristics of problem solving. The key here is the demonstrable formal double equivalence between bounded rationality and the behaviour of a Turing Machine during a formal (symbolic) computation and 'algorithmically choosing' and 'satisficing'.

### §2.2 *Procedural and substantive rationality*

The search for *computational efficiency* is a search for *procedural rationality*, and computational mathematics is a normative theory of such rationality. In this normative theory, there is no point in prescribing a particular substantively rational solution if there exists no procedure for finding that solution with an acceptable amount of computing effort.

—Simon (1976, p. 133)

The theory of computational efficiency is computational complexity theory. The part of computational mathematics that formalizes the notion of a normative theory of rationality is the computing activity of a Turing Machine, subject to the Church–Turing Thesis. The dichotomy between procedural rationality, underpinning Simon's kind of (classical) behavioural economics and the substantive rationality of orthodox behavioural economics is highlighted by the divide between the behaviour of an ideal computing machine – the Turing Machine – and that between one that is constrained by time and space constraints, encapsulating economic costs, formalized by computational complexity theory (reversing the two former dichotomies).

When we begin to claim that 'This decision maker is satisficing', the next question we may ask primarily becomes 'What are the procedures the decision maker uses?' instead of 'What does the decision maker choose?' The fundamental distinction between Simon's approach and the other theories that invoke behavioural traits, such as in Modern Behavioural Economics, is the insistence on 'methods' or 'procedures' involved in choosing and their centrality in the theory of decision making. The link between a procedurally rational choice and computation is present from the very outset in Simon's scheme. The insistence here is on the complexity of this decision process, in terms of the effort devoted to doing it.

### *§2.3 Heuristics*

> Most weak methods require larger or smaller amounts of search before problem solutions are found, but the search need not be blind trial-and-error – in fact, usually cannot be, for the search spaces are generally far too vast to allow unselective trial and error to be effective. Weak methods generally incorporate Polya's idea of *"heuristics"* – *rules of thumb* that allow search generators to be highly selective, instead of searching the entire space.
>
> —Simon (1983a, p. 4570; italics added)

Simon's use, refinement and explorations of formal decision making and formalizing problem solving were decisively influenced by Polya's 'little' classic of 1945 (Polya, 1945), from even before he completed Simon (1947). There is still no better description of the nature and scope of 'heuristics' than given in that Polya classic:[13]

> **Heuristic** or *heuretic*, or *'ars inveniendi'* was the name of a certain branch of study, not very clearly circumscribed, belonging to *logic*, or to *philosophy*, or to *psychology*, often outlined, seldom presented in detail, and as good as forgotten today. The aim of heuristic is to study the *methods and rules of discovery and invention* . . . .
>
>     . . .
>
> *Heuristic*, as an adjective, means *'serving to discover'*.
>
> (Polya, op. cit., pp. 112–3;
> bold emphasis in the original; italics added)

No one person made the notion of 'heuristic' to underpin (mathematical) logic, philosophy (of science) and (cognitive) psychology of the *sciences of the artificial* (Simon, 1996) and for 'serving to discover' (Simon, 1977; Langley et al., 1987) more than Herbert Simon. From an early reference to 'rules of thumb', surely derived from 'rules of anticipated reactions' in Simon (1947) and 'rule of action' (March & Simon, 1958) to fully fledged formal algorithms, via *heuristics* in Newell and Simon (1956) was *one of* the – many – computable and computational complexity theoretic paths Simon took.

Newell and Simon initiated the project of constructing a programme – an algorithm – which learns to play good chess, in 1954, while they pinned down the investigation of *heuristics* on proving theorems in *Principia Mathematica* to start with. The programme they designed was hand-simulated first and interpreted into machine language which gave birth to the *Logic Theorist*, which was their first example of human problem solving (Newell et al., 1958). However, it was subject to an uncharacteristically strong criticism from the otherwise enlightened Hao Wang:

> There is no need to kill a chicken with a butcher's knife. Yet the net impression is that Newell-Shaw-Simon failed even to kill the chicken with their butcher's knife. . . . To argue the superiority of 'heuristic' over algorithmic methods by choosing a particularly inefficient algorithm seems hardly just.
>
> (Wang, 1970, p. 227)

It was unfortunate that Wang had misunderstood Simon's stated priorities (Simon,1991, pp. 209–210) and the path to them, from the concept of 'rules of thumb'. Newell and Simon were involved in finding procedures used by human beings in solving problems and used this information to construct the programme *Logic Theorist*.

What are *heuristics*, if not algorithms? A perceptive remark on heuristics is that 'a method is simply a plan that you use twice' (Newell & Simon, 1972, p. 835), which, on the 'third' occasion approaches the formal status of an algorithm. That is, heuristics represents the methods that human beings actually use to search in a problem space. They are nothing but algorithms.[14]

Algorithms are formally connected to symbolic structures which are underpinned by computability theory. Physical, symbolic systems such as human beings and digital computers, as Newell and Simon pointed out, can process only a finite number of steps in any given interval of time. However, the finiteness to which the most general model of algorithms – Turing Machine – appeals is in many cases not strong enough to show the severe limitation that human minds have to confront (Newell & Simon, 1976, p. 120). Empirical boundaries correspond to the level of complexity that the human minds can actually handle (see also the contents of Simon's letter, referred to earlier, in note 6). A study of heuristics is crucial in order to understand how human beings handle problems whose complexity is beyond the empirical boundary. In other words, heuristics act as procedures that help reduce the problem to a level of complexity which can be handled algorithmically

The approach described in *Human Problem Solving* (Newell & Simon, 1972) that encompasses heuristics is underpinned by computational complexity theory, which in turn is based on computability theory. Moreover, the significance of heuristics is not revealed until some algorithmic impossibilities concerned with procedural decision making are formally proved. To further explore this connection, we need to examine the interconnections between the approaches of Turing and Herbert Simon to Machine and Human Problem Solving.

## §3  From Turing to Simon: problem solving and decision problems

> Given a Diophantine equation with any number of unknown quantities and with rational integral numerical coefficients: To devise a process according to which it can be determined by a finite number of operations whether the equation is solvable in rational integers.
>
> —Hilbert (1902, p. 451)

That's where it all began! This came to be known, famously, as *Hilbert's Tenth Problem* and, as a decision problem, could not be answered without a formal definition of 'a process according to which it can be determined by a finite number of operations', in other words, a formal definition of the intuitive notion of an algorithm. Until about 1936–1937, when the definitions of such a finite procedure was defined formally, mathematicians had only an *intuitive* notion of an algorithm.

I have always wondered, without any idea of a conjecture, why Simon did not try to tackle this problem – especially via the notion of a *heuristic* as used in problem solving.

Church defined algorithm (effective calculability) with the λ-calculus, and Turing defined it in terms of Turing Machines. They were *proved* to be equivalent definitions, and the intuitive notion of algorithm captured by these definitions imply the so-called Church–Turing Thesis. *If this thesis is true*, then the halting problem for Turing machines is **unsolvable**. Church (1938) mentioned that the intuitive notion of an effective procedure can be formalized in three different ways: Turing Machines (Turing, 1936; λ-definability, Church, 1936) and the general recursive functions (of Herbrand and Gödel, Kleene, 1936a). The equivalence of the three notions had been proved in Kleene (1936b) and Turing (1937). The equivalence of recursiveness and computability enables one to apply the definition of recursive function to prove more classes of computable functions. (Davis, 1982, chap. 3). The consensus on the notion of effective calculability was reached in the late 1930s, and this led to the development of computability theory.

Herbert Simon was fully aware of all these developments at a very early stage. Both Herbert Simon and Allen Newell were recipients of the ACM *Turing Award* in 1975 for their contribution to the human problem-solving approach, which they initiated in the mid-1950s together with Cliff Shaw. It is evident that their work, where computation plays an important role, was grounded on Turing's contributions:

Concurrently with Turing's work appeared the work of the logicians Emil Post and (independently) Alonzo Church. Starting from independent notions of logistic systems (Post productions and recursive function, respectively), they arrived at analogous results on *undecidability* and *universality* – results that were soon shown to imply that all three systems were equivalent. Indeed, the convergence of all these attempts to define the most general class of *information processing systems* provides some of the force of our conviction that *we have captured the essentials of information processing in these models*.

> (Newell & Simon, 1976, p. 117; italics added)

If there were any lingering doubts that Simon's boundedly rational agent, encapsulated in the formalism of an information processing system, is processing symbol sequences in the same way as a Turing Machine, subject to the same computational complexity norms, then the above observation should dispel them once and for all, at least we hope so. The *Human* Problem Solving information-processing system of **Herbert Simon** was exactly equivalent to the Mathematical Problem-Solving *Machine* constructed by **Alan Turing** – *if we can also suppose that heuristics are algorithms*.

Although Turing does not seem to have made an attempt to solve Diophantine decision problems in the above Hilbertian sense, he 'constructed' the hypothetical Turing Machine for solving another decision problem posed by Hilbert in 1928 (Turing, 1936), and theoretical developments based on Turing machines contributed eventually to the negative solution of *Hilbert's 10th problem*, 70 years after the question was posed (see Matiyasevich, 1994, for details). The decision problem that concerned Turing, in the specific context of *problem solving*, was general: Is there a systematic procedure to decide whether a given problem (puzzle) is solvable or not? This decision problem regards all those problems which can be transformed into what he called 'substitution puzzles'. The answer to this was proved to be negative by Turing. The negative solution to this decision problem indicates that we need to develop *specific* procedures in order to decide *specific* problems. There is no *general* solution – that is, algorithmic procedure – to any given problem. This has a direct bearing for the theories of decision making that rely on optimization, without addressing the procedural aspects. This is also why Simon, understanding the need for specific studies, indulged in simulation by computation, underpinned by *heuristic procedures*, to explore the structure of problem spaces – not only, indeed, not even, for popular reasons of cognitive computational constraints.

In order to understand how he arrived at the negative solution, it could be useful to take a close look at the problem setting – which also elucidates why, again even if in an *ex post* sense, Simon may have concentrated so much in understanding *Human Problem Solving* by studying games and puzzles:

> Given any puzzle [problem] we can find a corresponding substitution puzzle which is equivalent to it in the sense that given a solution of the one we can easily use it to find a solution of the other. If the original puzzle is concerned

with rows of pieces of a finite number of different kinds, then the substitution may be applied as an alternative set of rules to the pieces of the original puzzle. A transformation can be carried out by the rules of the original puzzle if and only if it can be carried out by the substitutions and leads to a final position from which all marker symbols have disappeared.

(Turing1954, p. 15; italics in the original)

He further wrote, "In effect there is no opposition to the view that every puzzle is equivalent to a substitution puzzle."[15] The production rules[16] that are introduced in Turing's example follow type 0 grammar,[17] though, the time at which Turing proposed it was before the Chomsky hierarchy was defined (Chomsky, 1956, 1959).

It is assumed that there exists a systematic procedure for deciding whether a puzzle is solvable or not. At the same time, this systematic procedure can be transformed into a substitution puzzle whose set of rules is $K$ (determined finite natural number). Naturally, $K$ has unambiguous moves, and it always comes out with final result no matter what $R$, the puzzle of interest, is. In particular, it will come out with, say $B$(lack), when $R$ belongs to class $I$, and $W$(hite) when it belongs to class $II$. Then, when we look at the puzzle $P(K,K)$[18] to be investigated, we will find inconsistent results. That is, we should be able to classify that $P(K,K)$ belongs to class $I$ or $II$. But according to the substitution puzzle $K$, it has the potential to result in both possibilities; as a result, we could not classify it into either one or the other of the two classes. This leads to a contradiction!

This demonstration towards showing that there is no general algorithm for deciding whether a puzzle is solvable or not suggests that we need to seek for separate algorithms in order to decide whether a kind of problem is solvable or not, given the initial puzzle and the desired outcome.

It was here where the formalized, machine-based problem-solving methods of Turing synchronized perfectly with the information processing system that was the human problem solver of Simon. Thus, it was also natural that the ground where bounded rationality and computability meet is clearly presented in Newell and Simon (1972), where symbolic systems can be adopted to understand human thinking, especially in the activities of information processing. In the theory of *Human Problem Solving*, the *vague* idea of an "environment" is precisely formulated into a "problem space" and a problem solver into an *Information Processing System*. In addition, in Simon's approach, the notion of "complex problems" needs to be given a *precise* definition, and it is done within the context of Turing's computability theory and computational complexity theory.

## §4    Herbert Simon's cognitively rational problem solver and computational complexity theory

Moreover, since *Homo sapiens* shares some important psychological invariants with certain nonbiological systems – the computers – I shall want to make frequent reference to them also. One could even say that my account will cover the topic *human* and *computer psychology*.

—Simon (1990, p. 3; italics added)

Simon stressed the infeasibility of a procedure of optimization by showing that digital computers which overpower human beings in terms of their physical computational capacity find their strength insignificant when confronted with the *complexity of real world problems* (Simon,1976, p. 135). Understanding our own limits is one of the lessons we obtain from digital computers. The same logic should be applied to economic decision makers, as Simon suggested in the following:

> The human mind is programmable: it can acquire an enormous variety of different skills, behaviour patterns, problem solving repertoires, and percep-
> tual habits. . . . . There seems to be no escape. If economics is to deal with uncertainty, it will have to understand how human beings in fact behave in the face of uncertainty, and by what *limits of* information and *computability* they are bound.
>
> (Simon, 1976, p. 144; italics added)

For empirical reasons, the unsolvability of a problem does not really stop people from looking for a solution for it, particularly not Herbert Simon. Sipser admirably summarizes the *pros* and *cons* of proving the unsolvability of a problem and then coming to terms with it:

> After all, showing that a problem is *unsolvable* doesn't appear to be any use if you have to solve it. You need to study this phenomenon for two reasons. First, knowing when a problem is *algorithmically unsolvable* is useful because then you realize that the problem must be simplified or altered before you can find an algorithmic solution. Like any tool, computers have capabilities and limitations that must be appreciated if they are to be used well. The second reason is *cultural*. Even if you deal with problems that clearly are solvable, a glimpse of the unsolvable can stimulate your imagination and help you gain an important perspective on computation.
>
> (Sipser, 1997, p. 151; italics added)

As I have stressed, Simon was concerned with both empirical and theoretical questions of decision making and he grounded himself, for tackling these questions *effectively*, on Turing Computability. He later looked for computational complexity in average cases or empirical complexity that is relevant for human problem solving. Now that we have seen that there exist algorithmically unsolvable decision problems, we can appreciate how Turing computability should be the outer limit for human rationality or machine computability. Anything that goes beyond Turing computability is clearly meaningless (especially for procedural decision making) since even the most powerful abstract computing machine cannot solve such a problem, even in principle. But this can only be an outer boundary of how far procedural rationality can go in theory because the notion of pure computability in theory does not take into account time and space limitations, which are essential to solve a problem or compute a function. They become particularly important in the case of human decision making. This only reinforces the conclusions and strengthens the concepts that Simon advocated. This was why Simon spent so much time in understanding the nature and structure of a problem – against the backdrop of a deep knowledge of the limits of computability – so that essentials need not be sacrificed in the simplifications that had to be achieved to make the unsolvable approach empirical solvability:

> How complex or simple a structure is depends critically upon the way in which we describe it. Most of the complex structures found in the world are enormously redundant, and we can use this redundancy to simplify their description. But to use it, to achieve the simplification, we must find the right representation.
>
> (Simon, 1962, p. 481)

The preceding observation can be interpreted in terms of computational complexity theory, where the complexity of a problem is determined by the time and space requirements of an algorithm that solves the problem.[19] There are three aspects of problem solving: the inherent solvability of a problem, the procedure to solve a problem and the complexity of the procedure. Provided we have Turing's abstract model of computation, we can use this idea to construct an abstract machine for solving a particular problem. We can then analyse the number of steps or memory that the algorithm would require, *approximately*, without going about to count the *precise* time and space required by the problems of the same kind. This helps us to have an idea of the associated difficulty of a problem we are dealing with before we really start to solve it. Computational complexity provides a more solid, inner boundary of bounded rationality with Turing computability as its outer boundary. Although the scale of time steps and space (memory) that computational complexity theory regards is normally pretty large, it is important to have a general idea of tackling a problem by knowing the complexity of the algorithm which solves it. In theory, the reducibility among problems is also used to study the complexity without actually constructing a real algorithm.

As far as problem solving is concerned, according to Turing's interpretation, a decision problem is to decide whether one can change a string of symbols to the desired string of symbols, by only using a set of rules that are given in advance. Knowing that a decision problem is unsolvable leads us to ask different questions and try to solve them; otherwise, it provides no practical help when we try to solve a problem. We need to find a set of rules for a substitution puzzle, that is an 'algorithm', to solve our problem. However, even if we have an algorithm to solve a certain kind of problem, it does not guarantee that we can solve the problem within the desirable period of time. If the problem involved is complex, it can demand immense amount of computation by the problem solver. Time complexity and space complexity are very useful and standard tools for providing measures of quantitative ideas on how much effort is needed for solving a problem.

When we have an algorithm for solving a problem, we can look at its general behaviour and analyse how many time steps and the space or memory it would require. Time complexity tells the number of steps needed for running an algorithm, and space complexity takes care of the memory needed. Time and space complexity are the functions of size of input, for example, playing a 3-disk *Tower of Hanoi*[20] needs much less time steps than does a 10-disk Tower of Hanoi. In many cases, it is very difficult to obtain the exact reduced form of time and space complexity of an algorithm. Therefore, in computational complexity, asymptotic notations, such as $O(n)$, are used to present the asymptotic behaviour of an algorithm as the asymptotic approximation of the true function behind it. When large input sizes are involved, exponential time grows drastically faster than polynomial time, and the problem becomes unmanageable, in precisely definable ways, very quickly.

It should be remembered that there exists always more than one method to solve a problem; therefore, the complexity of a problem is determined by the method that solves it.[21]

Space complexity[22] has attracted *relatively* less attention and effort compared to time complexity, despite the powerful result that PSPACE = NPSPACE.[23] By default, when the complexity of a problem is discussed, time complexity is the one that is referred to. Arguably, it is because whether **P = NP** is one of most popular unsolved problems. We, however, would like to emphasize, for the domain of *human* problem solving, *space complexity is at least as important as time complexity*. Although, there is no doubt that the architecture of human brain has the potential to store huge amount of knowledge, the amount of information that minds can process at a given moment is severely limited.

For example, it is very tough to calculate 4,593 * 3,274 in the mind for an ordinary person, unless this person has pencil and paper at hand or he or she is an expert in arithmetic calculations. Such calculation requires a certain amount of temporary memory which is a function of input size. In terms of time limitation, minds are constrained by attention span, apart from other externally imposed time constraints; for example, a chess player has to make a move in five minutes. How minds are constrained by time and memory varies with different contexts and structure of the problems and among different persons. Furthermore, these two dimensions should not be completely independent; that is, the memory constraints affect the time which is needed for solving a problem and vice versa. Therefore, it is important to investigate the time complexity of a problem (or an algorithm) together with the space complexity; consequently, we will be able to know what kinds of heuristics are needed based on these two dimensions. Space complexity is even more crucial when the problem concerned requires no aid of external memory.

In spite of the fact that the time and space complexity of an algorithm can be analysed, human beings are constrained very differently from (digital) computers. We normally have only a certain amount of time to make a decision, and we have very limited working memory (no matter expert or layman) to process this task, regardless of the presumably unlimited long-term memory. We are forced to use those algorithms which will be able to halt within a certain amount of time, by applying the knowledge and experience we have in the long-term memory. Although, we are often assigned to a task like 'find the best person for this job', we are not able to solve it as an optimization problem. At best, we will have the criteria for appropriate candidates and consider only a small group of people. Depending on the time and memory we are supplied with and the procedure we should go through, we have to be selective to different degrees.

Turing (1951) suggested that a machine should be programmed to learn to play the games like chess, GO and bridge. Chess is the recurring example and an important one for Simon; it is also one of the examples of **complex combinatorial problems**[24] which make brute-force algorithms infeasible. Even though the problem space of chess is closed and certain, the massive size of the game tree prevents human beings or even supercomputers to use brute search algorithm. Let us take the number of the possible continuations of chess, which is approximated in Shannon (1950), as an example. If we want to know, from the beginning of the game, whether Black or White has a winning strategy, we have roughly $10^{120}$ variations to calculate; when each branch reaches its end, we can see whether that branches leads to a win, a loss or a draw. Suppose we have a high-speed computer which uses only one microsecond ($10^{-6}$ a second) for one variation, for searching the whole problem space; it will take $10^{100}$ million years! Obviously, in real life, different actions should be taken, that is why we can always find plenty of chess tactical guides in the bookshops.

Finally, some notes on *satisficing* as an instance of the *satisfiability* problem[25] of computational complexity theory. Simon showed that Olympian rationality is a special case of bounded rationality by appealing to the act of *satisficing*. He suggested descriptively that a model of satisficing can be turned into optimizing by setting the aspiration level at an optimal level. This lucid point can be substantiated mathematically by applying the results in combinatorial complexity.

The formal decision problem framework for a boundedly rational information processing system can be constructed in one of the following ways: systems of linear Diophantine inequalities, systems of linear equations in non-negative integer variables, integer programming. Solving the former three problems are equivalent in the sense that the method of solving one problem provides a method to solve the other two as well. The Integer Linear Programming (**ILP**) problem and **SAT** can be translated both ways; that is, one can be transformed into another.

The satisfiability problem is one of the important problems in modern computer science. In Velupillai (2010), it is demonstrated that **SAT** problem is the meeting ground of Diophantine problems and satisficing, in turn, this connection leads to the conclusion that bounded rationality is the superset of Olympian rationality, which Simon had been advocating.

## §5  Concluding remarks: can we go beyond Simon?

So when we reach a bifurcation in the road of the labyrinth, 'something' chooses which branch to take. And the reason for my researches, and the reason why labyrinths have fascinated me, has been my desire to observe people as they encounter bifurcations and try to understand why they take the road to the right or to the left.
—Simon (1991, p. 179)[26]

We cannot only observe and be guided by the lessons Simon learnt, formalized and experimented with, as he observed boundedly rational agents negotiating the maze of life and its problems. We have to go beyond, standing on his mighty shoulders. How might we do it?

There may well be many ways to go 'beyond Simon'. We mention just one possibility, only because we think it encapsulates every precept we think Simon's vision worked with: the game of GO – as a Game, as a domain for the articulation of formal problem solving in both his and Turing's senses and, of course, as a means of playing the game with information processing systems!

The game of GO, thus, can be one of the possible problem-solving paradigms to go beyond Simon, yet remaining faithful to the research programme he developed. In a mathematical sense, GO is more flexible and general than chess because its board size can be, in principle, unlimitedly enlarged. The philosophy and heuristics of GO are not necessarily consistent with those of chess, which makes human problem solving more interesting. GO was also in the choice list of Simon, but Newell and Simon finally chose chess as their paradigmatic example of human problem solving.[27] We think they made the right decision for the pioneers they were.

It is here that we expect to be able to confront Simon's cognitive behavioural agent's actual performance, playing GO – instead of chess, as in Simon's life-long experimental basis for studying complex spaces and search strategies over them and for generating decision procedures as rules for implementation by an increasingly sophisticated set of algorithms. It will be natural, then, to model the 'increasing sophistication' of algorithms as evolutionary processes, underpinned by nearly-decomposable structures.

This game has already been studied by combinatorial game theory. GO has been shown to be PSPACE-hard *and* EXP-time complete, which means GO is in the exponential time class and it is proved that there can be no PSPACE algorithm for solving GO (Lichtenstein & Sipser, 1980; Robson, 1983). Problems in exponential time are considered to be among the most difficult problems. This result suggests that deciding whether black or white has winning strategy, at an arbitrary position, is practically infeasible. Clearly, any expectation for finding an optimal strategy to win in such a complex setting is both meaningless and futile. On the other hand, it also provides a perfect setting for studying 'actual' modes of decision making without being tied to the search for optimal strategies.

The theme of this chapter is that Simon's Behavioural Economics should be formally understood within the framework of computability theory and computational complexity theory. By extracting the procedural content of decision making, heuristics are considered as algorithms. In computational complexity theory, the complexity of a problem is analysed not only through the structure of task environments but also through the heuristics that problem solvers used to solve the problems. In this framework, we are able to show that bounded rationality via satisficing is the general notion of rationality.

If we view a piece of knowledge as an articulated paragraph, composed by words, which are, in turn, composed of symbols from a finite set, it becomes clear that it is never straightforward to understand or learn the knowledge by reading or memorizing it. We might have to follow the author with the same or different path on how the attained knowledge is reached. What matters is the knowledge generated in the mind, not the knowledge written. This is partly because a segment of words might have been a compression or definition of bigger segment of words. Tacit knowledge, too, played an important part in Simon's behavioural economics – as important a part as heuristics, and for the same reasons.

Simon's vision and definitions regarding bounded rationality were always intuitive and straightforward. He thus left a large canvas for others to build models based on bounded rationality. Simon's notions concerning bounded rationality can be interpreted more clearly in the light of alternative mathematical formalisms, those which are faithful to the notion of procedural decisions. Also, models should be constructed according to different situations and the actors who handle those situations. In this chapter, it is argued that the two aspects of human problem solving – the task environment (problem space) and problem solver (algorithm) should be distinguished and then studied.

By appealing to computability theory, it is shown that bounded rationality is a superset of Olympian rationality. Subsequently, the empirical boundary of rationality is further narrowed down to an inner boundary – the one established by computational complexity. Finally, it is suggested that Simon's empirical boundaries can be further approached – along the same methodology – by investigating the heuristics which are the algorithms (methods) that are used by human beings in problem-solving circumstances.

## Notes

1  An earlier version of this chapter appeared as Velupillai and Kao (2014).
2  Ray Solomonoff had presented one of his fundamental papers at the famous Dartmouth conference (1956) that initiated the formal research programme of artificial intelligence. Solomonoff's later papers, particularly Solomonoff (1964a, 1964b), were one of three pioneering approaches to algorithmic probability – the other two being Kolmogorov and Chaitin; Simon was fully aware of developments in algorithmic probability theory and its importance in the computational complexity of inductive processes, based on Turing's model of computation.
3  After further research, without the slightest doubt on the preceding assertion, I would like to add both Simon's intimate familiarity with, and appreciation of, Adriaan De Groot's extraordinary monograph on chess (De Groot, 1978 – but Simon was intimately familiar with the first English edition of 'more than 12 years' earlier). But, as pointed out in Chapter 4, in the context of discussing a Zeitgeist, it was not only Polya's classic and this one by De Groot that was important in shaping Simon's approach to human problem solving; it was also – and this is an informed conjecture – the 1945 translation of Duncker's monograph (Duncker, 1945) that was important. This is particularly so for understanding Simon's stance on heuristics versus algorithms in human problem-solving processes.
4  The two works that inspired and influenced him most decisively in these two respects – the study of causal structures and the linking of inductive inference with a formal notion of algorithmic complexity – were Goodwin (1947) and Solomonoff (1956, 1964a, 1964b). The former remained a central inspiration in Simon's sustained vision on problem simplification, search space decomposition and evolution, via an interpretation of

the notion of unilateral coupling in Goodwin (*loc. cit.*) with the formalism of *semi-* (or *nearly*) *decomposable* matrices, which would not have been alien to the author of the famous 'Hawkins–Simon' results (Hawkins & Simon, 1949). An early version of Solomonoff (1956) was, in fact, the only document 'submitted' by John McCarthy, in lieu of a post-conference report on the famous Dartmouth conference, in which both Simon and Solomonoff were two of the ten official participants. In fact, one of Simon's last writings, published, indeed, after his death (Simon, 2001), returned to the framework of Solomonoff's *Dartmouth contribution* to tackle issues that had been central to his scientific philosophy and outlook, from his Chicago University days, on linking scientific discovery with pattern recognition by means of a focus on parsimony in modelling. The notion of computational complexity that underpins our visions of Simon's cognitive behavioural economics is formally equivalent to Solomonoff's definition in that classic, later to be called algorithmic complexity (or Kolmogorov complexity). It was this latter notion that Simon used in his classic on *The Architecture of Complexity* (Simon, 1962, p. 478).

5 In the papers referred to earlier, I have gone into greater substantiation for this distinction, where Simon's cognitive behavioural economics is referred to as *Classical Behavioural Economics*.

6 Let alone *countably infinite* sets of alternatives!

7 It is precisely here that Simon first used the notion of *computability* explicitly (*loc. cit.*, footnote 2, p. 247, in the reprinted version in Simon, 1957).

8 A similar modelling logic can be found, *not surprisingly*, in a simple job search model in McCall (1970); 'not surprisingly' in view of Simon's prescient observation (*loc. cit.*, footnote 2, p. 247) of the role of aspiration levels in Wald's decision theory which was one fulcrum on which McCall developed his pioneering work in Search Theory. Wald's formalization via Markov Decision Processes, introduced by McCall, was later adopted as one of the three 'recursive' bedrocks of Newclassical *Recursive Macroeconomics* (Ljungqvist & Sargent, 2004) – the two other two recursive tools being (Kalman) filtering and (Bellman's) dynamic programming. None of these so-called recursive tools have anything to do with recursion theory.

9 These parameters are algebraic, rational numbers or other computable numbers.

10 It is an easy mathematical task to consider this in notions of *randomness* in *algorithmic* terms.

11 *Minmax* could, therefore, be such a *satisficier*, especially in a constructive context, such as in Euwe (2016).

12 Thus, obviating the need to consider the issue of the *Halting problem for Turing Machines* and the distinction between *recursive* and recursively enumerable sets.

13 I now think that Simon's way of interpreting and using the notion of heuristic owes as much to De Groot (op. cit.) and, hence, also Duncker (1945).

14 Today, as I complete this manuscript, I have a more nuanced, if also humbler, view and do not automatically reason as if heuristics are algorithms, *tout court*!

15 See Turing (1954, p. 13) for an example of a *substitution puzzle*.

16 Its formalism can be traced back to Post (1947).

17 Type 0 grammar is the superset of the hierarchy and includes all recursively enumerable languages. Turing Machines are the most general kind of symbol operators which are capable of recognizing the languages generated from all types of grammar.

18 To derive a contradiction via a *diagonal argument*.

19 The rigorous definitions of time and space complexity and those of different complexity classes can be found, for example, in chapters 7 and 8 in Sipser (1997). The notion of 'response time', for example, as defined and used in Luce (1986), is not amenable to an analysis of time complexity, based on a model of computation, as here.

20 A favourite example in Simon's pedagogy (see, e.g., Simon, 1975).

21 See Sipser (1997, pp. 229–231), for an example.

22 I refrain from investigating space complexity using *Busy Beavers* mainly because they are *uncomputable functions*. However, in related work within the ASSRU group,

structured searches for Busy Beavers as repositories of knowledge generators has been a standard exercise (cf. Zambelli, 2004).
23 This is implied by the first theorem in Savitch (1970).
24 See Guy (ed.), 1991.
25 The problem *Satisfiability* (**SAT**) is defined as follows: Given a Boolean formula (the Boolean formula is, itself, in the *Conjunctive Normal Form*) $\varphi$, determine whether there is an assignment that satisfies it (i.e., more formally, **SAT** is the set of all *satisfiable* Boolean formulas).
26 From the 'dialogue' with Jorge Luis Borges, held in Buenos Aires, in December, 1970 (see Simon, 1991).
27 The reasons for which are stated in (Newell & Simon, 1972, pp. 664–665). Given these reasons, we can only wonder whether they would have chosen the game of GO as their paradigm if they had been from the Orient!

# References

Chomsky, Noam (1956), There Models for the Description of Language, *IRE Transaction on Information Theory*, Vol. 2, No. 3, pp. 113–124.

Chomsky, Noam (1959), On Certain Formal Properties of Grammars, *Information and Control*, Vol. 2, pp. 137–167.

Church, Alonzo (1936), An Unsolvable Problem of Elementary Number Theory, *American Journal of Mathematics*, Vol. 58, No. 2, pp. 345–363.

Church, Alonzo (1938), The Constructive Second Number Class, *Bulletin of the American Mathematical Society*, Vol. 44, pp. 224–232.

Davis, M. (1982), *Computability and Unsolvability*, Dover Publications, Inc., New York.

De Groot, Adriaan (1978), *Thought and Choice in Chess* (Second Edition), Mouton Publishers, The Hague.

Duncker, Karl (1945), On Problem Solving (translated by Lynne S. Lees), *Psychological Monographs*, Vol. 58, No. 5, pp. iii–114.

Euwe, M (2016), Mathematics – Set-Theoretic Considerations on the Game of Chess, *New Mathematics and Natural Computation*, Vol. 12, No. 1, pp. 11–20.

Goodwin, Richard M. (1947), Dynamical Coupling with Especial Reference to Markets Having Production Lags, *Econometrica*, Vol. 15, No. 3, July, pp. 181–204.

Guy, Richard K. (ed.) (1991), *Combinatorial Games*, American Mathematical Society, Short Course, August 6–7, 1990, Columbus, Ohio, American Mathematical Society, Providence, Rhode Island.

Hilbert, David (1902), Mathematical Problems, *Bulletin of the American Mathematical Society*, Vol. 8, pp. 437–479.

Kao, Ying-Fang & K. Vela Velupillai (2012), Origins and Pioneers of Behavioural Economics, *Interdisciplinary Journal of Economics and Business Law*, Vol. 1, pp. 47–73.

Kao, Ying-Fang & K. Vela Velupillai (2015), Behavioural Economics: Classical and Modern, *The European Journal of the History of Economic Thought*, Vol. 22, No. 2, pp. 236–271.

Kleene, S. C. (1936a), General Recursive Functions of Natural Numbers, *Mathematische Annalen*, Vol. 112, pp. 727–242.

Kleene, S. C. (1936b), $\lambda$-Definability and Recursiveness, *Duke Mathematical Journal*, Vol. 2, pp. 340–353.

Langley, Pat, Herbert A. Simon, Gary L. Bradshaw & Jan M. Zytkow (1987), *Scientific Discovery: Computational Explorations of the Creative Process*, The MIT Press, Cambridge, MA.

Lichtenstein, D. and M. Sipser (1980), Go Is Polynomial-Space Hard, *Journal of the Association for Computing Machinery*, Vol. 27, No. 2, pp. 393–401.

Ljungqvist, Lars & Thomas J. Sargent (2004), *Recursive Macroeconomic Theory* (Second Edition), The MIT Press, Cambridge, MA.

Luce, Duncan (1986), *Response Times: Their Role in Inferring Elementary Mental Organization*, Oxford University Press, Oxford.

March, James G. (1978), Bounded Rationality, Ambiguity and the Engineering of Choice, *The Bell Journal of Economics*, Vol. 9, No. 2, pp. 587–608.

March, James G. & Herbert A. Simon (1958; 1993), *Organizations* (Second Edition), Blackwell Publishers, Oxford.

Matiyasevich, Yuri (1994), *Hilbert's Tenth Problem*, MIT Press, Cambridge MA.

McCall, John J. (1970), Economics of Information and Job Search, *The Quarterly Journal of Economics*, Vol. 84, No. 1, pp. 113–126.

Newell, Allen and Herbert A. Simon (1956), The Logic Theory Machine, *IRE Transactions on Information Theory IT-2*, Vol. 3, pp. 61–79.

Newell, Allen and Herbert A. Simon (1972), *Human Problem Solving*, Prentice-Hall, Inc., Englewood Cliffs, NJ.

Newell, Allen & Herbert A. Simon (1976), Computer Science as Empirical Inquiry: Symbols and Search, *Communications of the ACM*, Vol. 19, No. 3, pp. 113–126.

Newell, Allen, Herbert A. Simon & J. Cliff Shaw (1958), Elements of the Theory of Human Problem Solving, *Psychological Review*, Vol. 65, No. 3, pp. 151–166.

Polya, G. (1945), *How to Solve It: A New Aspect of Mathematical Method*, Princeton University Press, Princeton, NJ.

Post, Emil L. (1947), Recursive Unsolvability of a Problem of Thue, *The Journal of Symbolic Logic*, Vol. 12, No. 1, pp. 1–11.

Robson, J. M. (1983), The Complexity of Go, *Information Processing*, Vol. 83, pp. 413–417.

Sargent, Thomas J. (1993), *Bounded Rationality in Macroeconomics*, Clarendon Press, Oxford.

Savitch, W. J. (1970), Relationships between Nondeterministic and Deterministic Tape Complexities, *Journal of Computer and System Sciences*, Vol. 4, pp. 177–192.

Shannon, C. E. (1950), Programming a Computer for Playing Chess, *Philosophical Magazine*, Vol. 41, No. 314, pp. 256–275.

Simon, Herbert A. (1947), *Administrative Behavior* (Second Edition), The Free Press, New York.

Simon, Herbert A. (1955), A Behavioral Model of Rational Choice, *Quarterly Journal of Economics*, Vol. 69, No. 1, pp. 99–118.

Simon, Herbert A. (1956), Rational Choice and the Structure of the Environment, *Psychological Review*, Vol. 63, No. 2, pp. 129–138.

Simon, Herbert A. (1957), *Models of Man*, John Wiley & Sons, Inc, New York.

Simon, Herbert A. (1958; 1982), The Role of Expectations in an Adaptive or Behavioristic Model, in: *Expectations, Uncertainty, and Business Behavior*, edited by M. J. Bowman, reprinted as Chapter 7.11, pp. 380–399, in: *Models of Bounded Rationality, Volume 2: Behavioral Economics and Business Organization*, The MIT Press, Cambridge, MA.

Simon, Herbert A. (1962), The Architecture of Complexity, *Proceedings of the American Philosophical Society*, Vol. 106, No. 6, pp. 467–482.

Simon, Herbert A. (1972), Theories of Bounded Rationality, pp. 161–176, in: *Decision and Organization*, edited by C. B. Radner & R. Radner, North-Holland, Amsterdam.

Simon, Herbert A. (1975), The Functional Equivalence of Problem Solving Skills, *Cognitive Skills*, Vol. 7, pp. 268–288.

Simon, Herbert A. (1976), From Substantive to Procedural Rationality, pp. 129–148, in: *Method and Appraisal in Economics*, edited by Spiro J Latsis. Cambridge University Press, Cambridge.

Simon, Herbert A. (1977), *Models of Discovery – and Other Topics in the Methods of Science*, D. Reidel Publishing Company, Dordrech & Boston.

Simon, Herbert A. (1983a), Discovery, Invention, and Development: Human Creative Thinking, *Proceedings of the National Academy of Sciences*, Vol. 80, pp. 4569–4571.

Simon, Herbert A. (1983b), *Reason in Human Affairs*, Basil Blackwell, Oxford.

Simon, Herbert A. (1990), Invariants of Human Behavior, *Annual Review of Psychology*, Vol. 41, pp. 1–19.

Simon, Herbert A. (1991), *Models of My Life*, The MIT Press, Cambridge, MA.

Simon, Herbert A. (1996), *The Sciences of the Artificial* (Third Edition), The MIT Press, Cambridge, MA.

Simon, Herbert A. (1997), *Models of Bounded Rationality – Volume 3: Empirically Grounded Economic Reason*, The MIT Press, Cambridge, MA.

Simon, Herbert A. (2001), Science Seeks Parsimony, Not Simplicity: Searching for Pattern in Phenomena, chapter 3, pp. 32–72, in: *Simplicity, Inference and Modelling: Keeping It Sophisticatedly Simple*, edited by Arnold Zellner, Hugo A. Keuzenkamp & Michael McAleer, Cambridge University Press, Cambridge.

Sipser, Michael (1997), *Introduction to the Theory of Computation*, PWS Publishing Company, Boston.

Solomonoff, Ray J. (1956), *An Inductive Inference Machine*, Manuscript, Dartmouth.

Solomonoff, Ray J. (1964a), A Formal Theory of Inductive Inference: Part I, *Information and Control*, Vol. 7, pp. 1–22.

Solomonoff, Ray J. (1964b), A Formal Theory of Inductive Inference: Part II, *Information and Control*, Vol. 7, pp. 224–254.

Turing, Alan M. (1936), On Computable Numbers, with an Application to the Entscheidungs Problem, *Proceedings of the London Mathematical Society*, Vol. 42, No. 2, pp. 230–265.

Turing, Alan M. (1937), Computability and λ-Definability, *The Journal of Symbolic Logic*, Vol. 2, No. 4, pp. 153–163.

Turing, Alan M. (1951), Intelligent Machinery, a Heretical Theory, *Philosophia Mathematica*, Vol. 4, No. 3, pp. 256–260.

Turing, Alan M. (1954), Solvable and Unsolvable Problems, *Science News*, Vol. 31, pp. 7–23.

Velupillai, Kumaraswamy (2000), *Computable Economics*, Oxford University Press, Oxford.

Velupillai, K. Vela (2010), *Computable Foundations for Economics*, Routledge, London.

Velupillai, K. Vela & Ying-Fang Kao (2014), Computable and Computational Complexity Theoretic Bases for Herbert Simon's Cognitive Behavioral Economics, *Cognitive Systems Research*, Vol. 29–30, September, pp. 40–52.

Wang, Hao (1970), *Logic, Computers, and Sets*, Chelsea Publishing Company, New York.

Zambelli, Stefano (2004), Production of Ideas by Means of Ideas: A Turing Machine Metaphor, *Metroeconomica*, Vol. 55, Nos. 2–3, pp. 155–179.

# 7 *Notes* on hierarchic, *near*-decomposable, causal, evolutionary dynamics

## The Architecture of Complexity

(An earlier concise version of this chapter appeared in the **OECD BLOG**, of January 2017.)

### §1 Representations and causality, near decomposability and evolution[1]

> In everyday language, that – i.e., 'time . . . [seeming] to run *in two directions at once* – sounds nonsensical. But within the mathematical formalism of quantum theory, *ambiguity about causation emerges* in a perfectly logical and consistent way.
> —**NATURE** (Vol. 546, No. 7660, p. 590; italics added)

Simon, for almost the whole of his scientific life – that is, for a little more than half a century – tried to dispel *ambiguity* in *causal structures*, 'classically' conceived, but did not neglect its *emergence* in social structures. This he did with notions of *representations* that were, in a Brouwer–Wittgenstein sense of wordless, logicless *mental pictures*. Simon's work in understanding the impossible diagrams – pictures, sketches – of Neckar, Escher, Penrose & Penrose and Reutesvärd were in terms of such mental pictures, representing them (see **Models of Thought**, *Vol. 1*, 1979, especially §6, and **Models of Thought**, *Vol. II*, 1989, especially ch. 6.3).

I can do no better – here, especially – than quote extensively from Simon's 'mature' reflections of his past thoughts and practices, in representing problems for purposes of solving by means of heuristics:

> What kind of *representations* do scientists use in thinking about their research problems, and where do these *representations* come from?
> . . . .
>
> Let me return to my main topic of providing anecdotal evidence about the *problem-solving process* used in *scientific discovery* with an example . . .
> Economists frequently use what they call 'partial equilibrium analysis.' to avoid talking about everything at once by making a host of ***ceteris paribus*** assumptions. They examine the impact of a disturbance upon a small sector of the economy while assuming no interaction with the rest of the economy. . . .
> Thoughts of these kinds . . . went through my mind while I read, in the early 1950s, a paper by Richard Goodwin, *Dynamical Coupling with Especial Reference to Markets Having Production Lags* . . . I recall conceiving of *a*

*large dynamic system divided into sectors*, with strong interactions among the components in each sector, and weak interactions among sectors. . . .

I held a vague mental image of *the matrix of coefficients of the dynamic system* . . . At some point, I saw that the rows and columns of the matrix could be arranged in a number of diagonal blocks with large coefficients in them, and only small coefficients outside the diagonal blocks. The matrix was *nearly* 'block diagonal.'

. . .

At some later point, I acquired *a metaphor*. I *visualized* a building divided into rooms, each room divided, in turn, into cubicles.

(Simon, 1991, 1996, pp. 375–377; bold italics in the original)

Pictorially, or figuratively, the 'large dynamical system' (Figure 7.1[2]) and 'a building divided into rooms' (Figures 7.2 and 7.3),[3] each resulting in block-diagonal matrices, and, hence, nearly decomposable, evolutionary, dynamical systems, can be represented as follows:

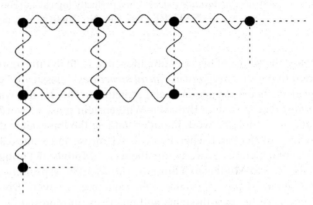

*Figure 7.1* 'Large [Strongly and Weakly Coupled] Dynamical System'

|     | A1  | A2  | A3  | B1  | B2  | C1  | C2  | C3  |
|-----|-----|-----|-----|-----|-----|-----|-----|-----|
| A1  |     | 100 |     | 2   |     |     |     |     |
| A2  | 100 |     | 100 | 1   | 1   |     |     |     |
| A3  |     | 100 |     |     | 2   |     |     |     |
| B1  | 2   | 1   |     |     | 100 | 2   | 1   |     |
| B2  |     | 1   | 2   | 100 |     |     | 1   | 2   |
| C1  |     |     |     |     | 2   |     | 100 |     |
| C2  |     |     |     | 1   | 1   | 100 |     | 100 |
| C3  |     |     |     |     | 2   |     | 100 |     |

*Figure 7.2* Matrix Arrangements of Rooms in a Building

| A1 | B1 | C1 |
|----|----|----|
| A2 |    | C2 |
| A3 | B2 | C3 |

*Figure 7.3* Block Diagonal System of Rooms

And so we have *Hierarchical* in 1950 (Simon, 1977, p. 180 & ch. 4.1 & 4.4), Near Decomposable from about 1949 (Hawkins & Simon, 1949; Simon, 1977, ch. 4.3; Simon, 1991, p. 377; Goodwin, 1947) and *Causal* (Simon, 1952a, 1977, ch. 2.1 & 2.2) dynamical systems, underpinning the reasonably rapid evolution of a series of stable *complex structures*.[4]

As an aside, the *cybernetic* vision (Simon, 1952b) of an interregnum became the fully fledged digital computer basis of boundedly rational *Human Problem Solvers* implementing *Heuristic Search Procedures* to prove, for example, axiomatic mathematical theorems (in the monumental **Principia Mathematica** of Russell and Whitehead) substantiating Newell's entirely reasonable claim that 'Herb had put it all together at least 40 years ago' (Newell, 1989, p. 400; italics added).

## §2 Hierarchy, complexity and the *Architecture of Complexity*

> Episodes . . . . can be *hierarchical*, with one episode *embedded in another*.
> —Newell and Simon (1972, p. 480; italics added)

The final appearance, in the public domain, of the classic on *The Architecture of Complexity* (Simon, 1962 – henceforth referred to as *AoC* – no pun with the *Axiom of Choice* is intended), appeared (very slightly revised) as the last chapter of the third edition of **The Sciences of the Artificial** (Simon, 1996), with the subtitle 'Hierarchic Systems'. The original paper was read on 28 April 1962 – which would have been Ludwig Wittgenstein's 73rd birthday. So, it is appropriate that Simon acknowledges allegiance, in Simon and Newell (1956), referred to in the lead footnote in Simon (1962), to that much-quoted Gibbsian aphorism – *Mathematics is a **Language*** – whereas Wittgenstein (1953, §109), did his best to free Philosophy from the '*bewitchment of intelligence by **language***' (emphases added)! For my purposes here, *given the kind of scientist Simon was*, I assume the word **ARCHITECTURE** can be interpreted in any of its standard *design process* senses, whilst keeping in mind that it could also mean *the product* of the design *process*.

In defining the notion of *complexity*, in *AoC* (pp. 467–8), Simon eschews formalisms and relies on a rough, working concept of complex systems that would help identify examples of observable structures – predominantly in the behavioural sciences – that could lead to theories and, hence, theorems, of *evolving dynamical systems* that exhibit properties that are amenable to design and prediction using the *hilfenkonstruktion* of *hierarchy, near decomposability* and *causality*. Thus, the *almost* informal definition[5] is (p. 468; italics added)

> [*r*]*oughly*, by *a complex system* I mean one made up of a large number of parts that interact in a *nonsimple* way. In such systems, the whole is more than the sum of the parts, . . . , in the *pragmatic* sense that, given the properties of the parts and the laws of their interaction, it is not a trivial matter to *infer* the properties of the whole. In the face of *complexity*, an in-principle reductionist may be at the same time a *pragmatic holist*.

Simon was always a *pragmatic holist*, even while attempting the reduction of the behaviour of complex entities to *parsimonious* processes that would exhibit the properties of 'wholes', based on *nonsimply interacting* 'parts', that may themselves be *simple*. In many ways, *AoC* both summarized Simon's evolving (*sic*!) visions of a quantitative behavioural science, which provided the foundations of administering complex, hierarchically structured, causal organisations, by boundedly rational agents implanting – with the help of digital computers – procedures that were, in turn, reflections of human problem-solving processes. But it *also presaged* the increasing precision of predictable reality – not amounting to non-pragmatic, non-empirical phenomena – requiring an *operational description of complex systems* that were the observable in nature, resulting from the evolutionary dynamics of hierarchical structures. Thus, the final – fourth – section[6] of *AoC* (p. 477, ff.) 'examines the relation between complex systems and their descriptions' – for which Simon returned to Solomonoff's pioneering definition of *algorithmic information theory* (Simon, 2004, p. 34).[7]

   *AoC* was equally expository on the many issues with which we have come to associate Simon's boundedly rational agents (and institutions) *satisficing* – instead of optimizing, again for pragmatic, historically observable, realistic reasons – using *heuristic search processes* in *Human Problem-Solving* contexts of behavioural decisions. The famous distinction between *substantive* and *procedural* rationality arose from the dichotomy of a state versus process description of a world 'as sensed and as acted upon' (p. 479, ff.), in *AoC*.[8]

   Essentially *AoC* is suffused with pragmatic definitions and human procedures of realistic implementations, even in the utilizing of digital computers. Computability theory assumes the Church–Turing Thesis in defining algorithms. The notion of computational complexity is predicated upon the assumption of the validity of the Church–Turing Thesis. Simon's algorithms for *human problem solvers* are *heuristic search processes*, where no such assumption is made. Hence, it is not surprising that a feeling of *ennui* engulfed him in his later years (Simon, 2004, p. 47; italics added):[9]

> The field of computer science has been much occupied with questions of *computational complexity*, the obverse of computational simplicity. But in the literature of the field, 'complexity' usually means something quite different from my meaning of it in the present context. Largely for reasons

of mathematical attainability, and *at the expense of relevance*, theorems of computational complexity have mainly addressed worst-case behaviour of computational algorithms as the size of the data set grows larger. In the limit, they have even focused on computability in the sense of Gödel, and Turing and the *halting problem*. I must confess that these concerns *produce in me a great feeling of ennui*.[10]

For Simon, who did *not* work within the standard Church–Turing Thesis of orthodox *Recursion Theory*, boundedly rational *Information Processing Systems*, satisficing, whilst implementing *Heuristic search processes* over uncountable infinite spaces, suitably constrained – say, by invoking (implicitly) Gödel's completeness theorem for propositional logic – to discover theorems and solve problems made 'decisions that are far beyond any of the (standard or orthodox) levels of complexity'.

However, let me conclude with a relevant observation by Gandy (1996, p. 136; italics added):

> [M]achines of the kind I am imagining would display the effects of consciousness – the ability to concentrate attention on a particular part or aspect of their input, the ability to reflect on and to alter the *behaviour of subsystems* in their *hierarchic structure*, and even, in a restricted way, an ability to *adapt* their social *behaviour*.[11]

## Notes

1  I had originally intended to devote some space to what has come to be known as the *Hawkins–Simon* condition (for square matrices), but the more general properties of non-negative square matrices have become, now, standard fare in mathematical economics. Although Simon's pioneering contributions to the near-decomposability/evolution nexus may benefit from a historic narrative, starting with Simon's contribution to, and understanding of, the structure and properties of square matrices, I shall not take up the issue of the Hawkins–Simon conditions. In any case, I have done so in other, not-very-recent writings – ante-dating my serious interest in Simon's contributions.

2  Goodwin's prescient observation for the long-run behaviour of this kind of coupled-oscillator is worth noting (Goodwin, 1947, pp. 201–202; italics added):

> Even more remarkable is the fact that it is *no longer simply periodic*; it does not repeat itself, even with no outside disturbance or natural damping. Except by accident the various periods will not dovetail, because they are not integral multiples of one another, and hence in each cycle they will join in a new way, *resulting in an ever-changing wave shape*.

The perceptive reader will recognize the similarity with the Fermi–Pasta–Ulan (FPU) system and the results of experiments with such representations which did not able one to infer easy stability properties of ostensible attractors.

3  Figure 7.3, therefore, is a hypothetical *nearly-decomposable system*. In terms of a heat-exchange metaphor (or transfer of 'disturbances to a system of oscillators', as in Figure 7.1), A1, A2 and A3 may be interpreted as representing cubicles in one room; B1 and B2 similarly as cubicles in a second room; C1, C2 and C3 as cubicles in a third room,

    and the whole represented as matrix entries of heat diffusion coefficients (or system vibration/oscillations) between cubicles as *block diagonal* (or nearly decomposable).

4  It is not without significance that almost all these pioneering articles are reprinted in Simon (1977), and moreover, the hierarchy and near-decomposability classics appear in section 4 of this collection with the heading *COMPLEXITY*!

5  It parallels the much-hyped 'modern definition', subscribed to by *aficionados* of the *Santa Fe methodology*, in many ways – except that it does *not* extol the virtues of *disequilibrium emergence of wholes*, from the interaction of a large number of parts, with *stable* (in the sense of, say, De Finetti, 1975, §8.4; Feller, 1971, ch. VI) statistical distributions.

6  The first section of *AoC* 'offers some comments on the frequency with which *complexity* takes the form of *hierarchy*', the second 'theorizes about the relation between the structure of a complex system and the time required for it to *emerge* through *evolutionary processes* and the third 'explores the dynamic properties of hierarchically organized systems and shows how they can be *decomposed into subsystems* in order to analyse their behavior' (p. 468, all the italics are added).

7  Solomonoff (1964) was first presented at the celebrated *Dartmouth* conference of 1956, where Simon was also present, which initiated the field of *artificial intelligence*.

8  Anyone who studies the example of *Hora* and *Tempus* (pp. 470–1) may, justifiably, wonder whether it is not (yet another) instance of the famous first three chapters of Book I of the *Wealth of Nations*! However, Simon's example is in the context of hierarchical systems – but, then, why does *Tempus* not hire a telephonist to 'answer the phone' and avoid the falling 'into pieces' of partly assembled watches? Because such a hiring increases the *degree of hierarchy*, which, thereby, *increases the number of interacting subsystems*, leading to 'larger' descriptive complexities.

9  This is, in more stark and explicit ways, the same reflections expressed by Simon in the letter to me (written after reading my book on **Computable Economics**, a first draft of which was completed in 1991 when I was 'only' 43 years of age. Perhaps he was being 'kinder and gentler' to me!). Excerpts from the letter, reflecting the mild version of the above ennui, are given, below.

10  In the letter Simon wrote me (& Leijonhufvud; cf. Appendix 4 of this book), his equivalent, but much milder, sense of *ennui* was expressed as follows (italics added):

> There are many levels of complexity in problems, and corresponding boundaries between them. Turing computability is an outer boundary, and as you show, any theory that requires more power than that surely is irrelevant to any useful definition of human rationality. A slightly stricter boundary is posed by computational complexity, especially in its common "worst case" form. We cannot expect people (and/or computers) to find exact solutions for large problems in computationally complex domains. This still leaves us far beyond what people and computers actually CAN do. The next boundary, but one for which we have few results except some of Rabin's work, is computational complexity for the "average case", sometimes with an "almost everywhere" loophole. That begins to bring us closer to the realities of real-world and real-time computation. Finally, we get to the empirical boundary, measured by laboratory experiments on humans and by observation, of the level of complexity that humans actually can handle, with and without their computers, and – perhaps more important – what they actually do to solve problems that lie beyond this strict boundary even though they are within some of the broader limits.
>
>     The latter is an important point for economics, because *we humans spend most of our lives making decisions that are far beyond any of the levels of complexity we can handle exactly*; and this is where satisficing, floating aspiration levels, recognition and heuristic search, and similar devices for arriving at good-enough

decisions take over. A parsimonious economic theory, and an empirically verifiable one, shows how human beings, using very *simple procedures*, reach decisions that lie far beyond their capacity for finding *exact solutions* by the *usual maximizing criteria*.

11  This observation is also relevant for **Problem 18**, on the *Limits of Intelligence*, in Smale (1998, p. 13), as discussed in Chapter 11.
12  Simon died on 8 February 2001; this may have been his last *written* paper before death intervened, I think unexpectedly (see the attached letter from Simon, dated 25 May 2000).

# References

De Finetti, Bruno (1975), *Theory of Probability: A Critical Introductory Treatment*, Vol. 2, John Wiley & Sons, Ltd., London.

Feller, William (1971), *An Introduction to Probability Theory and Its Applications: Volume 11* (Second Edition), John Wiley & Sons, Inc., New York.

Gandy, Robin (1996), Human versus Mechanical Intelligence, chapter 7, pp. 125–136, in: *Machines and Thought – the Legacy of Alan Turing*, Vol. 1, edited by Peter Millican & Andy Clark, Oxford University Press, Oxford.

Goodwin, Richard M. (1947), Dynamical Coupling with Especial Reference to Markets Having Production Lags, *Econometrica*, Vol. 15, No. 3, July, pp. 181–204.

Hawkins, David & Herbert A. Simon (1949), Note: Some Conditions on Macroeconomic Stability, *Econometrica*, Vol. 17, No. 3/4, July–October, pp. 245–248.

Newell, Allen (1989), Putting It All Together, chapter 15, pp. 399–400, in: *Complex Information Processing: The Impact of Herbert A. Simon*, edited by David Klahr & Kenneth Kotovsky, Lawrence Earlbaum Associates Publishers, Hillsdale, NJ.

Newell, Allen & Herbert A. Simon (1972), *Human Problem Solving*, Prentice-Hall, INC., Englewood Cliffs, NJ.

Simon, Herbert A. (1952a), On the Definition of the Causal Relation, *The Journal of Philosophy*, Vol. 49, No. 16, July 31, pp. 517–528.

Simon, Herbert A. (1952b), On the Application of Servomechanism Theory in the Study of Production Control, *Econometrica*, Vol. 20, No. 2, April, pp. 247–268.

Simon, Herbert A. (1962), The Architecture of Complexity, *Proceedings of the American Philosophical Society*, Vol. 106, No. 6, December, pp. 467–482.

Simon, Herbert A. (1977), *Models of Discovery – and Other Topics in the Methods of Science*, D. Reidel Publishing Company, Dordrecht-Holland.

Simon, Herbert A. (1979), *Models of Thought*, Vol. 1, Yale University Press, New Haven.

Simon, Herbert A. (1989), *Models of Thought*, Vol. 2, Yale University Press, New Haven.

Simon, Herbert A. (1991), *Models of My Life*, Basic Books, New York.

Simon, Herbert A. (1996), *The Sciences of the Artificial* (Third Edition), The MIT Press, Cambridge, MA.

Simon, Herbert A.[†12] (2004), Science Seeks Parsimony, Not Simplicity: Searching for Pattern in Phenomena, chapter 3, pp. 32–82, in: *Simplicity, Inference and Modelling: Keeping it Sophisticatedly Simple*, edited by Arnold Zellner, Hugo A. Keuzenkamp & Michael McAleer, Cambridge University Press, Cambridge.

Simon, Herbert A. & Allen Newell (1956), Models: Their Uses and Limitations, pp. 66–83, in: *The State of the Social Sciences*, edited by Leonard D. White, University of Chicago Press, Chicago.

Smale, Steve (1998), Mathematical Problems for the Next Century, *The Mathematical Intelligencer*, Vol. 20, No. 2, pp. 7–15.

Solomonoff, Ray J. (1964), A Formal Theory of Inductive Inference, *Information and Control*, Vol. 7, pp. 1–22, 224–254.

Wittgenstein, Ludwig (1953), *Philosophical Investigations* (translated by from the German, *Philosophische Untersuchungen* by G. E. M. Anscombe), Basil Blackwell, Oxford.

# 8 Gandy's *Mechanisms* Modelling the *Rationality* of Organizations by March & Simon*

## §1 An extended preamble

> The metaphor of *chess, cryptarithmetic*[1] and the *Tower of Hanoi* serving as the *green peas, Drosophila* and *E. coli* of cognitive science is as near to literal truth as it is to fancy.[2]
>
> —Simon (1989,[3] p. 394; italics added)

I have chosen to begin with this quote to emphasize Herbert Simon's lifelong commitment to the interlocking nature of *theory* and *empirics*[4] – but also of *learning about thinking procedures* in formulating *search heuristics* for *discovering solutions to problems* in economics, psychology and computer science.[5]

Simon worked with, and invoked, 16 (or 17, if 'causal' is distinguished from 'causal ordering') scientific *concepts*,[6] which he defined precisely between 1947 and 1989 (although his scientific contributions were spread over almost 70 years, 1935–2004, even if death intervened, cruelly, in 2001): *decision making,[7] human choice, rationality, causality and causal ordering*, near decomposability, *hierarchical systems*, (*cybernetic) feedbacks* (of 'classical' control systems), *heuristics, problem solving, bounded rationality, satisficing, discovery, surprise, information processing systems* (**IPS**), *evolution* and *complexity*. He invoked one or another collection of these concepts – sometimes implicitly but often explicitly – to study, above all, the *Rational Mechanisms in Organizations*.

Concepts, *concept formation*[8] and their roles in *information processing* theories of behaviour, thinking, problem solving, discoveries and, above all, the functions and mechanisms of *Administrative Organizations* (the phrase in Simon's first published book of 1947 – exactly 70 years ago) was based on the rationality of *mechanisms*, that is, of discovering and theorising about the rational structure of the *mechanisms* that underpin individual and organizational behaviour.[9]

I would like to add that my assertion applies to *all* of Simon's research work, as far as I could come to terms with the massiveness of it – *except* his significant contributions to the size distribution of firms and the skewed nature of them, which he modelled as being driven by model(s) of *stochastic* processes. But in view of Bartlett's reflections (Bartlett, 1990), Tong's important work (Tong & Lim, 1980), Simon's own comments in the **Raffaele Mattioli Lectures** (Simon, 1997, pp. 174–175) and the methodological message of Gregg and Simon (1967), I feel confident in stating, as a *conjecture* in, that such empirical distributions *can* be generated by *coupled-deterministic-nonlinear dynamical systems*. These systems, in turn, can also be viewed as the attractors of rational mechanisms in the dynamics of organization behaviour, as they evolve merge and 'disappear'.

It behooves me to mention that Allen Newell (1989, p. 400) refers to *bounded rationality* as 'the central idea' in Herbert Simon. I, on the other hand, claim that the concept of *heuristics*, via structured *search processes*[10] – for Simon, from Selz (cf. Newell & Simon, 1972, p. 874) and the Wurzberg school of an early form of cognitive science, unlike from Polya (1945) for Newell – in *decision making* is 'central', simply because – eventually – *Problem Solving and Discovery* by agents and institutions (particularly tied to evolutionary survival by the latter), with or without the bounded rationality–satisficing nexus, became the guiding discipline for his research. Since scholars such as Dahl and Newell *disagree* on what was – is – 'central' to Simon's research activity, my emphasis on *heuristics* as *the* central idea, partly based on my quotation from Simon (1996), on the title page, cannot be considered too controversial.

This chapter is structured as follows: The next section is on Simon's development of the notion of *Organizations* in terms of Gandy's (1980) notion of a *Mechanism*, modified and extended – especially with *parallel processing* considerations – by Shepherdson (1975, 1995), capable of computation in the sense of *Turing computability* (Turing, 1936). I shall, for the purposes of this chapter, concentrate on March and Simon (1993), in particular, chapters 6 and 7, of this classic, which I believe invokes all the preceding 16 (or 17) concepts to define, understand and develop a computational – that is, programmed – procedural, evolutionary theory of *Organizations*.[11] Apart from the additional structure due to the *four principles of mechanisms* due to Gandy (ibid.), it is analogous to the way I identified the choice activity of a rational individual with the computing process of a Turing Machine (Velupillai, 2000, ch. 3). Thus, the main result of this section – indeed, the only mathematical theorem in this chapter – is the *uncomputability* (or *undecidability*) of the *decision mechanism of an Organization* (as described in March & Simon, *ibid.*). Hence, Simon had no hesitation in attributing, to the processes of choice, problem solving and discovery, by *Organizations*, structured the way identified in this classic, bounded rationality and satisficing by individuals and groups of individuals, motivated – that is, having 'utility' functions – by formalized, orderable desires.

The notion of *size* of an *Organization* is almost as elusive as the *smile on the Cheshire Cat*! An *Organization* is never defined, or discussed, in *static* terms by Simon – it is intrinsically dynamic, often also evolutionary. *Size* (and its 'dual', *shape*) is quintessentially a *static* concept (which is why Klee & Minty, 1972, were able to use the *concept* of *worst-case alternative*[12] to demonstrate the computational complexity of the simplex algorithm). As one of two conjectures in §3, I suggest a dynamic definition of size – as if it is possible to encapsulate the pattern of an *evolving* jigsaw puzzle – based on *Ramsey's Theorem*.[13] For someone like

Herbert Simon, who was intrigued by combinatorial games, this must – at least – appeal in an amusing sense (although we suggest it seriously).

In the same (concluding) §3, I also suggest that a perspective of Simon's notion of problem solving by, and discovery in, organizations should be encapsulated in *deterministic, nonlinear, dynamical systems*. Simon's massive *oeuvre* is dominated by *linear dynamics*, although he seemed to want to 'break loose' and venture towards the weird and wonderful, untameable world of nonlinearity. Since the notion of size in the first conjecture of this section is dynamic, the algorithmic computational processes – whether under types of the Church–Turing Thesis or some variant of the search processes underpinning heuristics – should be generated also by a dynamic process – where the changing notion of size is reflected in the *non-equilibrium, nonlinear dynamics* of a *generative process*. A part of the meaning of this is implied by the *basins of attraction of attractors* of the discrete, nonlinear, dynamical system of the generative process is *algorithmically undecidable*. This is suggested as a conjecture in the concluding section and goes, I think, part of the way towards 'pulling the threads together' in a coherent way.

## §2  Rational mechanisms in computable organizations

> A theory of. . . organization cannot exist *without* a theory of rational choice. . . .
> [A] theory of rational choice can hardly exist *without* a theory of organization.
> —Simon (1957, p. 196; italics added)

One of the curiosities of Simon's two influential books on *Administrative Behavior* and *Organizations* (jointly with James March), published in 1947 and 1958 (first editions), respectively, is that neither of them contain any mathematical formalism. This is a curiosity only because many of Simon's essays of the intervening period were deeply mathematical, formally mathematical logical and also underpinned by some deep knowledge of the philosophy of science, at least of the logical positivistic variety.

The apparent curiosity disappears if one considers *Models of Man* (Simon, 1957) as a mathematical companion volume,[14] *ex post* for *Administrative Behaviour* (the mathematical appendix that was part of the unpublished thesis, on which the book was based, did not appear in the published book; by comparison also see Takahashi (2015) – although I do NOT agree with this author's stance on Simon *vs* Barnard; see the following) and *ex ante* for *Organizations*.[15]

Before I continue with the main theme of this section, it is necessary to point out that *bounded rationality* is *not* the 'capacity' of Barnard, as Takahashi (*op. cit.*) alleges or the kind of 'thing' economists define (e.g., Radner, 1975; Sargent, 1993; see also Gigerenzer & Selten, 2001, p. ix; Kao & Velupillai, 2015, §4.1). The most enlightening way to make the point we wish to make was that which was emphasized by Newell (1989, p. 400; italics added):

It is an interesting side note that Herb did *not* succumb to the temptation of a *capacity theory*. A common response to limited processing is to posit a resource, call it *rationality juice*. A person has only a limited *supply* of this juice, and what is used for purpose P cannot be used for purpose Q. Then, the analyst regains the ability to apply *optimization theory* by assuming that the person will always distribute his limited rationality juice *optimally* among his options. Many have succumbed to positing such overall resource limits (by this or any other name). In my opinion, it has shielded them from discovering the real character of the *mechanisms of cognition*, which have shape as well as volume. Instead, *Herb went for the details of the specific mechanisms involved*. There is nothing in Herb's story that I know of that says why this happened.

In going 'for *the specific mechanism*', Simon chose the dynamic, process-oriented path – as he had done since 1935 – and eschewed the orthodox way of static optimization, under given constraints.

The path from rational economic, administrative and thinking man to the *rational organizations man*[16] was *via* a dismissal – almost with disdain, as 'fundamentally wrongheaded' – of all 'classical' approaches to administrative and organizational rational behaviour. By this I mean 'all' approaches to individual, social or group rational behaviour, relying on 'traditional' game theory – that is, on variations of the notions broached in von Neumann/Morgenstern's classic of 1944,[17] statistical decision theory, orthodox – formal or informal – economic theory and 'Modern Behavioural Economics'[18] and that which emanated from an ostensibly different social choice theory.

The formulation of *Rational Mechanisms in Organizations* – at least in March and Simon (*ibid.*) – is built on the foundations of a decision making of programmed activity, solving problems posed to it and choosing to solve problems, using heuristic search processes to discover solutions, by a causally structured hierarchical system of organizations, coupled internally so that nearly decomposable, complex, evolutionary linear dynamics[19] allows serial and parallel processing of data can be empirically analysed.

Thus, every one of the 16 (or 17) concepts I specified in §1 of this chapter happens to be utilized, both theoretically and empirically, to define and determine the functions of the rational organizational mechanism. That this is not only for merely surviving in a market of more or less competition, by business organizations, in an advanced industrial economy, but also for its innovative evolution. This fact can be gleaned from a careful perusal of *Organizations*, especially chapters 6 and 7. Given the constraints of space, I choose to substantiate my above assertion with a few quotes from the relevant chapters of the book I am 'celebrating':

• *Most human decision-making, whether individual or organizational, is concerned with the discovery and selection of satisfactory alternatives*; . . .

(p. 162; italicized original)

- In organizations there is a considerable degree of *parallelism* between the *hierarchical* relations among members of the organization and the hierarchical relations among program elements.

(p. 171; italics added)

- [T]he central theme of [chapter 6 is] that the basic features of organizational structure and *function* derive from the characteristics of *human problem-solving processes* and *rational human choice*.

(p. 190; italics added)

- The five 'characteristic features' of the 'simplified models' [in chapter 6, p. 191; italics added] are:
  1  'Optimization is replaced by *satisficing* – . . . .'
  2  'Alternatives . . . . are *discovered, sequentially* through *search processes*.'
  3  [Repertoires] are developed by organizations . . . and serve as the *alternatives of choice* in recurrent situations.'
  4  Each specific action programs deals with *restricted range* of situations and a *restricted range* of consequences.'
  5  Each action program . . . executed semi-independently of the others – they are only *loosely coupled together*.'
- [A] mosaic of programs constitute the great bulk of human behavior in organizations.

(p. 193)

[A] *theory of choice* without *a theory of search* is inadequate.

(p. 194; italics added)

- [I]n the solution process several aspects may be dealt with separately – sequentially or simultaneously – in different parts of the organization.

(p. 200; italics added)

- [W]e have invoked the principle of *bounded rationality* as an important force making for *decentralization*; but we have not made any use of the distinction between *programmed* and *unprogrammed decision-making*.

(p. 232; italics added)

I can now state Gandy's four principles for the characterization of mechanisms to show that the *Organization*, particularly as described and developed in March & Simon (*ibid*), in activating the programmed part of its rational choice process, discovers, by calculating, using search heuristics, sequential and parallel processing digital computers, solutions to problems posed to it. Thus, Gandy's *Thesis M* (op. cit., p. 124; italics in the original):

*What can be calculated by a machine is computable.*

I would like to add that Gandy means, 'machine computable', in the sense of *computable by a Turing Machine*. In addition, it must be pointed out that the 'machine' Gandy envisaged, satisfying the four principles which we shall state, shortly, was a 'discrete deterministic mechanical device', entirely consistent with interpreting the programmed part of the *Organizations* in March and Simon in terms of discrete, deterministic, nonlinear dynamical system.

### Gandy's four principles (pp. 129–141, Gandy, *ibid.*)

I    *The form of description*: Any machine M can be described by giving a structural set of state-descriptions, together with a structural function. Given an **initial state** of the device, its subsequent states can be iterated forward.

II   *The Principle of the* **Boundedness** *of the* **Hierarchical** *States of the Computing Device.*

III  *The Principle of Unique Reassembly of the Structure and Function of the Computing Device, by means of the defining states.*

IV   *The Principle of Local* **Causality**.

A device or an institution – like the programmed part of the organization in March and Simon (*ibid.*) – can be said to compute the same way as a Turing Machine does – but not only of number-theoretic functions; any set of symbols can be the input – sequentially and simultaneously (in a parallel fashion) – to the device. I can, then, state as a lemma, analogous to proposition 3.1 in Velupillai (*op. cit.*),

*Lemma*

> The process of rational choice by an *Organization* is equivalent to the computing activity of a mechanical device and its mechanism satisfying *Gandy's four principles*.

*Proof*

> By explicit construction (as in the proof of the analogous proposition 3.1 in Velupillai, *ibid.*).

I now state what I consider the main – only – result of this chapter and an outline of its proof.

*Theorem*

> Given a class of choice functions that do generate preference orderings (pick out the set of maximal alternatives) for any rational agent, or group of agents, there is no effective procedure to decide whether or not any arbitrary choice function is a member of the given class.

*Proof*

> We can assume that the class of choice functions can be effectively encoded and, therefore, those choice functions that are rationalizable

are also effectively encodable. Moreover, the class of choice functions considered is not necessarily countably infinite. In other words, we now have a subset of the class of Gandy devices, satisfying the four principles earlier, computing members from the class of all symbol sequences to evaluate truth values for (classes of) binary relations. But no non-trivial property of this subset of Gandy machines, that is, the class of rationalizable choice functions, is effectively decidable. In particular, there is no effective procedure to decide whether or not any arbitrary given choice function is a member of the given rationalizable set.

*Remark I*

This is the technical reason for the programmed part of an organization to work with *boundedly rational* agents/group of agents, *satisfying*, in their activities.

*Remark II*

Thus, there is an inherent element of unpredictability, even in the activity of the programmed part of the organization (this is quite separate from the uncertain consequences of the actions of the nonprogrammed part of the organization).

*Remark III*

These two remarks, and the theorem earlier are the reasons why March and Simon able to state the following (*ibid.*, p. 161; italics added):

What kinds of *search* and other *problem-solving* activity are needed to *discover* an adequate range of alternatives and consequences. . . . In particular, finding the *optimal alternative* is a radically different problem from finding a *satisfactory alternative*.

Finally, I would like to point out that Simon, in particular, 'tamed' the uncomputable and undecidable results of the lemma and theorem (given earlier) and their consequences as stated 'formally' as the preceding three 'Remarks', by working inside a domain where Gödel's Completeness result was valid for Propositional Logic.[20] I can add that this underpins the results in Newell and Simon (*op. cit.*, part 3) and is the basis for the letter exchanges between Russell and Simon, of 1956/57 (see, Simon, 1996, pp. 207–209).

## §3 Conjectures and concluding notes

Up to this point we have invoked the principle of *bounded rationality* as an important force making for *decentralization*; but we have not made any use of the distinction between programmed and unprogrammed *decision-making*. . . . Whether prices are *effective* devices for *decision-making* has to be determined by examining [empirically] *the equilibrium* toward which they will lead the system. . . .
—March and Simon (1993, p. 232; italics added)

These words, in the final pages of *Organizations*, by March and Simon, are about the feasibility of the empirical determination of the basin of attraction – using the standard terminology of formal dynamical systems theory – of effective prices, More important, from the point of view of Simon's epistemology and methodology, it is about rules for the *empirical determination* of *effective* concepts that are relevant for the processes that an Organizations activates and initiates. Emphasizing, as Simon did, the empirical testing of theoretical results was how I started this paper; it is, therefore, appropriate that my concluding section returns to this theme.

I would like to conclude with two conjectures on issues that were central in *Organizations*; their *size* and the recursive (un)decidability of the deterministic, discrete, non-linear dynamics of the programmed part of an organization.

Before I proceed with the conjectures, I should state that the recursive (un) decidability of the dynamics of the programmed part entails unpredictability of this entirely deterministic division of an organization. In other words, the unpredictability of the evolutionary dynamics of an organization does not depend exclusively on the non-programmed part of the problem-solving activities of an organization.

As for the *size* of an organization, an observation of Simon's view may well be appropriate here:

> *[O]rganization size* and degree of integration, and the *boundaries* between organizations and markets, are *determined by rather subtle forces*.
> (Simon, 1991, p. 41; italics added)

Search for a 'computable' definition of the *size* of an organization is like looking for an identifiable pattern to follow, in reassembling[21] an *evolutionary* or changing jigsaw puzzle. To conjecture a resolution of this puzzle – knowing that Simon was fond of, and was an expert in, solving puzzles – begin with a 'party problem' version of what became Ramsey's Theorem, which I conjecture should be the (changing) measure of the *intractable size* of an organization.

How many people does one have to invite, to make sure that at least $k$ people would *all* know each other, or at least $l$ people would not all know each other? The answer, as Simon – a maestro of chess and the *Tower of Hanoi* solution algorithms – would *easily* have calculated, in the case that $k = 3$, $l = 3$, is 6!

The *eponymous* Ramsey, in trying to solve Hilbert's *Entscheidungsproblem* – resolved by his young fellow King's College, Cambridge, member Alan Turing just half a decade after Ramsey's untimely death at the age of 30 – stated what has become famous as the *Ramsey Theorem* (adapted for application to define the *size* of an organization of the March/Simon type – see Ramsey, 1930; Soifer [ed.], 2011, for formal definitions).

An organization, by definition, has a *finite* number of members – either individual or as members of a *finite* number of groups, say, each group defining a division of the organization. Denote this finite set by $A$, say. Suppose we take a subset, of, say, $k$ elements of $A$ and call it $B$ (members of $B$ are labelled in any form). Partition this subset of the original finite set into a (finite) class, say $C_i$, $i = 1, 2, \ldots, m$, such that each member of the partition has an equal, finite number of members as the total number in the original set, $A$. Now make sure that every subset of the original set of members $A$, containing as many members as each $C_i$, for all $i = 1, 2, \ldots , m$, is a member of one, and only one $C_i$, for all $i = 1, 2, \ldots , m$. Suppose there is a subset of members, say, $H$, such that every $k$-element subset of the original set A, which is made up of elements of $H$, is a member of, say, $C_k$. Then a notion of the structure of the original organizations is preserved under the finite partition, $A$.[22]

### Conjecture 1: definition of size of a given organization

$k$ is the *size* of the given organization.

Two remarks, regarding this conjecture, are in order.

First, as the organization evolves, or changes, because of mergers or internal reorganization, or new recruitments because of 'expansion' (not evolution), then the measure of its *size* changes. Thus, as March and Simon repeatedly emphasize in their classic, some relative stability of the function and structure of the given organization must be a prerequisite for any kind of coherent analysis.

Second, I have conjectured that there is a duality relation between the Busy Beaver's noncomputable activity and the apparently intractable measure $k$, when it is 'large' – even as low as greater than only 5. But the noncomputability of the Busy Beaver is relative to the Church–Turing Thesis and does not take into account the kind of parallel processing that a Gandy Mechanisms is capable of, when computing. Therefore, it is possible to wonder whether Simon may not use the structured search processes determining his use of *Heuristics* to solve problems, to find a way to 'tame' the intractable behaviour of the *Busy Beavers*; in this case, $k$ will also become 'tamed'![23]

Finally, I have observed, after years of study of Simon's many-splendoured research contributions, that he has exploited, to the extent possible, the power of linear continuous, and discrete, dynamics of systems of any finite order. His starting point, though, seems to have been the nature and structure of computer programs.

Suppose, we 'go' the 'other way' (see also Bartlett, 1990; Tong & Lim, 1980) – that is, start from dynamical systems that are discrete, deterministic – as all computer programs are – and non-linear. Suppose these systems are given initial values to start their dynamics. Is it possible to ask whether the basins of attraction of the limit sets of these dynamical systems are algorithmically determinate? The well-known answer to this question is in the negative. Faced with such a negative solution, I conjecture that Simon would have considered it a challenge to make this undecidable answer decidable. This is the contrary to the way he defined bounded rationality and satisficing – but in this case, too, his search for a heuristic that would answer in a finite time and in a determinate way – even if intractable time and space.

I conclude, therefore, with our second conjecture:

### Conjecture 2: on the undecidable dynamics of the evolution of an organization

The programmed part of a given organization's dynamics has algorithmically undecidable *basins of attraction*.

Herbert Simon, with or without the intellectual assistance of James March (or Allan Newell – or any of the other more than six dozen collaborators), would have tried his very best, as the *Scientist* who is a *Problem Solver*, using the structured search processes of *Heuristics*, would have tried his best to make the issue one of algorithmic decidability.

## Notes

\* An earlier version of this chapter was co-authored with Edgardo Buciarelli.

1 An inessential remark may be warranted here: there are minor infelicities in the vast reference list (#268!) of Newell and Simon (1972), an example of this (triviality) is the title of Brookes (1963) has a hyphen in the word for *cryptarithmetic* (cf. pt. 2 of Newell/Simon, *op. cit.*) – as *Crypt-Arithmetic*, known in much earlier times as *Arithmetical Restorations* (Brookes, *op. cit.*, p. 4, see also, Knuth (1997), page 324, where *Alphametics* and *cryptarithm* are mentioned as alternative names).

2 The interested reader can obtain a good introduction to the genetic concepts from Mukherjee (2016); the cognitive scientific aspects of *chess*, *cryptarithmetic* and the *Tower of Hanoi* are part of Simon's *oeuvre*, but see, in particular, parts 4 and 2 of Newell & Simon (1972) and chapter 4.8 of Simon (1989), respectively.

3 The title of this paper presages that of the *Afterword* in Simon (1991; 1996), *The Scientist as Problem Solver*, to which we will return later.

4 The roles played by Mendel's *green peas*, Morgan's *drosphila* and Monod's *Escherica (E-) coli experiments* in underpinning the *theories* (cf. Mukherjee, 2016) they formulated are salutatory lessons for anyone trying to understand Simon's scientific life of research. I do not make a hard-and-fast distinction between *empirics* and *experiments*, either methodologically or epistemologically.

5 It was important to understand the processes a human rational agent uses to solve puzzles and (parlour) games, and he considered chess, the word-puzzles of *cryptarithmetic* and the *Tower of Hanoi* as quintessential examples of this activity. In this he was very similar in the emphasis the almost playfully innocent Alan Turing gave to chess and GO. We surmise that both Simon and Turing would have welcomed Kasparov (2017) and Hassabis (2017), in the way machine models have been constructed to learn, mimic and defeat Grandmasters in chess and GO.

6 See Simon (1947), page 37.

7 As the then doyen of Political Science, Robert Dahl, pointed out, perceptively (Dahl, 1957, p. 245; italics added):

[T]he *concept* at the center of his theory is '*decision making*'.

This is in contrast to his lifelong collaborator – and friend – Allen Newell's view (see the following)!

8 Frege's classic of 1879 was titled **Begirffsschrift** (cf. van Heijenoort [ed.], 1967, pp. 1–82).

9 Analogous to the *Cowles Foundation Monograph* that became Arrow (1951), where *socially rational behaviour* was underpinned by *individual rationality* – produced when Simon was also a member of the *Cowles Foundation*.

10 I confess that it was only relatively recently that a realization of the difference between Simon and Turing (1954), in their respective approaches to *Problem Solving – Human* and *Machine* or *Formal*, respectively – became clear to me. Simon's notion of *algorithm* does not assume the *Church–Turing Thesis* (cf. also Simon, 2004), especially page 47 – published only after he died), but nor is it of the *Constructive Mathematical* variety; if anything, it is cognitive (psychological), inspired by Selz and Duncker.

'Challenging' Newell's view, based on decades of friendship and co-authorship, is not something I indulge in lightly, but the subject requires a detailed exposition, which I must reserve for another time.

11  For ease of expositions I shall *henceforth* refer to March and Simon (1958) *and* **Models of My Life** (1991), with the date of the second editions (1993, 1996 and the MIT Press edition, respectively).

12  See also Simon (2004), page 47. We have absolutely no doubts whatsoever that Simon would be exhilarated with the recent work of Spielman & Teng, reported by Cipra (2006) on deemphasizing the idea of defining and measuring computational complexity by notions of worst-case alternatives.

13  Alternatively, it is possible to use the concept of a *Busy Beaver Game*, which – according to Velupillai – has a kind of *duality* relationship with *Ramsey's Theorem*.

14  Although Simon (1952; 1953) is republished in Simon (1957), I have wondered whether the second part of the former could have been the missing Mathematical Appendix of Simon (1947)!

15  There is *no* reference to **Models of Man** in **Organizations**, although the latter was published one year after the former, but many of the essays, relevant for the mechanisms of rationality in organizations, in the former, were individually referred to in the latter. Also, *omniscient [Rational] man* in **Models of Man** (p. 202), became *Olympian Rationality* in Simon (1983, p. 19). Incidentally, Dahl (op. cit., p. 245) refers to Simon's *act* of '*creative destruction*' (Schumpeter, 1942, pp. 82–83) in his (largely successful) attempts to construct a *Science* of the *Principles of Administrative Behavior* – an act which Simon achieved – in my opinion – by laying the *foundations of a Science of Organization Behaviour* with what I call the construction of a *Rational Mechanism of Organizations* as *Computational Devices* in the sense of Gandy (ibid.).

16  Surprisingly, I have never encountered this particular phrase in any of Simon's works, but I would like to hasten to add that it does not mean it cannot be found *somewhere* in them!

17  There is a curious misprint in referring to the date of this classic's original publication, on page 202 of Simon (1957) – where, obviously, by '1945' is meant '1944'!

18  As Simon wrote in footnotes 2 and 3, respectively, on page 202, in Simon (*ibid.*; italics added):

> I must add that I agree with *neither* Edwards *nor* Savage in their assessment of the import and implications of these developments (in 'the theory of decision making').

and

> [I] cannot think of a more appropriate word [than '*wrongheaded*'] to describe the cheerful and buoyant obstinacy with which my friends in economics and statistics defend their *myth of omniscient man*.

These enlightened, if also cheerfully caustic, standpoints of Simon are dissected and explored in detail in Kao and Velupillai (*op. cit.*). That which is currently – fashionably – referred to as *behavioural economics* (Kao & Velupillai refer to this as *Modern Behavioural Economics*, **MBE**) goes back to the early works on the decision theory of Ward Edwards, based on the subjective probability theory of Leonard Savage, and became *subjective expected utility* (**SEU**) theory. None of this, in particular, MBE theory, is computable in *any* sense, with or without an assumption of the Church–Turing Thesis or any formalization of Simonian *Heuristics*. The probability theory that underpins MBE is not based on the theories of Savage (and there is *no* mention of Keynes – of the **Treatise on Probability** – Ramsey or de Finetti in von Neumann/Morgenstern).

19  It must be noted – contrary to 'popular' misconceptions – that *complexity* and *linear dynamics* are not antithetical notions, as evidenced by the framework and results of Turing (1952).
20  I became aware of the framework and results in the important paper by Laita et al. (2007) *after* the first draft of this chapter was completed. But I am heartened by the reinforcement their framework provides for my stance, on Simon's approach to problem solving and discoveries, *via* search processes underpinning the *Heuristics* of human decision-making. Indeed, the title of the first draft of this paper had the phrase *Decidable Discoveries* to circumvent the *undecidable* result of the earlier theorem. In other words, I want to emphasize that Simon searched iteratively, often modifying what he called the task domain (of a division of the organization), to make undecidabilities yield decidable results (see also Cohen, 1987, ch. 11; Franzén, 2005, ch. 2 & 7).
21  Recall the third of the four Gandy Principles, on the *unique reassembly* of the structure and function of a computing device, which I postulate an organization of the March/Simon variety is.
22  Endowing the set $H$ with a recursive structure, as in Jockusch (1972), makes my conjecture compatible with Gandy's notion of *Mechanisms*.
23  Incidentally, I am surprised that the *Clay Millennium Problems* (see Carlson et al., 2006) do not include anything about Ramsey Theory (or the *Busy Beaver* – although they do make the $P \stackrel{?}{=} NP$ issue one of those celebrated problems).

# References

Arrow, Kenneth Joseph (1951), *Social Choice and Individual Values*, Monograph 12, Cowles Foundation for Research in Economics at Yale University, John Wiley & Sons, Inc., New York, NY.

Bartlett, M. S. (1990), Chance or Chaos?, *Journal of the Royal Statistical Society*, Series A, Vol. 153, No. 3, pp. 321–347.

Brookes, Maxey (1963), *150 Puzzles In Crypt-Arithmetic*, Dover Publications, Inc., New York.

Carlson, J., A. Jaffe & A. Wiles (eds.) (2006), *The Millennium Prize Problems*, Clay Mathematics Institute/American Mathematical Society, MA/RI.

Cipra, Barry (2006), Smooth(ed) Moves, pp. 112–122, in: *What's Happening in the Mathematical Sciences*, edited by Dana Mackenzie & Barry Cipra, American Mathematical Society, Providence, RI.

Cohen, Daniel E. (1987), *Computability and Logic*, Ellis Horwood Limited, Chichester.

Dahl, Robert A. (1957), Review of Administrative Behaviour & Models of Man (by Herbert Simon), *Administrative Science Quarterly*, Vol. 2, No. 2, September, pp. 244–248.

Franzén, Torkel (2005), *Gödels Theorem: An Incomplete Guide to Its Use and Abuse*, A K Peters, Wellesley, MA.

Frege, Gottlob (1879; 1967), *Begriffsschrift: eine der arithmetischen nachgebildete Formelsprache des reinen Denkens* (translated by Stefan Mauer-Mengelberg, in: J. van Heijenoort, ed., 1967).

Gandy, Robin (1980), Church's Thesis and Principles for Mechanisms, pp. 123–148, in: *The Kleene Symposium*, edited by J. Barwise, H. J. Keisler & K. Kunen, North-Holland Publishing Company, Amsterdam.

Gigerenzer, Gerd and Reinhard Selten (eds.) (2001), *Bounded Rationality: The Adaptive Toolbox*, The MIT Press, Cambridge, MA.

Gregg, Lee William & Herbert Alexander Simon (1967), Process Models and Stochastic Theories of Simple Concept Formation, *Journal of Mathematical Psychology*, Vol. 4, No. 2, June, pp. 246–276.

Hassabis, Demis (2017), Artificial Intelligence: Chess Match of the Century, *Nature*, Vol. 27, April, pp. 413–414.

Jockusch, Carl Groos, Jr. (1972), Ramsey's Theorem and Recursion Theory, *The Journal of Symbolic Logic*, Vol. 37, No. 2, June, pp. 268–280.

Kao, Ying-Fang & K. Vela Velupillai (2015), Behavioural Economics: Classical and Modern, *European Journal of the History of Economic Thought*, Vol. 22, No. 2, pp. 236–271.

Kasparov, Gary & Mig Greengard (2017), *Deep Thinking: Where Machine Intelligence Ends and Human Creativity Begins*, Public Affairs, New York, NY.

Klee, Victor & George J. Minty (1972), How Good Is the Simplex Algorithm?, pp. 159–175, in: *Inequalities III, Proceedings of the Third Symposium on Inequalities*, UCLA, September 1–9, 1969 (dedicated to the memory of Theodore S. Motzkin), edited by Oved Shisha, Academic Press, New York, NY.

Knuth, Donald Erwin (1997), *The Art of Computer Programming – Volume 4A: Combinatorial Algorithms, Part 1*, Addison-Wesley, Upper Saddle River, NJ.

Laita, Luis M., Eugenio Roanes-Lozano & Luis de Ledesma Otamendi (2007), What Machines Can and Cannot Do, *Revista de la Real Academia Ciencias, Serie A, Matemáticas*, Vol. 101, No. 2, pp. 133–157.

March, James G. & Herbert A. Simon, with the collaboration of Harold Guetzkow, (1958; 1993), *Organizations* (Second Edition), Blackwell Publishers, Oxford.

Mukherjee, Siddhartha (2016), *The Gene: An Intimate History*, The Bodley Head, London.

Newell, Allen (1989), Puttimg It All Together, chapter 15, pp. 399–400, in: *Complex Information Processing: The Impact of Herbert Simon*, edited by David Klahr & Kenneth Kotovsky, Lawrence Earlbaum Associates, Inc., Hillsdale, NJ.

Newell, Allen & Herbert Alexander Simon (1972), *Human Problem Solving*, Prentice-Hall, Inc., Englewood Cliffs, NJ.

Polya, George (1945), *How to Solve It: A New Aspect of Mathematical Method*, Princeton University Press, Princeton, NJ.

Radner, Roy (1975), Satisficing, *Journal of Mathematical Economics*, Vol. 2, No. 2, pp. 253–262.

Ramsey, Frank Plumpton (1930), On a Problem of Formal Logic, *Proceedings of the London Mathematical Society*, Series 2, Vol. 30, No. 4, pp. 338–384.

Sargent, Thomas John (1993), *Bounded Rationality in Macroeconomics*, Clarendon Press, Oxford.

Schumpeter, Joseph Alois (1942), *Capitalism, Socialism and Democracy*, Harper & Brothers, New York, NY.

Shepherdson, John C. (1975), Computation over Abstract Sructures: Serial and Parallel Procedures and Friedman's Effective Definitional Schemes, pp. 445–513, in: *Logic Colloquium '73 – Proceedings of the Logic Colloquium*, edited by H. E. Rose & John C. Shepherdson, Bristol, July, North-Holland Publishing Company, Amsterdam.

Shepherdson, John C. (1995), Mechanisms for Computing Over Arbitrary Structures, pp. 537–555, in: *The Universal Turing Machine a Half-Century Survey* (Second Edition), edited By Rolf Herken, Springer-Verlag, Wien.

Simon, Herbert Alexander (1947), *Administrative Behavior: A Study of Decision-Making Processes in Administrative Organization* (Foreword by Chester Barnard), The Macmillan Company, New York, NY.

Simon, Herbert Alexander (1952; 1953), A Comparison of Organisation Theories, *The Review of Economic Studies*, Vol. 20, No. 1, pp. 40–48.

Simon, Herbert Alexander (1957), *Models of Man: Social and Rational* (Mathematical Essays on Rational Human Behavior in a Social Setting), John Wiley & Sons, Inc., New York, NY.

Simon, Herbert Alexander (1983), *Reason in Human Affairs*, Basil Blackwell, Oxford.

Simon, Herbert Alexander, (1989), The Scientist as Problem Solver, chapter 14, pp. 375–398, in: *Complex Information Processing: The Impact of Herbert A. Simon*, edited by David Klahr & Kenneth Kotovsky, Lawrence Erlbaum Associates, Publishers, Hillsdale, New Jersey.

Simon, Herbert Alexander (1991; 1996), *Models of My Life*, The MIT Press, Cambridge, MA.

Simon, Herbert Alexander (1991), Organizations and Markets, *Journal of Economic Perspectives*, Vol. 5, No. 2, Spring, pp. 25–44.

Simon, Herbert Alexander (1997), *An Empirically Based Microeconomics*, Cambridge University Press, Cambridge.

Simon, Herbert Alexander (2004), Science Seeks Parsimony, Not Simplicity: Searching for Pattern in Phenomena, chapter 3, pp. 32–82, in: *Simplicity, Inference and Modelling: Keeping It Sophisticatedly Simple*, edited by Arnold Zellner, Hugo A. Keuzenkamp & Michael McAleer, Cambridge University Press, Cambridge.

Soifer, Alexander (ed.) (2011), *Ramsey Theory: Yesterday, Today and Tomorrow*, Birkhäuser, Dordrecht.

Takahashi, Nobuo (2015), Where Is Bounded Rationality From?, *Annals of Business Administrative Science*, Vol. 14, No. 2, pp. 67–82.

Tong, H. & S. M. Lim (1980), Threshold Autoregression, Limit Cycles and Cyclical Data, *Journal of the Royal Statistical Society*, Series B, Vol. 42, No. 3, pp. 245–292.

Turing, Alan M. (1936), On Computable Numbers, with an Application to the Entscheidungs Problem, *Proceedings of the London Mathematical Society*, Series 2, Vol. 42, pp. 230–265.

Turing, Alan M. (1952), The Chemical Basis of Morphogenesis, *Philosophical Transactions of the Royal Society of London: Series B, Biological Sciences*, Vol. 237, No. 641, August 14, pp. 37–72.

Turing, Alan M. (1954), Solvable and Unsolvable Problems, *Science News*, edited by A. W. Haslett, Vol. 31, February, pp. 7–23.

van Heijenoort, Jean (1967), *From Frege to Gödel: A Source Book in Mathematical Logic, 1879–1931*, Harvard University Press, Cambridge, MA.

Velupillai, Kumaraswamy (2000), *Computable Economics – the Arne Ryde Memorial Lectures*, Oxford University Press, Oxford.

# 9  Towards a *Classical**

# Behavioural Finance Theory

Herb had it all put together *at least* 40 years ago [i.e., in1949, or earlier*] – . . . .
The central idea is *bounded rationality* – there are limits on man as a decision
maker and these limits, especially those of **cognitive processing** in all its varied
forms, loom large in man's **behaviour**. . . . This central scientific proposition has
remained without revision.

—Newell (1989, p. 400; bold italics, added)

## §1  Introductory quasi-historical notes

[I]t really seems as though old Hegel, in the guise of the World Spirit, were direct-
ing history from the grave and, with the greatest conscientiousness, *causing everything to be re-enacted twice over, once as grand tragedy and the second time as
rotten farce*. . . .

—*Engels*, **Letter to Marx**, *3 December, 1851*(italics added)

There are, broadly conceived, *four*[1] powerful and substantial approaches to (Mathematical) Finance Theory – whether in an aggregative or disaggregative form.

I characterize the first as the theory of finance underpinned by the conjunction
of *subjective expected utility* (SEU) and the *efficient market hypothesis* (EMH),
buttressed by the *stochastic calculus of Ito* (stochastic) *integrals* and, hence,
largely based on the formalism of stochastic differential equations. Barberis and
Thaler (2005, p. 1) refer to this approach as 'the traditional finance paradigm' and
that 'which seeks to'

understand financial markets using models in which agents are 'rational'.

They add that this 'rationality means two things': first, these 'rational agents'
behave in consonance with the tenets of 'Bayes's Law',[2] in *updating* their 'beliefs',
as 'new' relevant information arrives *sequentially*. Second, these 'rational agents'
act consistently with the postulates of SEU.

Second, closely related to the first but eschewing the *orthodox probabilistic
framework*, whether subjective, logical or objective, is the work pioneered by Shafer and Vovk (2001), of mathematical finance theory, with a basis in Kolmogorov's

*algorithmic complexity theory*. This, in turn, has its origins in von Mises's attempt at characterizing *place selection functions* – of a rigorous *selection of a particular sequence* – Ville's definitive demonstration of lacunae in the von Mises definition and the resulting emergence, in this work, of defining *martingales* in terms of the *impossibility of a gambling system*, violating a concept of fair game in a two-person, full-information, alternating sequence – that is, an *Arithmetic Game*. The Ito integral, avoiding the Ito lemma, via a deft use of heuristic arguments, enables Shafer and Vovk to derive an *Arithmetic Game* variation of the *Ito stochastic integral* and, hence, the *finance theoretic stochastic differential equation* (Shafer & Vovk, 2001, ch. 14).

In a nutshell, this kind of *Arithmetic Game* approach, without a basis in any notion of probability at its foundation, is founded on two precepts:

- That which is the centrepiece of the von Mises concept of the fundamental nature of a random sequence, summarised by his 'slogan': Erst das Kollektiv – dann die Wahrscheinlichkeit

    (von Mises, 1972, p. 21; see also p. 30)

- The idea of *incompressible sequences*, from *algorithmic* or Kolmogorov complexity theory, which in turn is based on *recursion* (or *computability*) theory and with an assumption of the *Church-Turing Thesis*

    (Li & Vitanyi, 1993, p. 95, ff.)

Third, there is the lineage that emanates from Louis Bachelier (1900), developed by Maury Osborne (1959) and Benoit Mandelbrot (1963). Brownian motions, fractal structures and *stable*[3] *distributions* (Feller, 1971, p. 169, ff.) of the dynamics of sequences of financial variables, viewed as generated by random mechanisms, is at the basis of this approach. Although interesting, and even iconoclastic, ultimately it is a reaffirmation of the 'traditional finance paradigm', albeit with 'new' mathematical tools.[4]

Finally, I come to the 'new' financial paradigm of *Behavioural Finance*, paying close attention to Thaler's important observation (Thaler, 2005, ed., p. xi, footnote):

Behavioural economics (of which *behavioural finance is a subset*) builds upon (does *not* replace) standard economic analyses.

Thaler is considered – for Thaler (1980) – the 'founding father' of *Modern Behavioural Economics* (**MBE**), see Camerer et al. (2004, p. xxii).[5] The reason for referring to MBE as a 'bicycle repair shop' for 'correcting anomalies as *counterexamples*' [*ibid.*, p. 6; italics added], with modified versions of the *same* tools and concepts of 'standard economic analyses', is Thaler's earlier observation.

Thaler (1993, p. xvi) adds, perhaps 'with tongue in cheek', that '[orthodox] financial economists did not know how to spell the word *anomaly*.' The phrase 'anomalies as counterexamples' strengthens Thaler's observation, if 'counterexamples' are interpreted in terms of (classical) analysis (Geldbaum & Olmsted, 2003) – but this is *different* from *Brouwerian* '*counterexamples*' in constructive mathematics (van Dalen, 1999).

One additional infelicitous – if not an outright *incorrect* – claim by Thaler should be mentioned. In the opening paragraph of Thaler (1993, p. xv; italics added), it is claimed that

> a reading of a standard finance textbook. . . can create the impression that financial markets are *nearly* devoid of human activity. There is great attention to *methods of computing* important numbers . . . and even a primer on how to price options. But *virtually no people*. Very little in the text would be changed if *all* the people in both the corporate sector and the financial sector were replaced by *automatons*.[6]

First of all, trivially, there is a rigorous distinction between 'nearly' and 'all' – but let that infelicity pass. Second, and more seriously, Thaler makes an incorrect assertion about *automatons* – not something Simon ever made; it is not true that 'very little . . . would be changed if all the people . . . were replaced by automatons'. Whether 'little', 'very little' or 'any' difference is made depends entirely on *the kind of automatons* used, for replacing nearly all, or all, the people. Third, related to the second incorrect assertion, the kind of behavioural finance advocated by Thaler and company, is as cavalier about the foundations of the methods of computations used to 'compute numbers'.

In fact, *all* of the so-called agents populating behavioural finance *can be replaced* by suitably defined automatons! Where they cannot be so 'replaced', the ambiguity of the predicted solutions would not be very different from those of the 'standard paradigm' for financial economics.

On the whole, I subscribe wholeheartedly to the Gigerenzer and Gaissmaier (2011, p. 452) characterization of *behavioural finance* as being based on the 'heuristics-and-biases program' of Tversky and Kahneman (1974), which is founded upon the '*two-systems theories of reasoning*' (*ibid.*, p. 452).[7] This is akin to Clower's *dual-decision hypothesis* in questioning the Walrasian microfoundations of Keynesian macroeconomics (with exceptional rigour) – except for *five* crucial *ad hockeries* in this alternative to the standard paradigm of the individual's *mind* to be underpinned by

- the *psychological* foundations of this 'heuristic-and-biases' program;
- the *probabilistic* – and, hence, *theoretical statistics* – bases of the Tversky–Kahneman program;
- the inattentive details of the (mathematical) *logic*, that *reason* is supposed to be disciplined by, for its activation (substantially or procedurally);
- no basis, in any of the computational exercises or experiments, in any kind of rigorous *theory of computation* – whether of the recursion theoretic, interval arithmetic, the so-called scientific computation, constructive or the idea of computation over a *ring of integers* (associated almost exclusively the

Smale school's attempt to link dynamical systems and complexity theories) viewpoints – and, hence, vacuous as a basis for any kind of complexity theoretic pronouncement; and
• thoroughly inadequate integration of bounded rationality and satisfiability in an 'optimal' decision theoretic framework.

These five *ad hockeries* do **not** exhaust the analytic infelicities of the framework of *behavioural finance*. Despite these infelicities, and an adherence to the discredited falsifiability hypothesis of Popper, the practitioners – and theorists – of behavioural finance are recommended (*sic!*) a four-step 'recipe'[8] for 'this line of research' (Camerer et al., *ibid.*, p. 7).

Finally, it is easy to show, by recursion theoretic arguments, that it is *impossible* – that is, *algorithmically undecidable* – to *construct* preferences, even if they are finitely countable, contrary to the claims of behavioural finance theorists (e.g., Payne et al., 1992).

### Mathematical appendix to §1

There are numerous other paradoxical beliefs of this society [of economists], consequent to the difference between *discrete numbers* . . . in which data is recorded, whereas the *theoreticians* of this society *tend to think in terms of real numbers* . . . No matter how hard I looked, *I never could see any actual real [economic] data that showed that [these solid, smooth, lines of economic theory]. . . actually could be observed in nature. . . .*

If you think in terms of *solid lines* while the practice is in terms of *dots and little steps* up and down, this misbelief on your part is worth, I would say conservatively, to the governors of the exchange, at least eighty million dollars per year.
                                                    – Osborne (1977; 1995, pp. 16–35; italics added)

Osborne's perceptive observation should be taken seriously – but is *not* done so by any of the four (or five) 'paradigms' mentioned earlier. In the following statements of the two theses, it is assumed that the financial data that being analysed is depicted as *sequences*.[9]

### The Church's Thesis[10]

*Every formalizable rule is reducible to a recursive procedure.*[11]

### Remark 1

'Formalizable' in the strict metamathematical sense, for example, as in Kleene (1967). It is possible, with this version – of the one popularly known *Church – Turing Thesis* – it may be possible to encapsulate even Simon's notion of *Heuristic Search Processes*. It may be noted that I have avoided using the notion of *effectivity* and *calculable* in the statement of this thesis.

*Remark 2*

Gandy's important caveats to what Church and Turing had in *mind* (*sic!*) is worth remembering (Gandy, 1980, pp. 123–124; italics added):

> Both Church and Turing had in mind calculation by an abstract human being using some mechanical aids (such as paper and pencil). The word "abstract" indicates that the argument makes *no appeal to the existence of practical limits on time and space*. The word "effective" in the thesis serves to emphasize that the *process of calculation is deterministic* – not dependent on guesswork – and that it must *terminate after a finite time*.

*Remark 3*

Simon's construction of computer programs, for human problem solving, made sure that machine implementation was not 'abstract' – that is, '*the existence of practical limits on time and space*' was explicitly acknowledged, but he did work with deterministic processes of calculations that *terminated after a finite time*. This was the primary reason for Simon's *Heuristic search processes* was not underpinned by any form of the Church–Turing Thesis.

*Remark 4*

'Termination after a finite time' – or, equivalently, search spaces that were finitely constrained – did not mean *countably* infinite sequences only, in the case of Simon.

*The Kolmogorov/Chaitin/Solomonoff/Martin-Löf Thesis:*

Every random *sequence* is reducible to an algorithmically irreducible arithmetic *sequence*, and these sequences are (at most) countable infinite.

*Remark 5*

The sequences have to be *countably infinite* and *recursively enumerable* but *not recursive*.

*Theorem 1*

Only *incompressible sequences* are capable of representing *no arbitrage behaviour* by *rational agents*.

*Proof*

By standard definitions of the italicized terms.

*Corollary 1*

The Efficient Market *Hypothesis* (EMH) is relevant only for *incompressible sequences*.

*Proof* (outline)

It is easy to show (*sic!*) – *rigorously*[12] – that *any* economic concept of efficiency is *non-effective* in the sense of computability theory. The statement of the corollary follows immediately.

*Corollary 2*

The *Efficient Market Hypothesis* is *uncomputable*.

*Proof* (outline)

There are two ways to prove this corollary. Either by way of using the idea of the non-effectivity of any economic concept of efficiency or by considering a 'market' as playing a game – in the sense of Shafer and Vovk – against nature.

## §2 *Heuristics*[13] as a basis for CBFT in Human Problem Solving

The "all-or-none" law of these activities, and the conformity of their relations to those of the *logic of propositions*, insure that the relations of psychons are those of the *two-valued logic of propositions*. Thus *in psychology*, introspective, behavioristic or physiological, *the fundamental relations are those of two-valued logic*.
—McCulloch and Pitts (1943, p. 131; italics added)

McCulloch and Pitts, Selz and Polya form the triptych that were *cognitive psychological* foundation on which Simon (together with Newell) explored *decision procedures* – optimal or not – as *Human Problem-Solving* exercises of *discovery*, with *heuristic* search strategies, buttressed by experimental studies of *perceptions*, in suitable *representations*. The cognitive psychological foundations of human problem solving were circumscribed by the *rational economic person's bounded rationality*, implementing decision procedures, *constrained by*[14] seeking *satisficing* – not necessarily optimal – outcomes.[15] I should add that Simon never referred gender neutrally to rational administrative *man*, the rational organisation *man* or the rational economic *man*. He contrasted the bounded – or limited – rationality of these concepts with the *Olympian Rationality* (Simon, 1983, p. 19) of orthodox economic theory.

Because of Camerer et al.'s (*ibid.*, p. xxii, and Kao & Velupillai, *op. cit.*) claim of Thaler (1980) being the origins of *Modern Behavioural Economics*, I have referred to Simon's way of doing – and defining (Simon, 1955) – behavioural economics as *classical*. In this spirit, and consequent on Thaler's definition (see the earlier discussion) of (modern) behavioural finance (**MBF**) as a subset of (modern) behavioural economics, I shall refer to Simon's alternative as *Classical Behavioural Finance Theory* (**CBFT**).

Although I agree entirely with the Gigerenzer/Gaissmaier characterization of *behavioural finance* as being based on the 'heuristics-and-biases program' of Tversky and Kahneman (1974), founded on the '*two-systems theories of reasoning*' (see the earlier discussion), it might be useful to point out that the fleshing out of this programme was in terms of *perceptions, representations, framing* and so on – which I have referred to as the 'positive heuristics', in the Lakatosian sense, of **MBF**.

It pains me, therefore, to know that practitioners and theorists at the frontiers of **MBF** either have no knowledge of Simon's pioneering, early – and sustained – contributions to these auxiliary concepts to his *computational cognitive psychological* bases for **CBFT**, or seem to belittle its relevance, even for **MBF**.

I shall only refer to some of the classic work by Simon – experimentally, theoretically and empirically – on these auxiliary concepts, like representations, framing, perceptions, verbal protocols, and the like – whilst requesting the reader to remember that Simon never formulated theoretical problems without assuring their solutions, after examining the experimental or empirical limitations of their impact on individual and collective actions – for example, in the latter case, within well-defined organizations (March & Simon, 1958; 1993).

As for *representations, framing* and *perceptions*, I can do no better than refer anyone interested in examining Simon's pioneering – and priority – writings and work to Simon (1977), particularly, to the last two chapters in section 4, the first three chapters of section 5[16] and the first five chapters of section 6. In particular, I hope it is noted that the first chapter of section 6, on the *Axioms of Newtonian Mechanics*, was published in 1947 – the same year as the first edition of **Administrative Behavior**!

As for *perceptions*, and the *cognitive mechanisms* that were called forth so that the *psychological underpinnings of behaviour* could be bared, I can do no better than refer to the chapters in sections 5 and 6 of **Models of Thought**, *Volume 1* (Simon, 1979). Whereas, at least in the 'early work [of] Kahneman, Tversky, and others [of **MBE** persuasion] viewed cognitive biases as judgemental kin of . . . *optical illusions*' (Camerer et al., 2004, p. 13; italics added), Simon, with experimental ingenuity and theoretical originality showed how such apparent 'illusions' – as the *Neckar cube*, the *Reutesvärd & Penrose/Penrose* and *Escher impossible* diagrams[17] – could be explained by re-interpreting (i.e., *re-framing* and using, if necessary, oblique coordinate systems) the r*epresentations* of reframed perceptual mechanisms of the structure of cognitive architectures. These exercises are beautifully explained in the first chapter of section 6 of Simon (*ibid.*).

Experimental work in perceptions, following the work of Adrian De Groot, and the Dutch school, was in terms of interpreting – again with appropriate representations and reframing – eye movements, in committing to memory chess positions and movements, by the play of a variety of Grand Masters against lesser-able players. Chapters 3, 4 and 5, of section 6 in Simon (*ibid.*) are exemplary examples of what can be learned and then used in re-programming machines 'who' can *learn* to play 'against' Grand Masters at their own, or approaching that, levels. This was, of course, an application of Simon's evolving attitude and mastery of programming in an artificial intelligence context of learning and an expertise of machines endowed with this ability. It was not brute-force application of memory powers of machines that was being exploited in his programming of learning machines – and this is why I say that he would have welcomed the recent results in chess and GO, of Machines prevailing over Kasparov and Sedol.

I come, now, to the key concept that underlies **CBFT** – *HEURISTIC*. There many ways in which this concept has been defined, used – and even abused. I am *tempted*, following Machlup (1958), to call it a 'weaselword' – akin to the way words such as structure, dynamics, stability, linear, non-linear, emergence, complexity and so on are used, and *misused*, in microeconomics (and macroeconomics).

I shall, however, not – for now – give in to temptation! The term has been used fruitfully, in many scientific contexts. In my own opinion, the way the concept of *heuristics* was used by Appel and Haken, in their *computer-aided-proof* of the celebrated four-*colour-conjecture* (Saaty & Kainen, 1977; 1986), was closest to Simon's way of applying it in search processes for problem solving. That there was no reliance on any version of the *Church–Turing Thesis*, in the algorithms Appel and Haken devised is an added factor in the similarities between the way Simon used the notion of *heuristics* in constructing search processes over spaces that were large. Again, the way Appel and Hagen restricted the nodes that had to be examined, by means of *heuristical* limits (whose fertility and 'correctness' was evidenced by their ultimate success in 'proving' the conjecture) was very similar to the way Simon used the *bounded rationality* of agents and institutions, who were *satisficing* – not necessarily optimising.

In Gigerenzer and Gaissmaier (op. cit., pp. 454/5), there is an excellent discussion of heuristics as applied in behavioural economics, in general, and in behavioural finance, in particular. They go on to a felicitous definition of the term as follows (*ibid.*, p. 454; italics added):

> A heuristic is a strategy that *ignores part of the information*, with the goal of making decisions more quickly, frugally, and/or accurately than more complex methods.

They are careful to add the caveat (*ibid.*, p. 454) that the preceding definition is adopted, *pro tempore*, for the purposes of the *Review* in question. For *my* purposes, this 'definition' must be understood in conjunction with the equally important observation by Gigerenzer and Selten (2001, p. ix; italics added):

> *Bounded rationality*, needs to be, but it is *not yet, understood*.

But, surely, successful *formalization* – consistent with Simon's theoretical strictures and empirical constraints – is one way of *understanding* the concept? Moreover, the concept itself cannot be understood, in what I call the Simon-sense, without also a concomitant formalized definition of *satisficing*. I believe I have tried to achieve these aims, with some success – in the sense that it has enabled me to study some of Simon's procedures and approaches to heuristic search, in spaces of definably large computational complexity, to solve decision problems (cf. Velupillai, 2010, ch. 2).

Finally, I must also point out that Simon's boundedly rational agents, satisficing in their *heuristic search processes* over (quantitatively) large feasible spaces, acting as *human information processers*, did so in a non-stochastic setting:

The models describe individuals, so that the hard part is to say with precision what is common to all *human information processors*. With this approach it does not seem natural to assume that *human behaviour* is fundamentally *stochastic*, its regularities showing up only with *averaging* (as in *statistical learning theory*); rather, like Freud's dictum that *all behaviour is causal* seems the natural one, and *only reluctantly* do we assign some aspects of *behaviour to probabilistic generators*.

(Newell & Simon, 1972, p. 10; italics added)

It must be remembered, too, that Simon worked in the domain of propositional *logic* – although he had definite views on extending his solutions to predicate *logic* – and, hence, implicitly accepted Gödel's *completeness* theorem and Church's *undecidability* result for this *logic*.[18]

I can, then, conclude this section with a 'thesis', an assumption and a theorem:

### Simon's Thesis

*Heuristic Search Processes* over problem spaces of *boundedly rational* human agents are constrained by *satisficing* – that is, there is 'natural' stopping rule for the computational processes that are implemented.

### Assumption 1

All sequences considered by Simon are *choice sequences* in the Brouwerian constructive sense.

### Remark 6

Hence, the sequences confronting Simon's information processing systems, implementing search processes, are uncountably infinite.

Hence,

### Theorem 2

Simon's *boundedly rational* agents, *satisficing*, are *equivalent to* the *creating subject* of Brouwerian constructive mathematics.

### Proof

First, it must be noted that the thesis and assumption ensure that *no* notion of an algorithm is used in the statement of the theorem. Second, the *constraint*s on the rational agent imposed by bounded rationality and satisficing are equivalent to those imposed on the activities of the creating subject in Brouwerian constructive mathematics. The conclusion of the theorem follows.

Thus, the *boundedly rational* agents, *satisficing*, are *creating subjects* implementing *heuristic search processes* in *discovering solutions* to decision problems in **Classical Behavioural Finance Theory**. Nothing can be further from the 'heuristics-and-biases' programme of Tversky and Kahneman, which is the guiding principle of modern behavioural finance theories.

## §3  Vistas for a future for *CBFT*

> With recent developments in our understanding of *heuristic processes* and their simulation by digital computers, the way is open to deal scientifically with *ill-structured problems* – to make the computer coextensive with the human mind . . .
>
> The revolution in *heuristic problem solving* will force man to consider his role in a world in which his intellectual power and speed are outstripped by the *intelligence of machines*. Fortunately, the new revolution will at the same time give him a deeper understanding of the *structure and workings of his own mind.*
>
> —Simon and Newell (1958, pp. 9–10; italics added)

Before I conclude with the *Vistas for a Future for CBFT*, I must tackle the issue of *Constructive Finance Theory*, mentioned in note 1 of this chapter. *The fundamental theorem of asset pricing* is the fulcrum around which the *constructive development of reverse mathematics* can be considered a contribution to mathematical finance theory.

The theorem itself is stated as follows:

### Fundamental theorem of asset pricing

The absence of *an arbitrage trading strategy is equivalent to the existence* of a *martingale measure.*

### Remark

- $p \in$ P is a *Martingale measure*, if $A \cdot p = 0$, where $\mathbf{P} = \{p \in \Re^n \mid \sum_{i=1}^{n} p_i = 1$ and $0 < p_i, \forall i \}$.
- A is an $R^{m \times n}$ matrix, where each entry of the matrix $a_{ij}$ is given by the difference between the price at 'time' 1 minus that at time 0, of asset $i$ in case $j$.
- $\xi \in \Re^m$ is an *arbitrage trading strategy* if $\xi \cdot A > 0$.

Now, the *absence* of an arbitrage trading strategy is (formally) equivalent to the impossibility of a gambling strategy and, hence, the *existence* of a martingale measure, in the former case, is the same as the *existence* of incompressible sequences.

In other words, the fundamental theorem of asset pricing is equivalent to the existence of the impossibility of a gambling system, in the strict sense of Shafer and Vovk.

The definitions of a *martingale measure* and that of *incompressible sequences* are *not* based on *heuristic search processes* and, hence, have nothing whatsoever to do with *classical behavioural finance theory* (and, of course, even less with **MBFT**).

Three of Simon's important priorities must be remembered, if **CBFT** is to be developed in a sense faithful to the developments he would have envisaged.

First, it must be emphasized that Simon thought of Microeconomics as one, unified, subject. He never differentiated it between behavioural microeconomics and *any* kind of general microeconomics – and similarly for behavioural finance, although he *may* have agreed with the latter being a subset of the first of the former two. And, for him, there was no question of doubting that both of these subjects were subsets of the broader filed of cognitive psychology, in general, and the study of the nature, structure and scope of the thinking mind.

Second, he would have continued to enrich both behavioural economics and behavioural finance theories, empirically, experimentally and theoretically, by studying *generalizations* and *extensions* of the metaphors of *chess, cryptarithmetic* and the *Tower of Hanoi* as cognitive psychological paradigmatic examples. He called the three, respectively, as the '*sweet peas*', *Drosophila* and *E. coli* of *cognitive science*' in Simon (1989, p. 394; italics added). Thus, he would have welcomed – both for its own achievements and as an example of what he stood for, in making the study of one's own mind deeper – from the point of view of cognitive psychology – by the advancing powers of *intelligent machines* – the successes of AI-based[19] machine models of chess and GO, against Kasparov and Sedol.

Third, he believed, and acted on the belief, in *Alan Turing's* celebrated *aphorism* – in a postcard to Robin Gandy, in 1954, he wrote,

Description must be *non-linear*, prediction must be *linear*.

Almost all his living life, he worked with descriptive, adaptive (i.e., capable of), computer programs that were *linear* – without ever forgetting that a generalization to *non-linear descriptive models* was both desirable and necessary. Hence, the emphasis on *linear deterministic difference equations* as formally equivalent to the dynamics of adaptive computer programs he – together with many collaborators, to solve diverse problems – constructed. Hence his expressed disinterest in the celebrated $\mathbf{P} \overset{?}{=} \mathbf{NP}$ question – since it is a non-issue in the case of *linear* dynamical systems.

However, towards the end of his life, particularly in his essay in memory of *The Legacy of Alan Turing*[20] (Simon, 1996) and in the *Raffaele Mattioli Lectures* (Simon, 1997, especially pp. 174–175), Simon broached, and took firm initial steps, towards *non-linear* descriptive models of human behaviour in microeconomics, based on a variety of cognitive psychological structures.

These three generalizations to *heuristic search processes*, where *boundedly rational* and *satisficing* agents, as *information processing systems*, solving *human decision problems*, transform – progressively – *ill-structured problems* to the domain of *solvability* of *well-structured problems*.

This is the path that Herbert Simon showed us – especially for Classical Behavioural Economics and *classical behavioural finance theory*. If we hurry, we may catch up to him, still walking on that path – but way ahead of us.

## Notes

♣ The meaning of 'classical', in this context, is explained in Kao and Velupillai (2015). *Classical Behavioural Finance Theory* is referred to, in the sequel, as **CBFT**.

♥ I suggest '*at least* 45 years ago', which makes it '1944, or earlier' (see Simon, 1991, pp. 83 & 87 ff., despite Takahashi, 2015).

1   There is also the formally *Constructive* (Bishop style but supplemented by Markov –
    algorithmic methods – approaches) *Finance theory*, but it is *not behavioural* in any
    sense in which this term can be interpreted. I shall return to this theme in the concluding
    section of this chapter.

2   My acquaintance with this celebrated result is as *Bayes's Theorem, Bayes's Rule* or
    *Bayes's Postulate* (De Finetti, 1970, p. 13; Feller, 1968, p. 124; Savage, 1972, p. 44,
    ff.) – but *never* as 'Bayes's *Law*'. I am, moreover, not convinced that theoreticians of
    'modern behavioural finance' have fully mastered the subjective/personalistic prob-
    ability bases of de Finetti and Savage, particularly with respect to the distinction
    between *finite* and *countable additivity* of the events over which these two kinds of
    probabilities are defined by these two pioneers (cf. in particular, de Finetti, ibid., §.3.11;
    Savage, ibid., p. 44; and the Appendix to Chapter 3 of this book).

3   'Stable' in the special sense in which is defined by Feller (*op. cit.*). This is not the
    definition – static or dynamic – that is usually invoked in (any kind of mathematical or
    quantitative) economics, micro, macro, game theoretic or even from the point of view
    of non-game theoretic industrial organization theory. Neither is it the kind of definition
    used by experimental economists – say Plott.

4   See *Theorem 1* in the mathematical appendix to this section. Incidentally, Maury
    Osborne is, arguably, (one of) the founder(s) of *Econophysics*.

5   They claim (in 2004!), in addition, that (*op. cit.*, p. xxi; italics added)

    [t]wenty years ago [i.e., 1984], behavioural economics did *not* exist as a field.

    I suppose Thaler (1980) is 'the first genuine article in Modern Behavioural Econom-
    ics' (*ibid.*, p. xxii) is *only* true in hindsight! Herbert Simon and Ward Edwards must be
    'turning in their graves.'

6   This is analogous, but not equivalent, to Simon's criticism of the Neoclassical empha-
    sis on *firms* and its negligence of a theory of *organizations* and the motivations of
    'people' who are behavioural actors within these institutions (Simon, 1991).

7   All the other concepts – for example, framing, representations and so on – are, at best,
    *positive heuristics*, in the sense of Lakatos.

8   The use of the word painstakingly is gratuitous, in the second step of the implementa-
    tion of the 'recipe' (although the time sequence of the four-step recipe is unclear).

9   If they are to be considered *random sequences*, then they are subject to the von Mises
    'slogan', made rigorous by *Kolmogorov/Chaitin/Solomonoff/Martin-Löf thesis,* noted
    earlier – which may be called a *theorem*, if the concept of *thesis* – or *natural law*, as
    Emil Post referred to it – is pushed 'back' to another foundational level. 'Law', here, is
    not meant in the same sense of Thaler's reference to Bayes's *Law*.

10  I would have preferred to state this thesis as *Turing's Theorem*, separating it from *Church's
    Thesis* (as in Gandy, 1980), but for reasons of space – the proof of the theorem would
    require a disproportionate amount of space – and simplicity, I refrain from doing so.

11  This is a modified version of Beeson's (1985, p. 55) statement of the *rule*.

12  I don't think I have a complete formal grasp of what this term means!

13  I have been greatly helped by reading Dr N. Dharmaraj's contribution to the *Herbert
    Simon Birth Centennial Special Issue* of **Computational Economics (Dharmaraj,
    2017)**, and for invaluable instruction on the nature and scope of the origins of *Heu-
    ristics* in the work of Allen Newell and Herbert Simon. I believe his arguments lend
    support to my interpretations.

14  The *constrained by* is, in my interpretation, the *stopping rule* of the heuristic search
    processes that *discover proofs* (of theorems), *laws* (Newton's, Kepler's Kirchhoff's)
    and so on. It is literally the stopping rule, say, of a Turing Machine – except that Simon
    does not (and never did) work within the framework of the Church–Turing Thesis.

15  I completely disagree with the downplaying of *bounded rationality* and *satisficing*,
    bordering on rank inaccuracies, in the references to these two concepts (and the notion

of *procedural rationality*) in Camerer et al. (*op. cit.*, e.g., pp. 4 & 38) and Barberis and Thaler (2005, e.g., p. 2). Incidentally, although Barberis and Thaler refer to Arrow (1986), in the context of rationality assumptions being (in)sufficient for predicting (individual) behaviour (*ibid.*, p. 64), they have obviously missed the point about 'the assumption of computability' in economic hypotheses – I would add, also, behavioural finance theoretic hypotheses – as 'the next step in analysis', in the concluding paragraph of this pioneering paper (Arrow, *op. cit.*, p. S398).

16  Whilst noting that chapter 4 of this section is a reasoned critique of the English version of Popper's falsification 'manifesto' on **The Logic of Scientific Discovery**. Incidentally, in view of the importance of Gödel's eventually unpublished manuscript on Carnap (Rodríguez-Consuegra, ed., 1995, pt. II, ch. 4), it is useful to know that this book is (partly) dedicated to *Rudolf Carnap* (whose mild manner was no match for Popper's aggressive behaviour).

17  To the best of my knowledge Simon was not aware of the priority of *Oscar Reutesvärd* over Penrose and Penrose. I may take this opportunity to note that I bought one of the celebrated *impossible triangle* drawings of Reutesvärd from the great man himself, more than 45 years ago, and lectured on such 'illusions' as theoretically difficult *dynamical system* problems of *perceptual mechanisms*, because of *non-linearities*. I had, then, in the early 1980s, very little mastery of the connections between *dynamical systems* and *knots* – a link that was fruitfully and brilliantly exploited by Alan Turing in his past published work (Turing, 1954). Reutesvärd himself explained the origins of his lifelong preoccupation with drawing a variety of impossible diagrams in terms of *Japanese perspective* – which is very different from 'Western' *perceptual mechanisms*.

18  See the fruitful triptych that the *mind* uses to try to solve problems, which eventually leads to Gigerenzer and Gaissmaier (op. cit., p. 452) to characterize MBE as the 'heuristics-and-biases program'.

19  After all, Simon was one of the founders of an enlightened, humane – if not also *human* – variant of *Artificial Intelligence*, at the historic Dartmouth Conference, of 1956.

20  He concluded this essay with the memorable observation (ibid., p. 101):

> If we hurry, we can catch up to Turing on the path he pointed out to us so many years ago.

What was the 'path [Turing] pointed out to us so many years ago', if not the one on which Simon walked – sometimes ran – and many of us still shun, for it is non-smooth and ill lit.

# References

Arrow, Kenneth J. (1986), Rationality of Self and Others in an Economic System, *The Journal of Business*, Vol. 59, No. 4, Pt. 2, October, pp. S385–S399.

Bachelier, Louis (1900), Théorie de la Spéculation, *Annales de l'Ècole Normale Supérieure*, Sér. 3, Vol. 17, pp. 21–86.

Barberis, Nicholas & Richard Thaler (2005), A Survey of Behavioral Finance, chapter 1, pp. 1–75, in: *Advances in Behavioral Finance*, Vol. 2, edited by Richard H. Thaler, Russell Sage Foundation, New York.

Beeson, Michael J. (1985), *Foundations of Constructive Mathematics*, Springer-Verlag, Berlin.

Camerer, Colin F., George Loewenstein & Matthew Rabin (eds.) (2004), *Advances in Behavioral Economics*, Princeton University Press, Princeton, NJ.

de Finetti, Bruno (1970), *Theory of Probability*, Vol. 1, John Wiley & Sons., London.

Dharmaraj, Navaneethakrishnan (2017), Human Problem-Solving: Standing on the Shoulders of Giants, *Computational Economics, Special Issue Commemorating the Birth Centennial of Herbert Simon*, Forthcoming.

Feller, William (1968), *An Introduction to Probability Theory and Its Applications*, Vol. 1 (Third Edition), John Wiley & Sons, Inc., New York.

Feller, William (1971), *An Introduction to Probability Theory and Its Applications*, Vol. 2 (Second Edition), John Wiley & Sons, Inc., New York.

Gandy, Robin (1980), Church's Thesis and Principles for Mechanisms, pp. 123–148, in: *The Kleene Symposium*, edited by J. Barwise, H. J. Keisler & K. Kunen, North-Holland Publishing Company, Amsterdam.

Geldbaum, Bernard R. & John M. H. Olmsted (2003), *Counterexamples in Analysis*, Dover Publications Inc., Mineola, NY.

Gigerenzer, Gerd & Wolfgang Gaissmaier (2011), Heuristic Decision Making, *Annual Review of Psychology*, Vol. 61, pp. 451–482.

Gigerenzer, Gerd & Reinhard Selten (eds.) (2001), *Bounded Rationality: The Adaptive Toolbox*, The MIT Press, Cambridge, MA.

Kao, Ying-Fang & K. Vela Velupillai (2015), Behavioural Economics: Classical and Modern, *The European Journal of the History of Economic Thought*, Vol. 22, No. 2, pp. 236–271.

Kleene, Stephen Cole (1967), *Mathematical Logic*, John Wiley & Sons, Inc., New York.

Li, Ming & Paul Vitanyi (1993), *An Introduction to Kolmogorov Complexity and Its Applications*, Springer-Verlag, New York.

Machlup, Fritz (1958), Structure and Structural Change: Weaselwords and Jargon, *Zeitschrift für Nationalökonomie*, Bd. 18, H. 3, pp. 280–298.

Mandelbrot, Benoit B. (1963), The Variation of Certain Speculative Prices, *Journal of Business*, Vol. 36, No. 4, October, pp. 394–419.

March, James G. & Herbert A. Simon, with the collaboration of Harold Guetzkow, (1958; 1993), *Organizations* (Second Edition), Blackwell Publishers, Oxford.

McCulloch, Warren S. & Walter Pitts (1943), A Logical Calculus of the Ideas Immanent in Nervous Activity, *Bulletin of Mathematical Biophysics*, Vol. 5, No. 4, pp. 115–133.

Newell, Allen (1989), Putting It All Together, chapter 15, pp. 399–400, in: *Complex Information Processing: The Impact of Herbert Simon*, edited by David Klahr & Kenneth Kotovsky, Lawrence Earlbaum Associates, Inc., Hillsdale, NJ.

Newell, Allen & Herbert A. Simon (1972), *Human Problem Solving*, Prentice-Hall, Inc., Englewood Cliffs, NJ.

Osborne, Maury F. M. (1959), Brownian Motion in the Stock Market, *Operations Research*, Vol. 7, No. 2, March–April, pp. 145–173.

Osborne, Maury S. M. (1977; 1995), *The Stock Market and Finance from a Physicist's Viewpoint*, Crossgar Press, Minneapolis, MN.

Payne, John W., Jane R. Bettman & Eric J. Joohnson (1992), Behavioral Decision Research: A Constructive Processing Perspective, *Annual Review of Psychology*, Vol. 43, pp. 87–131.

Rodríguez-Consuegra, Francisco A. (ed.) (1995), *Kurt Gödel: Unpublished Philosophical Essays*, Birkhäuser Verlag, Basel.

Saaty, Thomas L. & Paul C. Kainen (1977; 1986), *The Four-Color Problem: Assaults and Conquest*, Dover Publications, Inc., New York.

Savage, Leonard (1954; 1972), *The Foundations of Statistics* (Second Revised Edition), Dover Publications, Inc., New York.

Shafer, Glenn & Vladimir Vovk (2001), *Probability and Finance: It's Only a Game!*, John Wiley & Sons, Inc., New York.

Simon, Herbert A. (1955), A Behavioral Model of Rational Choice, *Quarterly Journal of Economics*, Vol. 69, No. 1, February, pp. 99–118.

Simon, Herbert A. (1977), *Models of Discovery and Other Topics in the Methods of Science*, D. Reidel Publishing Company, Dordrecht-Holland.

Simon, Herbert A. (1979), *Models of Thought*, Vol. 1, Yale University Press, New Haven, CT.

Simon, Herbert A. (1983), *Reason in Human Affairs*, Stanford University Press, Stanford, CA.

Simon, Herbert A. (1989), The Scientist as a Problem Solver, chapter 14, pp. 375–398, in: *Complex Information Processing: The Impact of Herbert Simon*, edited by David Klahr & Kenneth Kotovsky, Lawrence Earlbaum Associates, Inc., Hillsdale, NJ.

Simon, Herbert A. (1991; 1996), *Models of My Life*, The MIT Press, Cambridge, MA.

Simon, Herbert A. (1996), Machine as Mind, chapter 5, pp. 81–102, in: *Machines and Thought: The Legacy of Alan Turing*, Vol. 1, edited by Peter Millican & Andy Clark, Oxford University Press, Oxford.

Simon, Herbert A. (1997), *An Empirically Based Microeconomics*, Cambridge University Press, Cambridge.

Simon, Herbert A. & Allen Newell (1958), Heuristic Problem Solving: The Next Advance in Operations Research, *Operations Research*, Vol. 6, No. 1, January–February, pp. 1–10.

Takahashi, Nobuo (2015), Where Is Bounded Rationality From?, *Annals of Business Administrative Science*, Vol. 14, No. 2, pp. 67–82.

Thaler, Richard H. (1980), Toward a Positive Theory of Consumer Choice, *Journal of Economic Behavior and Organization*, Vol. 1, No. 1, January, pp. 39–60.

Thaler, Richard H. (1993), Introduction, pp. xv–xxi, in: *Advances in Behavioral Finance*, edited by Richard Thaler, Russell Sage Foundation, New York.

Thaler, Richard H. (ed.) (2005), *Advances in Behavioral Finance*, Vol. 2, Russell Sage Foundation, New York.

Turing, A. M. (1954), Solvable and Unsolvable Problems, pp. 7–23, in: *Science News*, No. 31, edited by A. W. Haslett, Penguin Books, London.

Tversky, Amos & Daniel Kahneman (1974), Judgment Under Uncertainty: Heuristics and Biases, *Science*, New Series, Vol. 185, No. 4157, September 27, pp. 1124–1131.

van Dalen, Dirk (1999), From Brouwerian Counter Examples to the Creating Subject, *Studia Logica: An International Journal for Symbolic Logic*, Vol. 62, No. 2, *Selected Papers in Honour of Ettore Casari*, March, pp. 305–314.

Velupillai, K. Vela (2010), *Computable Foundations for Economics*, Routledge, Taylor & Francis Group, London.

Von Mises, Richard (1972), *Wahrsheinlichkeit, Statistik und Wahrheit*, Vierte Auflage durchgesehen von Hilda Geiringer, Springer-Verlag, Wien.

# 10 *Intuitionistic* foundations for economic theory

## A *Brouwer–Simon research programme*[*]

> [P]roblem solvers in domains like *physics* and *engineering* make extensive use of diagrams, a form of pictures, in problem solving, and many distinguished *scientists* and *mathematicians* (e.g., Einstein, Hadamard) have *denied* that they 'think in words.'
>
> – Larkin and Simon (1987, pp. 65–66; italics added)[1]

## §1 A prologue

> One can imagine a world in which this [noun-verb] distinction would not be very useful, a world in which clouds constantly forming and dissolving, for instance. Our world is quite different.
>
> – Simon (1979, p. 360)

More than a century ago, as Ehrlich (2006, pp. 1–2; italics added) pointed out, Russell was explicit in his dismissal of any philosophical or foundational enrichment – rigorous or not – of the nature of the triptych of the infinitesimal, the infinite and the continuum:

> In his paper *Recent Work On The Principles of Mathematics*, which appeared in 1901, Bertrand Russell reported that the three central problems of traditional mathematical philosophy – the nature of the infinite, the nature of the infinitesimal, and the nature of the continuum – had all been 'completely solved'. Indeed, as Russell went on to add: 'The solutions, for those acquainted with mathematics, are so clear as to leave no longer the slightest doubt or difficulty'. . . . According to Russell, the structure of *the infinite* and *the continuum* were completely revealed by Cantor and Dedekind, and the concept of *an infinitesimal* had been found to be incoherent and was 'banish[ed] from mathematics' through the work of Weierstrass and others.

Thus, arose the dominance, in the 20th century, of the mathematics, the mathematical logic, the mathematical philosophy and the foundations of mathematics, in terms of what may now be called the research programme of Frege and Cantor, Dedekind and Weierstrass, Peano and Zermelo, codified in Hilbert's program.

Brouwer, standing on the shoulders of Kronecker and Poincaré, Borel and Lebesque, underpinned by a (restricted) Kantian philosophy of intuition, single-handedly challenged the Hilbert programme and provided a coherent, deep and, ultimately, *languageless*, *logicless* (perhaps, even *negationless*) philosophical foundation for an intuitionistic constructive mathematics.

It is in this sense that I speak of *A Brouwer–Simon* **Program***me* (of research).[2]

Purely by 'chance' I became aware, trying to familiarize myself with the rudiments of category theory, as part of my development of constructive foundations for computable economics, that the foundations of *smooth infinitesimal analysis* was to be found in a version of *First-Order Intuitionistic Logic* and, in particular, there was a 'natural' abandonment of the *tertium non datur* (cf. Bell, 2008, ch. 8).

For convenient reference for the discussion in this paper, a concise statement of Heyting's *formal system* of first-order intuitionistic logic, to which his intuitionistic constructive mathematical *maestro*, Brouwer, did not wholly subscribe is as follows:[3]

## Axioms

$p \to (q \to p)$

$[p \to q \to r)] \to [(p \to q) \to (p \to r)]$

$p \to (q \to p \cap q)$

$p \cap q \to p \ p \cap q \to q$

$p \to p \cup q \ q \to p \cup q$

$(p \to r) \to [(q \to r) \to (p \cap q \to r)]$

$(p \to q) \to [(p \to \neg q) \to \neg p]$

$\neg p \to (p \to q)$

$p(t) \to \exists x p(x) \ldots \forall x p(x) \to p(y)$ (*x free in, and t free for x in p*).

$x = x \ldots p(x) \cap x = y \to p(y)$

## Rules of Inference

$$\frac{p, p \to q}{q} \text{ (all variables free in p also free in q)}$$

$$\frac{q \to p(x)}{q \to \forall x p(x)} \qquad \frac{p(x) \to q}{\exists x p(x) \to q} \text{ (x not free in q)}$$

But there was left a nagging feeling, expressed – as I now see it, incorrectly – by Bishop (1967, p. 6), that *the continuum was a personal 'bugaboo' of Brouwer*. Moreover, given my own suspicion of any reliance on the *Axiom of Choice* in the mathematization of economic theory, I was not sure of the relevance of the role the continuum could or should play in mathematical economics.

But suddenly – serendipitously – I came to realize that viewing the *Grundlagenstreit* as *Hilbert versus Brouwer* was a misleading approach! I was, instead, led to the realization that it was more enlightening to view Brouwer from the 'vantage' point of Simon's approach to the heuristics of problem solving by *information processing systems* of individuals and institutions, subject to *boundedly rational behaviour* of *satisficing* decisions procedures, particularly in the discovery of mathematical theorems (in propositional logic). This viewpoint, unusual though it was, helped me clarify the distinction between Brouwer, on one hand, and Markov (1954) and Bishop (1967), on the other. It also made me realize the intuitionistic irrelevance of the contraposition of *König's Lemma* as the *Fan theorem* (of Brouwer), of which I had learned from Dummett (1977, ch. 3, especially p. 71, ff.).

However, apart from a very brief mention in the latter part of this essay, these are issues I leave for a different exercise – or for others, more competent that I am, as well as much younger and fresh in mind than an aged man that I have become, to develop. In particular, I conjecture that much of the work of the ostensibly constructive work in financial economics I hope, is shown to be irrelevant from a Brouwer–Simon viewpoint – where I, unhesitatingly, classify Simon as an intuitive constructivist in the Brouwerian sense.

## §2   Intuitionistic logic, problem solving – 'in your spare time, please'

> *The calculus of problems is formally identical with the Brouwerian intuitionistic logic, which has recently been formalized by Mr. Heyting.*
> —Kolmogorov (1932; 1998, p. 328; italics in the original)

My interest in computable behavioural economics – or, as I have been referring to it as *Classical Behavioural Economics*, in recent years – has one of its anchorings in the formalization of *Problem Solving* by Turing (1954) and Simon (Newell & Simon, 1972), both of whom underpin the *problem solver* in terms of a Turing Machine.[4]

Hilbert had begun the search for a rigorous definition of problem, problem solving and, eventually also, the problem solver, by explicitly stating in his influential address to the Paris International Congress of Mathematicians in August, 1900, titled famously and simply *Mathematical Problems* (Hilbert, 1900, p. 444; last italics in the original):

> [T]he conviction (which every mathematician shares, but which no one has as yet supported by a proof) that every definite mathematical problem must necessarily be susceptible of an exact settlement, either in the form of an actual answer to the question asked, or by the proof of the impossibility of its solution and therewith the necessity failure of all attempts. . . .
>
> Is this axiom of the solvability of every problem a peculiarity characteristic of mathematical thought alone, or is it possibly a general law inherent in the nature of the mind, that all questions which it asks must be answerable? For in other sciences also one meets old problems which have been settled in a manner most satisfactory and most useful to science by the proof of their impossibility. . . .

This conviction of the *solvability of every mathematical problem* is a powerful incentive to the worker. We hear within us the perpetual call: There is *the problem*. Seek its solution. You can find it by pure reason, for in mathematics there is no *ignoramibus*.

In that same famous lecture, Hilbert had also stated,[5] clearly and unambiguously, the acceptable criteria for the '*solution of a mathematical problem*':

> [I]t shall be possible to establish the correctness of the solution by means of a *finite number* of steps based upon a *finite number* of hypotheses which are implied in the statement of the *problem* and which must always be exactly formulated. This requirement of logical deduction by means of a *finite number* of processes is simply the requirement of *rigour in reasoning*.
>
> (*ibid.*, p. 409; italics added)

When the field of computable economics was being developed (from about 1983), it was against the backdrop of viewing *economics as problem solving* in the preceding Turing–Simon sense, with foundations in computability theory, which was an outcome of Hilbert's inadvertent 'challenge'.

But it was only about a decade and a half later that I understood that *problem solving* – human or machine – had a natural 'habitat' in intuitionistic logic. That intuitionistic logic provided the natural foundations for *problem solving* was persuasively and rigorously put forth by Kolmogorov (1932; 1998; see the opening quote of this section) more than 80 years ago.[6]

In the earlier classic Kolmogorov also showed, without a shadow of a doubt, why Brouwer – in particular – was adamant on his refusal to accept the *tertium non datur* and the *law of double negation* in any 'reasoning' which goes beyond the finite:

> [W]ithout the help of the principle of excluded middle it is impossible to prove any proposition whose proof usually comes down to an application of the principle of *transfinite induction*. For example, a proposition of that kind is: every closed set is the sum of a perfect set and a denumerable set.
>
> The proof of such propositions is often carried out without the help of the principle of *transfinite induction*. But all these proofs rest upon *the principle of excluded middle, applied to infinite collections*, or upon *the principle of double negation*.
>
> (Kolmogorov, 1925; 1967, p. 436; italics added)

It was to Brouwer's credit that he was early able to intuit (*sic!*) the *transfinite* implications of the *unrestricted* use of the *tertium non datur* (and the law of double negation). In a problem-solving context, then, it was clear that it was *impossible to rely on classical logic* for studying solvability in a mathematical framework.[7]

This is especially to be remembered in any context involving intuitionism, particularly in its Brouwerian variants, since he – more than anyone else, with the possible exception of Wittgenstein – insisted on *the independence of mathematics from logic*. In Brouwer's enunciation of the famous *first act of intuitionism* (Brouwer, 1981), there is the uncompromising requirement for (his version of) constructive mathematics to be independent of 'theoretical logic' *and* to be '*languageless*':

> FIRST ACT OF INTUITIONISM Completely separating mathematics from *mathematical language* and hence *from the phenomena of language* described by theoretical logic, recognizing that intuitionistic mathematics is an essentially *languageless* activity of the mind having its origin in the perception of a move of time.
>
> (ibid., p. 4; italics added)

Imagine, therefore, the incredulity with which I read a leading advanced textbook (*sic*!) on **Real Analysis with Economic Applications** *asserting*, without any 'reservations' (Ok, 2007, p. 279; italics added), that

> [i]t is worth noting that in later stages of his career, he became the most forceful proponent of the so-called intuitionist philosophy of mathematics, which not only forbids the use of the Axiom of Choice but also rejects *the axiom* that a proposition is either true or false (thereby disallowing the method of proof by contradiction). The consequences of taking this position are dire. For instance, an intuitionist would *not accept the existence of an irrational number*! In fact, *in his later years, Brouwer did not view the Brouwer Fixed Point Theorem as a theorem*. (He had proved this result in *1912*, when he was functioning as a 'standard' mathematician)
>
> If you want to learn about intuitionism in mathematics, I suggest reading – *in your spare time, please* – the four articles[8] by Heyting and Brouwer in Benacerraf and Putnam. (1983)

I don't suppose I should be surprised at this kind of preposterously ignorant and false assertions, observations and claims. These are made in a new advanced text book on mathematics for graduate (economic) students, published under the imprint of an outstanding publishing house – Princeton University Press – and peddled as a text treating the material it does contain 'rigorously' (although the student is not warned that there are many yardsticks of 'rigour' and that which is asserted to be 'rigorous' in one kind of mathematics could be considered 'flippant and slippery' in another kind).

Yet, every one of the assertions in the above quote is false, and also severely misleading. Brouwer did not 'become the most forceful proponent of the so-called intuitionist philosophy of mathematics' in *later stages* of his career; he was an intuitionist long before he formulated and proved what came, later, to be called the Brouwer Fix-Point theorem (cf. Brouwer, 1907, 1908a, 1908b).

Just for the record, even the fixed-point theorem came earlier than 1912. It is nonsensical to claim that Brouwer did not consider the 'Fixed Point Theorem as a theorem'; he did not consider it *a valid theorem in intuitionistic constructive mathematics*, and he had a very cogent reason for it, which was stated with admirable clarity when he finally formulated and proved it, forty years later, within intuitionistic constructive mathematics (Brouwer, 1952). On that occasion he identified the reason why his original theorem was unacceptable in intuitionistic constructive – indeed, in almost any kind of constructive – mathematics, for example, in *Bishop-style constructivism*, which was developed without any reliance on a philosophy of intuitionism:

> [T]he validity of the Bolzano-Weierstrass theorem [in intuitionism] would make the classical and the intuitionist form of fixed-point theorems equivalent.
>
> (Brouwer, 1952, p. 1)

Note how Brouwer refers to a 'classical . . . form of the fixed-point theorem'. The *invalidity* of the Bolzano–Weierstrass theorem[9] in any form of constructivism is due to its reliance on the law of the excluded middle in an infinitary context of choices (cf. also Dummett, 1977, pp. 10–12). The part that invokes the Bolzano–Weierstrass theorem entails *undecidable disjunctions*, and as long as any proof invokes this property, it will remain unconstructifiable.

It is worse than nonsense – if such a thing is conceivable – to state that 'an intuitionist would not accept the existence of an irrational number'. Moreover, the law of the excluded middle is *not a mathematical* axiom; it is a logical law, which when *added* as an axiom to Heyting's system of first-order intuitionistic *logic* 'reduces' it to first-order *classical* logic.[10] In any case, the law of the excluded middle is accepted even by the intuitionists so long as meaningless – *precisely* defined – infinities are not being considered as alternatives from which to 'choose'.[11]

As for the un-finessed remark about the axiom of choice being forbidden, the author should have been much more careful. Had this author done his elementary mathematical homework properly, Bishop's deep and thoughtful clarifications of the role of a choice axiom in varieties of mathematics may have prevented the appearance of such nonsense (Bishop, 1967, p. 9):

> When a classical mathematician claims he is a constructivist, he probably means he avoids the axiom of choice. This axiom is unique in its ability to trouble the conscience of the classical mathematician, but in fact it is not a real source of the unconstructivities of classical mathematics. A choice function exists in constructive mathematics, because a choice is *implied by the very meaning of existence.*[12] Applications of the axiom of choice in classical mathematics either are irrelevant or are combined with a sweeping appeal to the principle of omniscience.[13] The axiom of choice is used to extract elements from equivalence classes where they should never have been put in the first place.

Unfortunately, core areas of mathematical economics and game theory, with impeccable orthodox sanction, are replete with even worse false claims and assertions about constructivity, intuitionism and computability. I chose the phrase 'even worse' most deliberately. The preceding inanities by Ok, admittedly in a textbook that may 'corrupt' the mind of fresh and innocent graduate students in economics, are just that: marginal textbook assertions that may pass – with luck – by the average reader without inflicting too much damage.

However, I chose the phrase 'even worse' also to highlight the fact that the above attitudes and lack of understanding of the basics of Brouwerian Intuitionistic Mathematics must mean economics cannot be studied as an activity in 'problem solving' and the economist viewed as a 'problem solver', in the precise Turing–Simon sense. Yet lip service is paid to 'problem solving' and the 'problem solver' in standard economics, as if they can be underpinned by a 'real analysis' based on set theory plus the axiom of choice.

On 8 September 1930 Hilbert gave the opening address to the German Society of Scientists and Physicians, in Königsberg,[14] titled: *Naturkennen und Logik*. This lecture ended famously echoing those feelings and beliefs he had expressed in Paris, 30 years earlier, (Dawson, 1997, p. 71; italics added):

> For the mathematician there is no Ignoramibus and, in my opinion, not at all for natural science either. . . . The true reason why [no one] has succeeded in finding an *unsolvable problem* is, in my opinion, there is *no unsolvable problem*. In contrast to the foolish Ignoramibus, our credo avers:
> We must know,
> We shall know.[15]

A day before that, on Sunday, 7 September, 1930, at the roundtable discussion on the final day of the Conference on Epistemology of the Exact Sciences, organized by the Gesellschaft für Empirische Philosophie, a Berlin Society allied to the Wiener Kreis, the young Kurt Gödel had presented what came to be called his *First Incompleteness Theorem*. In fact, in one fell swoop, Gödel had shown that it was *recursively demonstrable* that in the formal system of classical mathematics, assuming it was *consistent*, there were true but unprovable statements – that is, *incompleteness* and, almost as a corollary to this famous result, also that mathematics was *inconsistent*.[16] Two of the pillars on which Hilbert was hoping to justify formalism had been shattered.

There remained the third: *Decidability*. The problem of resolving this question depended on finding an acceptable – to the mathematician, metamathematician and the mathematical philosopher – definition of definite finitary method. It is on this 'altar' that standard mathematical economics falters – and it is this that underpins problem solving and the problem solver in the Turing–Simon sense; it is this that underpins the case for an *Intuitionistic approach to mathematical economics*.

## §3 Hilbert's programme

> Hilbert's program . . . . was driven by dual beliefs. On the one hand, Hilbert believed that mathematics must be rooted in *human intuition*. . . . It meant that intuitively bounded thought (*finitary* though, he called it) is trustworthy, and that mathematical

paradox can arise *only when we exceed those bounds to posit unintuitable* (i.e., *infinite*) *objects*. For him, *finite arithmetic* and *combinatorics* were the paradigm *intuitable* parts of mathematics, and thus *numerical calculation was the paradigm of finitary thought*. All the rest – set theory, analysis and the like – he called the 'ideal' part of mathematics. . . . On the other hand, Hilbert also believed that this ideal part was sacrosanct. No part of mathematics was to be jettisoned or even truncated. 'No one will expel us.' he declared, 'from the paradise into which Cantor has led us'[17]

—Carl Posy (1998, pp. 294–295; italics added)

So, where was the difference between Hilbert's programme and *Brouwer's Program*[18]? Let me first outline a version of the Grundlagenkrise from the point of view of the (pyrrhic?) triumph of the Hilbert programme – at least in mathematical economics.

Summarizing the tortuous personal and professional relationship between Brouwer and Fraenkel, van Dalen (2000, p. 309) concluded that

Fraenkel also should be credited for pointing out a curious psychological hypocrisy of Hilbert, who to a large extent adopted the methodological position of his adversary – 'one could even call [Hilbert] an intuitionist' – (Fraenkel, 1927, p. 154). Although the inner circle of experts in the area . . . had reached the same conclusion from time before, it was Fraenkel who put it on record.

So, why was there a *Grundlagenkrise*? Why, in early October 1928[19] did Hilbert write Brouwer as follows:

Dear Colleague,
Because it is not possible for me to cooperate with you, given the incompatibility of our views on fundamental matters, I have asked the members of the board of managing editors of the Mathematische Annalen for the authorization, which was given to me by Blumenthal and Carathéodory, to inform you that henceforth we will forgo your cooperation in the editing of the Annalen and thus delete your name form the title page. And at the same time I thank you in the name of the editors of the Annalen for your past activities in the interest of our journal.

Respectfully yours,
D. Hilbert

This letter,[20] written at the tail end of the *Grundlagenkrise*, marked the beginning of the end of it and silenced Brouwer[21] for a decade and a half. Why, if they were both 'intuitionists', did Hilbert and his 'Göttinger' followers, former students and admirers 'silence' him in this deplorably undemocratic way? Were they afraid of an open debate on the exact mathematical meaning of intuitionism and constructive mathematics? Did they take the trouble to read and understand Brouwer's deep and penetrating analysis of mathematical thinking and mathematical processes? There is sad, but clear, evidence that Hilbert never took the trouble to work through, seriously, with the kind of foundational case Brouwer was making; contrariwise, Brouwer took immense pain and time to read, work through an understand the foundational stance taken by Hilbert and his followers.

What were the issues at the centre of the *Grundlagenkrise*, leaving aside the personality clashes? As I see it there were three foundational issues, on all of which I believe Brouwer was eventually vindicated:

- The invalidity of the *tertium non datur* in infinitary mathematical reasoning
- The problem of *Hilbert's Dogma* – that is, 'existence ⇔ consistency' versus the constructivist credo of 'existence as construction', in precisely specified ways
- The problem of the continuum – and, therefore, the eventual place of Brouwer's remarkable introduction of *choice sequences* and the *ideal mathematician*[22] whose time seems to have come only in recent years

Carl Posy, reflecting on *'Brouwer versus Hilbert: 1907–1928'* (*op. cit.*), from a Kantian point of view[23] – both Brouwer and Hilbert had been deeply influenced by Kant, and Hilbert, after all, grew up in Königsberg, which Kant never left!! – summarized the outcome of the *Grundlagenkrise* in an exceptionally clear way, as follows (*ibid.*, pp. 292–3):

> [Hilbert] won politically. Although a face-saving solution was found, the dismissal [from the Editorial Board of the *Mathematische Annalen*] held. Indeed, Brouwer was devastated, and his active research career effectively came to an end.
>
> [Hilbert] won mathematically. Classical mathematics remains intact, intuitionistic mathematics was relegated to the margin. . . .
>
> And [Hilbert] won polemically. Most importantly . . . Hilbert's agenda set the context of the controversy both at the time and, largely, ever since.

Quite apart from whether Hilbert actually 'won', at least on the third front, – especially in the light of the subsequent quasi-constructive and partly intuitive 'revolutions' wrought by recursion theory and non-standard methods – there is also the question of *how* he won. The answer to this question of *how* is of relevance to the ways in which Simon's research programme in *behavioural economics* has been sidelined.

To suggest a tentative answer to this question, let me 'fast-forward' 40 years, to the trials and tribulations faced by Errett Bishop who re-constructed (*sic*!) large parts of classical mathematics, observing constructive discipline on the invalidity of the tertium non datur and non-admissibility of 'Hilbert's Dogma' in his classic and much-acclaimed **Foundations of Constructive Analysis** (Bishop, 1967). Bishop, too, faced similar personal and professional obstacles to those that Brouwer and his followers faced – although not to the same degree and not from the kind of officially formidable adversary like Hilbert. Anil Nerode, George Metakides and Robert Constable summarize the sadness with which Bishop, too, felt 'silenced' (Nerode et al., pp. 79–80):

After the publication of his book *Constructive Analysis* [in 1967], Bishop made a tour of the eastern universities . . . . . He told me then that he was trying to communicate his viewpoint directly to the mathematical community, rather than through the logicians. . . . After the eastern tour was over, he said the trip may have been counterproductive. He felt that his mathematical audience were not taking the work seriously. . . .

After the lecture [at Cornell, during the 'tour of the eastern universities] he mentioned tribulations in the reviewing process when he submitted the book for publication. He mentioned that one of the referee's reports said explicitly that it was a disservice to mathematics to contemplate publication of this book. He could not understand, and was hurt by such a lack of appreciation of his ideas. . . .

In the next dozen years his students and disciples had a hard time developing their careers. When they submitted papers developing parts of mathematics constructively, the classically minded referees would look at the theorems, and conclude that they already knew them. They were quite hesitant to accept constructive proofs of known classical results; whether or not constructive proofs were previously available. . . . Nowadays, with the interest in computational mathematics, things might be different. Bishop said he ceased to take students because of these problems. . . .

When Bishop was invited to speak to the AMS Summer Institute on Recursion Theory, he replied that the aggravation caused by the lecture tour a decade earlier had contributed to a heart attack, and that he was not willing to take a chance on further aggravation.

What is it about the adherence to the *tertium non datur* and to 'Hilbert's Dogma' that makes a whole profession so intolerant?[24] But obviously it is not only here that intolerance resides. Equally dogmatic, intolerant, voices were raised against Giuseppe Veronese's, admittedly somewhat less 'rigorous' – at least in comparison with the works of Brouwer and Bishop – pioneering work on the non-Archimedean continuum. In particular, Veronese's great Italian contemporary, Peano, mercilessly – and as intolerantly as Hilbert was against Brouwer – criticized and dismissed this work on the non-Archimedean continuum. Gordon Fisher, in his masterly summary of '*Veronese's Non-Archimedean Linear Continuum*' (Fisher, 1994), while acknowledging the 'tortured and ungrammatical style' of the writing of a massive book of no less than 630 pages (Veronese, 1891), noted that Peano's review of 1892 (Peano, 1892) was 'especially scathing' (Fisher, 1994, p. 127). Detlef Laugwitz, who did much to revive non-standard analysis, described the 'open controversy that blazed up', in 1890, 'when Veronese announced his use in geometry of infinitely large and small quantities' (Laugwitz, 2002, p. 102). When the German translation of the 1891 Italian edition appeared in 1894,

Cantor was doubly irritated. There was another approach to infinitely large integers; and, moreover, Veronese re-established the infinitely small which Cantor believed to have proved contradictory.

(*ibid.*, pp. 102–3; italics added)

A massive two-decade-long campaign against what has since become the eminently respectable field of non-standard analysis was launched by many of the mighty scholars of the foundations of mathematics: Cantor, of course, but also Peano and Russell.

## §4   The *Brouwer(–Simon) Programme* – languageless, logicless mathematical activity

> Brouwer's intuitionism is closely related to his conception of *mathematics as a dynamic activity of the human intellect* rather than the discovery of an immutable abstract universe. This is a conception for which I have some sympathy and which, I believe, is acceptable to many mathematicians who are not intuitionists.
>
> —Abraham Robinson (quoted in Dauben, *op. cit.*, p. 461; italics added)

*Brouwer's Programme* for an *Intuitionistic Constructive Mathematics* was underpinned, eventually, by

* a variant of Kantian Intuition of Time and its 'dynamics', as perceived by the human intellect;
* the 'construction' of an *Ideal Mathematician*, implementing the dynamics of time as a *mental construction*; and
* choice and *Lawless* Sequences.

Thus, in Brouwerian *Intuitionistic Constructive Mathematics*, the *concept of a process* is intrinsic; this is why I 'append' Simon's name to this programme of research. After all, Simon's information processing systems were *processors*, and the *bounded rationality* with which these processors implemented *satisficing* decisions in *problem solving* were uncompromisingly *process-oriented*![25]

A mathematics underpinned by these concepts and mental constructions did not require logic or language; mathematics was independent of, and prior to, logic and language (which had, to be sure, both mnemonic and communication value, as even emphasized by Brouwer's own enthusiastic involvement in the 'Significs' movement in Holland). Intuitionistic Constructive Mathematics, as conceived in Brouwer's program, was an autonomous mental activity, which did not require, as in Hilbert's program, any reliance on extraneous logical or linguistic props to bridge the gulf between finitary and infinatory processes.

In these senses, too, one can without any feeling of incongruence, speak of a Brouwer–Simon programme of research.

Where does computability theory fit in within the Hilbert–Brouwer divide? Or, what is the difference between recursion theory (computability theory) and constructive mathematics (especially of Brouwer's uncompromising *Intuitionistic* variety)? In the former the cardinal disciplining precept is the Church–Turing Thesis; this is not accepted in the Brouwer or Bishop variant of constructive mathematics. Why not? I think an answer can be found along the lines suggested by Troelstra (1977, pp. 3–4; italics added):

Should we accept the intuitionistic form of *Church's thesis*, i.e., the statement *'Every lawlike function is recursive'*?

There are two reasons for abstaining from the identification '*lawlike = recursive*':

(i)   An axiomatic reason: . . . [A]ssuming recursiveness means carrying unnecessary information around. In the formal development, there are many possible interpretations for the range of the variables for *lawlike sequences* . . . . .

(ii)  A second reason is 'philosophical': the (known) informal justifications of 'Church's thesis' all go back to Turing's conceptual analysis (or proceed along similar lines)

Turing's analysis strikes me as providing very convincing arguments for identifying 'mechanically computable' with 'recursive', but as to the identification of 'humanly computable' with 'recursive', extra assumptions are necessary which are certainly not obviously implicit in the *intuitionistic* (*languageless*) approach . . .

On the 'other hand,' Van Atten, in his most enlightening 'booklet' **On Brouwer** (2004, p. 33; italics added) has convincingly (at least to me!) pointed out that

[o]ne may, *like Markov and Bishop*, settle for just lawlike sequences (*defining 'lawlike' as 'recursive'*), but while *practical*, that also amounts to ducking the issue how to model the continuum.

The path opened up by the foundational results of Gödel, Church, Turing and Post made obsolete Hilbert's Program, without completely resolving the ambiguities surrounding 'Hilbert's Dogma'. I suspect, in view of Gödel's epistemology and his metamathematical results, we will forever remain unable to resolve its status unambiguously – also because Brouwer and the Brouwerians, as well as *non-Intuitionistic Constructivists*, like Bishop, refuse to compromise with *logic and language*.

The extent to which Hilbert was wedded to his mathematical ideology can be gauged from the fact that those who were close to Hilbert 'shielded' him from Gödel's remarkable results, presented at the very meeting where Hilbert had enunciated yet another of his paens to the Hilbert programme and to Hilbert's Dogma. He – Hilbert – came to hear of Gödel's Königsberg results 'only months later' and 'when he learnt about Gödel's work, he was angry' (van Dalen, 2005, p. 638), and van Dalen goes on (*ibid.*, p. 639; second set of italics, added):

Gödel's incompleteness theorems brought the second ending of the *Grundlagenstreit*. Where Hilbert had won the conflict in the social sense, he had *lost it in the scientific sense*.

Why, if Hilbert 'lost it in the scientific sense', do we, minor purveyors of the Hilbert programme as *Mathematical Economics* (*pace* the Bourbakians!), continue the advocacy of a scientifically lost cause? Perhaps we, as mathematical econo-mists are, after all, more enamoured of social approval than an adherence to a scientifically sanctioned norm!

My generation was educated from the wisdom and wit embodied in Samuel-son's *Foundations of Economic Analysis*. Paradoxically, it was the first serious book in economic analysis I was exposed to, and I remain firmly attached to it in intellectual fondness, even while discarding its mathematical philosophy. Like the dangerous epitaph to Marshall's **Principles**, 'borrowed', indirectly, from Hux-ley,[26] the one Samuelson borrowed from Willard Gibbs for *his* epitaph, set the tone and pace for the mathematization of economics:

> *Mathematics is a language.*[27]

Somehow, I detect the source for this vision in Frege's masterpiece, **Begriffss-chrift**, *a formula language, modelled on that of arithmetic, for pure thought*. Brouwer's whole point is that 'pure thought' does not need – indeed is positively harmed by – a 'formula language', particularly one that seeks to found a 'concept script' for 'pure thought'.

A commitment to an *Intuitionistic Approach to Mathematical Economics* means an explicit rejection of this vision. It is also an uncompromising endorsement of Simon's programme of research, developed over at least two decades, culminat-ing in *Classical Behavioural Economics*. The creating subjects of Brouwer, the choice sequences confronting them, the theorems that were proved, using methods that were considered *mental activities* have their correspondence with the *Simon's boundedly rational, satisficing, activities of information processing systems that implemented search processes to solve problems and discover theorems.*

## Notes

♣ An earlier version, drastically different, was presented as an invited contribution at the conference in honour of Professor Ali Khan, held on 3–4 May 2013, at Johns Hopkins University, Baltimore. It was mercilessly criticized by 'all and sundry' – mostly by those who did not even know that Scarf's algorithm for computing general economic equilibria were based on non-constructive – even uncomputable – 'mecha-nisms', but others, either ignorant of intuitionistic constructive mathematics, or of any variety of constructive mathematics – particularly Bishop's – joined in the copi-ous criticism.

1 See also Simon (1996), p. 375, ff.

2 Very reluctantly, I have refrained from calling it a *Brouwer-Wittgenstein-Simon Pro-gramme of Research*!

3 One obtains classical logic, from the earlier Heyting system, by adding either the *law of the excluded middle* (*tertium non datur*) or the *law of double negation* (which means that one is sanctioned, in orthodox mathematics, to invoke and use, indis-criminately, *transfinite induction* – which neither Brouwer nor – indeed – Simon, endorsed).

4 Simon refers to the problem solver as an *Information Processing System* (**IPS**), who is, essentially, a Turing Machine. My views are more nuanced, now (July, 2017).

5  Hilbert's vision of the *solvability* of *mathematical problems*, and *criteria for solvability*, were interpreted by Brouwer, correctly in my opinion, as a way of unconditionally accepting the untrammeled validity of the *tertium non datur*. Hence, of course, violating a basic tenet of intuitionistic logic.

6  A sequel to the classic that eventually led to the BHK – Brouwer – Heyting – Kolmogorov – system (Kolmogorov, 1925). To the best of my knowledge, Simon never referred to the BHK system.

7  Anyone, like me (sic!), who is familiar with the Tamil *epic* **Manimekalai** – especially the Bhikkuni's dialogue with Aravana Adigal and, hence, with at least a modicum of knowledge of *Buddhist Logic* – will read Brouwer (and Simon) with a great deal of sympathy, especially on the restricted validity of these two laws in decision processes of some rational content.

8  Given the shoddy scholarship displayed in this – and many other – assertions by Ok, it is not surprising he forgets (or, more likely, does *not* understand) to add Michael Dummett's important contribution, to the mathematical philosophy of intuitionism as the fifth article for 'spare time' reading from the fine collection in Benacerraf and Putnam.

9  For the 'benefit' of the absolute novice in these things, a simple version of this celebrated theorem is

Every bounded sequence **has** a convergent subsequence.

The word *has* is a euphemism for the many sins of *undecidable disjunctions* in the eyes of the constructive mathematician.

10  See also **§1. Prologue** earlier.

11  Even as early as in 1908, we find Brouwer dealing with this issue with exceptional clarity (cf. Brouwer, 1908b, pp. 109–110; bold emphasis, added):

Now consider the *principium tertii exclusi*: It claims that every supposition is either true or false; . . .

Insofar as **only finite discrete systems** are introduced, the investigation whether an imbedding is possible or not, can always be carried out and admits a definite result, so in this case the principium tertii exclusi is reliable as a principle of reasoning.

[I]n **infinite systems** the principium tertii exclusi is as yet not reliable.

12  See, also, Bishop and Bridges (1985, p. 13), 'Notes'.

13  Bishop (op. cit., p. 9), refers to a version of the law of the excluded middle as *the principle of omniscience*.

14  Where he was also honoured, in those enlightened pre-Nazi days, by being presented, by the Königsberg Town Council, with an 'honorary citizenship'. Incidentally, it is now Kaliningrad – and no longer part of Germany!

15  The marker that was placed over Hilbert's grave in Göttingen had etched on it the German original of these last two lines:

Wir müssen wissen.
Wir werden wissen.

16  This result, in its full formal version, is known as Gödel's *Second Incompleteness Theorem*: the *consistency* of a mathematical system cannot be proved *within* that system itself.

17  The exact quote is as follows (Hilbert, 1925, p. 191):

No one shall drive us out of the paradise which Cantor has created for us.

To this, the brilliant 'Brouwerian' response would have been (I conjecture), if I may be forgiven for stating it this way, by Wittgenstein (1939, p. 103) was

> I would say, 'I wouldn't dream of trying to drive anyone out of this paradise.' I would try to do something quite different: I would try to show you that it is not a paradise – so that you'll leave of your own accord. I would say, 'You're welcome to this; just look about you.'

18  To the best of my knowledge, no one has referred to Brouwer's 'programme of research' on refounding mathematics as an *intuitionistically based constructive activity* as 'Brouwer's Program' – nor of Simon, similarly, trying to refound economics in this way.

19  I am slightly unsure about the exact date, for which I am relying on van Dalen (2005). There seems to be a slight discrepancy in this connection. van Dalen (ibid., p. 599) reports that a telegram from Erhard Schmidt was delivered to Brouwer on 27 October 1928, asking him 'not to undertake anything before' talking to Carathéodory, who was on his way to meet Brouwer. This referred to two letters, from Göttingen, that had already been delivered to Brouwer before the arrival of Carathéodory, who duly arrived in Laren, where Brouwer was living, on 13 October 1928. One or the other dates has to be slightly incorrect!

20  This battle between the two protagonists in the *Grundlagenkrise*, Hilbert and Brouwer, was referred to as the '*Frosch-Mäusekrieg*' by Einstein in his letter to Max Born on 27 November 1928. Einstein, who was also a member of the editorial board of the *Mathematische Annalen*, did not support Hilbert's unilateral and extraordinary action to remove Brouwer from the board.

21  In van Dalen's poignant description, the once effervescent, immensely productive and active Brouwer (van Dalen, 2005, pp. 636–637)

> felt deeply insulted and retired from the field. He did not give up his mathematics, but he simply became invisible. . . . Even worse, he gave up publishing for a decade . . . His withdrawal from the debate did not mean a capitulation, on the contrary, he was firmly convinced of the soundness and correctness of his approach.

This is precisely the point of Viscount Morley's famous aphorism: '*You have not converted a man because you have silenced him*' (**On Compromise**, 1874).

22  Not dissimilar to the Turing Machine, at least in some senses.

23  As perceptively observed by Posy (*ibid.*, p. 292),

> From the start Hilbert and Brouwer – Kantian constructivists both – differed sharply about the foundations of mathematics. Brouwer was prepared to revise radically the content and methods of mathematics, while Hilbert's Program was designed constructively to secure and preserve all of 'classical' mathematics. Hilbert won.

Incidentally, Fraenkel's Lectures (Fraenkel, 1927) were delivered under the auspices of the *Kant-Gesellschaft, Ortsgruppe Kiel*.

24  As intolerant as those economists, obviously an overwhelming majority of practising economists, also called *orthodox*, who 'swear by' the triptych *rationality, equilibrium, optimality*. Simon, with *bounded rationality* and *satisficing* violated two of the three tenets of orthodoxy.

25  Thus, Simon's tireless advocacy of *procedural rationality*, as against the *substantive rationality* of orthodoxy.

26  *Natura non facit saltum.*

27  A few years later Samuelson expressed his displeasure in *not* excising *the indefinite article* from the Gibbs quote for the epitaph of the **Foundations**! Simon consistently used, and appealed, to *a symbolic* (and *pictorial*) *representation*, instead of language in its conventional senses.

# References

Bell, John L. (2008), *A Primer of Infinitesimal Analysis* (Second Edition), Cambridge University Press, Cambridge.

Bishop, Errett (1967), *Foundations of Constructive Analysis*, McGraw-Hill Book Company, New York.

Bishop, Errett & Douglas Bridges (1985), *Constructive Analysis*, Springer-Verlag, Heidelberg.

Brouwer, Luitzen E. J. (1907; 1975), Over de grondslagen der wiskunde [On the Foundations of Mathematics], *Academic Thesis*, pp. 11–104, in: *L. E. J. Brouwer Collected Works: Vol. 1 – Philosophy and Foundations of Mathematics*, edited by Arend Heyting, North-Holland/American Elsevier, Amsterdam & New York.

Brouwer, Luitzen E. J. (1908a; 1975), Over de grondslagen der wiskunde, [On the Foundations of Mathematics], pp. 105–106, in: *L. E. J. Brouwer Collected Works: Vol. 1 – Philosophy and Foundations of Mathematics*, edited by Arend Heyting, North-Holland/American Elsevier, Amsterdam & New York.

Brouwer, Luitzen E. J. (1908b; 1975), De onbetrouwbaarheid der logische principes [The Unreliability of the Logical Principles], pp. 197–111, in: *L. E. J. Brouwer Collected Works: Vol. 1 – Philosophy and Foundations of Mathematics*, edited by Arend Heyting, North-Holland/American Elsevier, Amsterdam & New York.

Brouwer, Luitzen E. J. (1952), An Intuitionist Correction of the Fixed-Point Theorem on the Sphere, *Proceedings of the Royal Society London*, Vol. 213, June 5, pp. 1–2.

Brouwer, Luitzen E. J. (1981), *Brouwer's Cambridge Lectures on Intuitionism*, edited by D. van Dalen, Cambridge University Press, Cambridge.

Dawson, John W. (1997), *Logical Dilemmas: The Life and Work of Kurt Gödel*, A. K. Peters, Wellesley, MA.

Dummett, Michael (1977), *Elements of Intuitionism*, Clarendon Press, Oxford.

Ehrlich, Philip (2006), The Rise of Non-Archimedean Mathematics and the Roots of a Misconception I: The Emergence of Non-Archimedean Systems of Magnitudes, *Archive for History of Exact Sciences*, Vol. 60, pp. 1–121.

Fisher, Gordon (1994), Veronese's Non-Archimedean Linear Continuum, pp. 107–145, in: *Real Numbers, Generalizations of the Reals, and Theories of Continua*, edited by Philip Ehrlich, Kluwer Academic Publishers, Dordrecht.

Fraenkel, Adolphe (1927), Zehn Vorlesungen über die Grundlegung der Mengenlehre, in: *Wissenschaft und Hypothese XXXI*, B. G. Teubner, Leipzig and Berlin.

Hilbert, David (1900; 1902), Mathematical Problems, *Bulletin of the American Mathematical Society*, Vol. 8, July, pp. 437–479.

Hilbert, David (1925; 1926), On the Infinite, pp. 183–201, in: *Philosophy of Mathematics – Selected Readings* (Second Edition), edited by Paul Benacerraf & Hilary Putnam, Cambridge University Press, Cambridge, 1983.

Kolmogorov, Andrei N. (1925; 1967), On the Principle of Excluded Middle, pp. 414–437, in: *From Frege to Gödel – a Source Book in Mathematical Logic, 1879–1931*, edited by Jean van Heijenoort, Harvard University Press, Cambridge, MA.

Kolmogorov, Andrei N. (1932; 1998), On the Interpretation of Intuitionistic Logic, chapter 25, pp. 328–334, in: *From Brouwer to Hilbert – the Debate on the Foundations of Mathematics in the 1920s*, edited by Paolo Mancosu, Oxford University Press, Oxford.

Larkin, Jill H. & Herbert A. Simon (1987), Why a Diagram Is (Sometimes) Worth Ten Thousand Words, *Cognitive Science*, Vol. 11, No. 1, January–March, pp. 65–100.

Laugwitz, Detlef (2002), Debates about Infinity in Mathematics around 1890: The Cantor-Veronese Controversy, Its Origins and its Outcome, *NTM Zeitschrift für Geschichte der Wissenschaften, Technik und Medizin*, Vol. 10, Nos. 1–3, pp. 102–126.

Markov, A. A. (1954), *Theory of Algorithms*, Academy of Sciences of the USSR, Moscow & Leningrad.

Nerode, Anil, George Metakides & Robert Constable (1985), Remembrances of Errett Bishop, pp. 79–84, in: *Errett Bishop – Reflections on Him and His Research, Contemporary Mathematics*, Vol. 39, American Mathematical Society, Providence, RI.

Newell, Allen and Herbert A. Simon (1972), *Human Problem Solving*, Prentice-Hall, Inc., Englewood Cliffs, NJ.

Ok, Efe A. (2007), *Real Analysis with Economic Applications*, Princeton University Press, Princeton, NJ.

Peano, Giuseppe (1892), Review of G. Veronese, Fondamenti di Geometria a più dimensioni, *Rivista di Matematica*, Vol. 2, pp. 143–144.

Posy, Carl J. (1998), Brouwer versus Hilbert: 1907–1928, *Science in Context*, Vol. 11, Part 2, pp. 291–325.

Simon, Herbert A. (1979), *Models of Thought*, Vol. 1, Yale University Press, New Haven, CT.

Simon, Herbert A. (1996), *Models of My Life*, The MIT Press, Cambridge, MA.

Troelstra, A. S. (1977), *Choice Sequences: A Chapter of Intuitionistic Mathematics*, Clarendon Press, Oxford.

Turing, Alan M. (1954), Solvable and Unsolvable Problems, *Science News*, No. 31, pp. 7–23.

van Dalen, Dirk (2000), Brouwer and Fraenkel on Intuitionism, *The Bulletin of Symbolic Logic*, Vol. 6, No. 3, September, pp. 284–310.

van Dalen, Dirk (2005), *Mystic, Geometer, and Intuitionist: The Life of L. E. J. Brouwer – Volume 2: Hope and Disillusion*, Clarendon Press, Oxford.

Veronese, Giuseppe (1891), *Fondamenti di geometria a più dimensioni e a più specie di unità rettilinee espositi in forma elementare*, Tipografia del Seminario, Padova.

Wittgenstein, Ludwig (1939), *Wittgenstein's Lectures on the Foundations of Mathematics – Cambridge, 1939, from the Notes of R.G. Bosanquet, Norman Malcolm, Rush Rhees, and Yorick Smithies*, edited by Cora Diamond, The University of Chicago Press, Chicago.

# 11 A *crooked path* along *The Gravel Walks*

> River gravel. In the beginning, that.
> High summer, and the angler's motorbike
> Deep in roadside flowers, like a fallen knight
> Whose ghost we'd lately questioned: '*Any luck?*'
> . . . .
>
> But the actual washed stuff *kept you slow and steady*
> As you went *stooping with your barrow full*
> . . . .
>
> So *walk on air against your better judgement*
> Establishing yourself somewhere in between
> Those solid batches mixed with grey cement
> And a tune called '*The Gravel Walks*' that conjures green.'
> —Seamus Heaney, The Gravel Walks (italics added)

In the half century of my life as an economist, the works, correspondence and lives of four Universalists has dominated my own interests – but also four others whose works, over the years, came gradually to influence me: Gunnar Myrdal, the *Universal Social Scientist* (Velupillai, 1990); Maynard Keynes, the *Universal Man*;[1] Paul Samuelson, the *Universal Economist* (Velupillai, 2018); and Herbert Simon, the *Universal Behavioural Scientist* (this whole monograph).

But the other four, those to whom I am equally indebted, for their ideas and methodologies, were *no less Universal* in the doctrines they advocated: Richard Goodwin, Piero Sraffa, Luitzen Brouwer and Alan Turing.[2]

They all uphold the tradition of a Leonardo da Vinci, in the sense of being latter-day *renaissance men* – the only difference being that I had the privilege of knowing all of them, personally, except Brouwer and Turing. There is, therefore, no excuse whatsoever for me *not* to be humble, be measured and careful in my claims and be unreservedly modest in any analytical framework I think I have constructed – especially if it is to be consistent with the impossible task of synthesizing the diverse strands of their methodological frameworks.

I hope this is the message in this monograph which is, after all, a focus only on one face of the octagon, but illuminated by the light I have discerned from the other seven sides.

So, *The Gravel Walks* have dominated my intellectual pursuits, in my search for a synthesis of the apparent diverse frameworks, these eight Universalists have fashioned, for an analytical understanding of dynamic mathematical behavioural economics, in a constructive and computable mode.

On 12 September 1996, the late Paul Samuelson wrote me as follows:

> You must fill me in on exactly how Goodwin contributed toward *solving Hilbert's 16th problem.*

Samuelson was referring to my claim that Le Corbeiller's student (Goodwin, too, was a 'student' of this great applied mathematician), Rui Pacheco de Figueiredo, in his Harvard applied mathematics doctoral dissertation, had used what he (and Le Corbeiller) had referred to as the 'Goodwin Oscillator' (one that, contrary to conventional wisdom, generated closed paths, that were stable) which was endowed with *only one-bend*[3] (unlike the van der Pol and similar oscillators). de Figueiredo had used this one-sided oscillator, as Goodwin referred to it, to solve, for the *Liénard (Nonlinear) Equation* and give an acceptable[4] answer – even if non-constructive in its proof – *to the second part of Hilbert's 16th Problem.*

The point was that a geometric construction that Goodwin had developed, for entirely economic reasons, had been used to resolve – even if only partly – a celebrated 'problem'. I asked myself, whether something similar could be said, or demonstrated, on the basis of one of many of Simon's innovative constructions. I confined myself to four of Simon's conceptual constructions: *Heuristics, Information Processing Systems, Bounded Rationality* and *Satisficing*; however, bounded rationality and satisficing underpinned the construction, definition and activities of the *Information Processing System.*

Hence, in Herbert Simon's world, **Human** *Problem Solving* was implemented by *Information Processing Systems*, utilizing *Heuristic* (algorithmic) *Processes.*

To try to find an application of the Simon conceptual constructions, in the attempt to *solve* one or another of the known *famous problems*, I 'scoured' the literature and decided (sic!) to look at the following list:

*   *Hilbert's Problems* – specifically, the *10th Problem*
        (cf. Hilbert, 1900; 1902; Davis, 1973; Matiyasevich, 1993)

*   The Clay Mathematical Institute's *Millennium Problems* – specifically that which was on the question of whether **P** $\doteq$ **NP**
        (Carlson et al., 2006, see, in particular, the chapter by Stephen Cook)

*   The *Four-Colour Problem* and the Appel-Haken *Computer Aided Proof* of *Guthrie's conjecture*, which became a *theorem*, and the *search* for its *mathematical* proof as the *Solution*
        (Appel & Haken, 1976; Saaty & Kainen, 1977; 1986)

*   Smale's *Mathematical Problems*[5] for the 21st century (Smale, 1998), especially *Problems 3 & 18, Does P = NP?* and the *Limits of Intelligence*, respectively.

For a very long time I had wondered how one would approach the unsolvability of *Diophantine equations* with the conceptual apparatus that Simon had provided – particularly whether an *Information Processing System* could, using *Heuristics* (in the way Newell & Simon had done, in their monumental text of 1972, *Human Problem Solving*), find a way to approach the issue in the way Davis, Putnam, Julia Robinson and, finally, Matiyasevich, had done.

Eventually, I came to the 'melancholy' conclusion that any method of solution of *exponential Diophantine equations* had to invoke a *formalized* process for the necessary proof and, therefore, I had to find an equivalence between *Heuristics* and a form of the *Church–Turing Thesis*. At this point, the *decidability* issue seemed tied to *Turing Machine Computability*, predicated on the (implicit) assumption of a form of the Church–Turing Thesis – and I was convinced that Simon's (and the constructivists – whether Brouwerian *Intuitionists* or Bishop-style mathematicians) disinterest in *proving* – using, in particular, *tertium non datur* – the *unsolvability of Hilbert's Tenth Problem* was entirely justified.

This was similar to the way I interpreted the *disinterest* – bordering on the proverbial 'deafening silence' – shown by Simon (and Newell) to the $\mathbf{P} \stackrel{?}{=} \mathbf{NP}$ question,[6] which was an important problem in both Smale's list of *Mathematical Problems for the Next Century* and the Clay Mathematical Institute's *Millennium Problems*.

Incidentally, Alan Turing used *Turing Machine Computability* – predicated on a variant of the Church–Turing Thesis (see, however, Chapter 8 of this book) – to make sense of the *Trefoil Knot* and introduce the *unsolvability* of the *Word problem*; 'unsolvability' requires a definition of 'solvability' and, hence, his (last published paper was titled) *Solvable and Unsolvable Problems* (Turing, 1954). I was wrong to think that Turing's machine computability was equivalent to Simon's *Human Problem Solving* by *Information Processing Systems*. The former was a question of *Machine Computable*; the latter was predicated upon *Heuristics* (of Search Processes, assuming Gödel's *Completeness Theorem* for Propositional Logic), or[7] an *intuitive understanding of Mental constructions of processes that solved problems* – in the sense of *Brouwer* (and *BHK*).

That leaves the *Computer Aided Proof* of the four-colour theorem – Guthrie's Conjecture – and *Problem 18: Limits of Intelligence*, in Smale's list, both of which, I think, could be approached via the conceptual tools constructed by Simon, that is, the use of *Heuristics* by *Information Processing Systems*.

It is serendipitous to remember that it is almost exactly 60 years since the *Dartmouth Conference*, which gave birth – by, among others, Herbert Simon – to the concept of *Artificial Intelligence* (and almost 20 years since Smale, 1998). However, priority – as handsomely acknowledged by Simon (1996) – in this respect, albeit with respect to *Machine Intelligence*, must go to Turing (1950).[8] Although Penrose (1989, 1994) *tries* 'to show some limitations of artificial intelligence' (Smale, ibid., p. 13), I subscribe to the cogent – computability-based – refutations of the Penrose thesis[9] given by Davis (1996) and Putnam (1995), respectively.

Smale (*ibid.*, p. 13; italics in the original), significantly, states *Problem 18; Limits of Intelligence*, as

*What are the limits of intelligence, both artificial and human?*

*Remark 1*

> I do *not* believe either Turing or Simon (or Brouwer, for that matter) sub-
> scribe to the view that there were *limits to intelligence*, in any determin-
> able sense.

*Remark 2*

> Both Turing and Simon defined, *pro tempore*, notions of intelligence (as
> a process), the former subject to a form of the Church–Turing Thesis,
> and the latter in terms of (formally undefined) Heuristic processes; in
> Brouwer's case, it was subsumed in his notion and concept of the *cre-
> ative mathematician*.

Hence,

*Conjecture 1*

> The problem of 'the limits of intelligence' is (algorithmically) *undecidable*.

*Remark 3*

> The proof is 'easy', provided one can 'accept', unambiguously, any of the
> (formal) definitions of *intelligence*, given by Turing or Simon.

Finally, there is the computer-aided proof of Appel and Haken (1976), of Guthrie's
Conjecture of the *planar* four-colourability of a map (Saaty & Kainen, 1986). I
think this computer-aided proof is reproducible, using Simon's notion of *Heuristics*, implemented by *Information Processing Systems* – and would be fully
endorsed by Herbert Simon. As Saaty and Kainen observe (*ibid.*, p. 95; italics
added),

> Appel and Haken began with an initial discharging *algorithm* and *succes-
> sively modified it*. This [modification] involved considering the possible fail-
> ure cases of each *algorithm*, which could occur because of the 'overcharging'
> of some vertex; i.e., transferring to a vertex with negative charge too much
> positive charge. *The enumeration of cases was done by a [digital] com-
> puter, changes were made, and then the new algorithm was again examined.*
> In other words, *the computer was used via man-machine interaction as a
> 'scratch pad'* in order *to find an appropriate discharging procedure.*
>   The next step in the *proof*, checking configurations for reducibility, also
> employed the computer . . . Human computation [alone] is simply too slow.
>   *[A]ny proof* of the four-color theorem . . . must be extremely complex,
> *requiring computer assistance.*

Reading *heuristics* for *algorithm* – Appel and Haken do not invoke (in fact, *cannot*) any form of the Church–Turing Thesis, and cannot implement any form of
the BHK process in their automated proof – and the *modification* is to be (partly

automated) by information processing systems, it is possible to show that this is exactly how Simon (and Newell) envisaged *Human Problem Solving*.

### Remark 4

Appel and Haken also invoke, felicitously, *Heuristic* notions, but in limiting the possible *probabilistic* alternatives in the proof process, thus reducing the cases to be considered; Simon's *Heuristics* are implemented in constrained deterministic spaces.

I can, therefore, conclude with a conjecture:

### Conjecture 2

The four-colour theorem *can* be proved *mathematically* – but with the *aid of a digital computer*.

### Remark 5

The proof of conjecture 2, I surmise, would be within a(n) (constrained deterministic) iterative space, subject to Gödel's Completeness Theorem for Propositional Logic, implementing Simon-type *Heuristics* by *Information Processing Agents*.

### Remark 6

The 'constraints' are determined by the *bounded rationality* of *Information Processing Systems, solving problems* by *satisficing*.

The *Crooked Path* along *The Gravel Walks* was a long journey, even if rewarding for the many illuminating, intellectual and humane insights. It remains unfinished and *incompletable* and is suffused with ambiguous unpredictabilities, with forks replete – often – with undecidable disjunctions. This is only an interim report, full of compromises and promises.

I am reminded of Hannah Arendt's (1998; 1958) poignant words, in *The Human Condition* (p. 232; italics added):

The central concept of the two entirely new sciences of the modern age, *natural science* no less than *historical*, is *the concept of process*, and the actual human experience underlying it is action. Only because we are capable of acting, *of starting processes* of our own, can we conceive of both nature and history as *systems of processes*.

It is no exaggeration to think that Herbert Simon is in that great tradition of thought, and action, which begins with **Vico** (*history as a process*), continues with **Newton** (*natural Science as a process*) and **Brouwer** (*mathematics as a mental process*), then begins *a new* 'modern age' with **Turing** who made *computation a process*. Herbert Simon fashioned behavioural sciences as a process, in this noble, centuries-old tradition. It is, now, a **Vico–Newton–Brouwer–Turing–Simon** tradition of a *new Modern Age*.

## Notes

1  The title of the book on Keynes, by Richard Davenport-Hines, is *Universal Man – The Lives of John Maynard Keynes* (cf. Velupillai, 2015).

2  They, too, have fashioned 'Universalities': *Universal Macroeconomic Dynamics* (Goodwin), *Universal Classical Economic Value Theory* (Sraffa), *Universal Intuitionistic Constructive Mathematics* (Brouwer) and *Universal Machine Computation* (Turing). The perceptive reader may have noticed that six, of the eight, are portrayed in the **ASSRU Logo** (cf. the Preface of this book). The time will come when the *hexagon* of people will become an *octagon*! By the way, there *is* such a thing as the *Universal Turing Machine* and, in my opinion, Sraffa's *construction* of the Standard Commodity, the *constructive proof* of its uniqueness and the Standard Ratio are a contribution to a *Universal* (Classical) Theory of Value. I also believe that the 'forced van der Pol' oscillator has *Universal* dynamic and algorithmic properties. The *Brouwer–Heyting–Kolmogorov* (**BHK**) methods of proof are *Universal*.

3  Goodwin (1950), developed the idea *entirely geometrically* (by 'free-hand' drawing of possible macrodynamics), when reviewing Hicks (1950), essentially showing that either the 'ceiling' or the 'floor' was *sufficient* to generate an endogenous closed path in a two-dimensional dynamical system.

4  I chose the word acceptable guardedly, mainly because of the controversy surrounding the (untenable) claims, in this regard, by a 'young' Uppsala (applied) mathematician.

5  *The Riemann Hypothesis* and what was *the second-part of Hilbert's 16th Problem* (neither still *completely solved*) – are included also in Smale's list as the 1st and the 13th Problem, respectively; the $P \stackrel{?}{=} NP$ question, the 5th in the *Millennium Problem* list is the 3rd in Smale's *Mathematical Problems for the Next Century*.

6  After all, **NP** stands for *non-deterministic, polynomial time* (**Turing**) *computability*! See also Simon's feeling of *ennui*, and the context in which it arose, described in Chapter 7 of this book.

7  *MY opinion* – not something I can unambiguously attribute to Herbert Simon.

8  In interpreting *Machine Intelligence* as *Mechanical Intelligence* – the title of one of the volumes of the Collected Works of A. M. Turing (1992, edited by D. C. Ince) – I can, at last, find a way to 'equate' Turing's *Machine-based solvability* and Simon's notion of *Human Problem Solving* (also emphasized by Simon, 1996). In this connection, see also Gandy (1996).

9  It must be remembered that Penrose believed – and reasoned on this belief – that the *mind resided in the brain* and, hence, 'is concerned with the brain' (Gandy, *op. cit.*, p. 135). Simon (1996, p. 81), is explicit in stating,

> I speak of 'mind' and not 'brain'.

And as Gandy points out (*ibid.*, p. 136; italics added),

> [P]enrose asserts forcefully that *consciousness is essential to rational thought*; I do not quite understand what he means by *consciousness*.

Gandy's modesty prevents him from asserting that 'rational thought' has nothing to do with 'consciousness'.

## References

Appel, K. & W. Haken (1976), Every Planar Map Is Four Colorable, *Bulletin of the American Mathematical Society*, Vol. 82, No. 5, September, pp. 711–712.

Arendt, Hannah (1998; 1958), *The Human Condition* (Second Edition), with an Introduction by Margaret Canovan, The University of Chicago Press, Chicago.

Carlson, J., A. Jaffe & A. Wiles (eds.) (2006), *The Millennium Prize Problems*, American Mathematical Society, Providence, RI.

Davis, Martin (1973), Hilbert's Tenth Problem Is Unsolvable, *The American Mathematical Monthly*, Vol. 80, No. 3, March 1, pp. 233–269.

Davis, Martin (1996), Is Mathematical Insight Algorithmic?, *Behavioral and Brain Sciences*, Vol. 13, No. 4, December, pp. 659–660.

Gandy, Robin (1996), Human versus Mechanical Intelligence, chapter 7, pp. 125–136, in: *Machines and Thought: The Legacy of Alan Turing*, Vol. 1, Oxford University Press, Oxford.

Goodwin, Richard M. (1950), A Non-Linear Theory of the Cycle, *The Review of Economics and Statistics*, Vol. 32, No. 4, November, pp. 316–320.

Hicks, J. R. (1950), *A Contribution to the Theory of the Trade Cycle*, Clarendon Press, Oxford.

Hilbert, David (1900; 1902), Mathematical Problems, *Bulletin of the American Mathematical Society*, Vol. 8, July, pp. 437–479.

Matiyasevich, Yuri (1993), *Hilbert's Tenth Problem*, with an Introduction by Martin Davis, The MIT Press, Cambridge, MA.

Penrose, Roger (1989), *The Emperor's New Mind: Concerning Computers, Minds and The Laws of Physics*, Oxford University Press, Oxford.

Penrose, Roger (1994), *Shadows of the Mind: A Search for the Missing Science of Consciousness*, Oxford University Press, Oxford.

Putnam, Hilary (1995), *Review* of Shadows of the Mind, *Bulletin of the American Mathematical Society*, Vol. 32, No. 3, July, pp. 370–373.

Saaty, Thomas L. & Paul C. Kainen (1977; 1986), *The Four-Color Problem: Assaults and Conquest*, Dover Publications, Inc., New York.

Simon, Herbert A. (1996), Machine as Mind, chapter 5, pp. 81–102, in: *Machines and Thought: The Legacy of Alan Turing*, Vol. 1, Oxford University Press, Oxford.

Smale, Steve (1998), Mathematical Problems for the Next Century, *The Mathematical Intelligencer*, Vol. 20, No. 2, pp. 7–15.

Turing, Alan M. (1950), Computing Machinery and Intelligence, *Mind*, New Series, Vol. 59, No. 236, October, pp. 433–460.

Turing, Alan M. (1954), Solvable and Unsolvable Problems, *Science News*, Vol. 31, February, pp. 7–23.

Turing, Alan M. (1992), *Mechanical Intelligence: Collected Works of A. M. Turing*, edited by D. C. Ince, North-Holland, Amsterdam.

Velupillai, Kumaraswamy (1990), Gunnar Myrdal: The Universal Social Scientist (1898–1987), presented at the *Colloque Myrdal*, Montreal, January, 1989; in: *Gunnar Myrdal et son Oeuvre*, edited by Giles Dostaler, Diane Éthier & Laurent Lepage, Economica, Paris.

Velupillai, K. Vela (2015), Universal Man: The Lives of John Maynard Keynes: A Review Note, *Economic and Political Weekly*, Vol. 51, No. 6, February 6, pp. 35–38.

Velupillai, K. Vela (2018), Macroeconomics of the Universal Economist, Invited Contribution, in: Preparation for *Eminent Economists: Paul Samuelson*, edited by Richard Anderson, William Barnett & Robert Cord, Palgrave Macmillan, London.

# Appendix 1

## Labyrinths and mazes without Minotaurs – Borges's library, Simon's mazes and Turing's librarian[1]

### A *'fictional'* preamble

> Here there is a play on words. In English, the word for 'labyrinth' is *maze* and for 'surprise,' *amazement*. There is a clear semantic connotation as well.
> This is the form in which I perceive life: a continual amazement; a continual bifurcation of the labyrinth.
> —Borges in Simon (1991, p. 177; italics in the original)

In his dialogue with Simon, initiated and conducted, at the latter's request, in December 1970, at Borges's 'beautiful high-ceilinged baroque office in the *Biblioteca Nacional*', the celebrated Argentinian began by wondering why Simon was interested in having the conversation, in the first place. The preceding reflection on *the amazement of life's mazes* was in response to Simon's answer to this initial question by Borges (*loc. cit.*, p. 176; italics added[2]):

> I want to know how it was that the *labyrinth* entered into your field of vision, into your concepts, so that you incorporated it in your stories.

In the letter to Borges, requesting a meeting during his visit to Buenos Aires in December, 1970, Simon acknowledged that he had been particularly inspired by 'La Biblioteca de Babel' – *The Library of Babel*[3] – to which he had been introduced by Ed Feigenbaum,[4] during one of his regular sojourns at RAND in the academic year 1960/61, through having brought to his attention the collection *Ficciones*.

However, the metaphor of *a journey through a maze* had already played a significant role in Simon's pioneering formulation of behavioural decision processes by *satisficing boundedly rational agents* (Simon, 1957), thus providing his effective alternative to the orthodox vision of *Olympian, Omniscient*, rational agents (Simon, 1983, p. 19), optimizing beyond all formal and realistic constraints, even while playing lip service to the framework of 'constrained optimization'; it was as if engineers were designing perpetual motion machines, despite the elementary *laws* of Newtonian mechanics and (phenomenological) thermodynamics.

Many, even enlightened scholars, who dispute orthodox formalizations of rationality and the underpinning they provided for human decision making, particularly in the social and humanistic fields, associate '*mechanical*' and '*machines*' with varieties of determinism.[5] Simon, following in the noble footsteps of Turing, had begun, just at this time, his later lifelong research focus on trying to model and understand 'the implication of a belief in the possibility of computer simulation of human thought for free will'[6] – considered by all shades of authoritative, orthodox, thinking (sic!) to be incompatible with machine modelling of thought – in the specific context of problem solving by bounded rational, satisficing, human decision makers, viewed as *Information Processing Systems*.

This was the way – in my opinion, but with suitable 'generalizations' of the notion of algorithms – Simon synthesized Turing's notions of *solvability and unsolvability* in the context of problem solving and Shannon's parallel, pioneering, work on *information processing and the limits of a transmitting channel's capacity*.[7] Bringing together, effectively, the way the *Halting Problem for Turing Machines* (as a theorem) made it possible to encapsulate the nature of free will in decision making, in the context of (human) problem solving, with the limits of information processing by *mechanical* channels in the sense of Shannon (and later Hamming), was one of Simon's greatest insights and contributions to what I have come to call *Classical Behavioural Economics* (Kao & Velupillai, 2012).

The mistaken belief that any reference to machines or mechanical precluded any notion, concept or possibility of discussing or formalizing 'free will', the indeterminacy of human 'choice', whether in the context of finite or infinite – countable, uncountable or whatever – was put to rest in different ways by *Turing, Shannon, Simon* and *Borges*.

Thus, the final answer, this time in answering the question Borges posed Simon, on the nature of his work, Simon was able to state:

> This is the form in which I conceive *free will*: it resides in the fact that *I* am that which acts when I take a given action. And the fact that something has caused this behavior in no manner make me (the I who acts *unfree*).
>
> So when we reach a bifurcation in the road of the labyrinth, 'something' chooses which branch to take. And the reason for my researches, and the reason why *labyrinths* have fascinated me, has been my desire to observe people as they encounter *bifurcations*[8] and try to understand why they take the road to the right or to the left.
>
> (Simon, 1991, p. 179; bold italics, added)

Surely, choices at these 'bifurcations' points or 'forks' – are the ones Turing (1939, §4) referred to as *Oracles*[9] – and, in the current terminology of Turing Machine based computability theory, they are *non*-deterministic paths of a tree (say, in a graph). These are what lead to the great problem of $P \stackrel{?}{=} NP$.

In the next section, against the backdrop provided in this 'fictional' preamble, a concise description of the way Simon used the metaphor of a journey through a maze – a labyrinth – to formalize his pioneering alternative to orthodox formulations of Olympian, Omniscient, rational behaviour; the former in a natural and intrinsic procedural way – one actually travels through the labyrinth, with or without the benefits of possessing *Ariadne's Thread* – and the latter in a fictitious world of *as if* mongering.

In the section on **Turing's** *Librarian* **in Borges'** *Library of Babel*, inspired by Bloch (2008), I weave a few unpredictable themes, based on Borges' imagined lives of the librarians in his *Library of Babel*, using Turing's remarkable theorem on the Halting Problem for Turing Machines that makes nonsense of the varied deprecations of noble claims by Turing, Simon and Borges on thoughts and thinking by simulating machines or minds (whether they are the same, or one can be studied by simulating the other or whatever, remains, in fact, *undecidable* in any formal sense).

The final, ultra-brief, section, outlines, speculatively, what I think we as non-orthodox, interdisciplinary economists can learn, at least in the form of metaphors, from repeated and unceasing reading of Borges's apparently paradoxical stories – none of which are remotely formal in any mathematical sense, but almost all of which are infused with deep mathematical insights.

## A classical behavioural economist's journey in *a maze*

> Classical economic theory assumes that decision makers, whether groups or individuals, know *everything* about the world and use it all to calculate the optimal way to behave. . . . *This is a ridiculous view of what goes on.*
>
> To go into a firm and evaluate the actual decision-making process, you must find out what information they have, *choose* to focus on, and how they *actually process that information.* That's what I've been doing all these years. *That's why my AI work is a natural continuation of what I did earlier in economics.* It's all an attempt to see *how decision making works:* first at the individual level – how is it possible to solve problems with an instrument like a human brain? – and at the group level, although I've never gotten back to that level.
>
> – Simon (1994; italics added.)

By his own admission (see Part II, Simon, 1991), 1956, was a watershed year that saw the publication of the article in which the maze metaphor was utilized effectively (Simon, 1956), to launch the boundedly rational agent, satisficing, as an Information Processing System solving problems, that is, towards the monumental treatise on *Human Problem Solving* (Newell & Simon, 1972). The Olympian rational agent of orthodox theory – even the ostensibly extended behavioural agent *of Modern Behavioural Economics* of Ward Edwards who, also 'emerged' at about the same time (Kao & Velupillai, *op. cit.*) – who, in any case, *almost* never played any role in Simon's work before the watershed year, completely disappeared from the world of Simon's behavioural sciences from that time onwards. There was never any infinite horizon, utility maximizing paradigm in Simon's contribution after the maze metaphor helped him launch his (classical) boundedly rational, satisficing, behavioural agent, procedurally searching for an acceptable path along the labyrinth that was the life of decision making.

As he characterized it,

> In my 1956 paper, 'Rational Choice and the Structure of the Environment,' I wove around *the metaphor of the maze* a formal model of how an organism (a person?) could meet a multiplicity of needs and wants at a satisfactory level and survive without drawing upon superhuman powers of intelligence and computation. The model provided a practicable design for a creature of *bounded rationality*, as all we creatures are.
>
> (Simon, 1991, p. 175; italics added)

From the weaving of a formal model of decision making, around the metaphor of a maze, Simon next took the imaginative – even audacious – step of writing a story: *The Apple: A Story of a Maze*. It illustrated his theory of human decision making, as a process of learning heuristics, eventually formalizable as *o-machines*, during the life of a reasonably 'intelligent' – albeit isolated from other human interactions – agent, traversing *endlessly* through the mazes of a labyrinth.

The structure of the maze that housed Hugo, the protagonist in The Apple, had great mathematical similarities to the *Library of Babel*, especially its never-ending potential paths and the unmentioned length of life that Hugo could expect to live, if – indeed – life and death made any sense to him. In other words, it is not clear whether Hugo had any perception of ageing, although he obviously felt the passage of diurnal time.

Hugo's focus, in addition to the internal ruminations that result in learning from his daily experiences of journeying through the maze that makes up the labyrinth – although there is a Minotaur he is searching for, to slay, ultimately – is the environment. Here, Hugo is assumed to have a single, fixed, aspiration level for food, but as he realizes that there are different ways to satisfy this aspiration, he develops a certain sophistication in his taste (not realizing, of course, that he may or may not have intrinsic, mutable taste buds with which he may or may not have been genetically endowed). But the alternative 'menus' are located in such a way that Hugo has to walk in the maze, where there are branches at each bifurcation. Hugo has a finite number of possible alternative routes to choose, from any bifurcation, which leads him to one or another of a finite variety of locations of alternative menus. Over time, Hugo develops likes and dislikes – what the economist may refer to as 'preferences', so they are not given at the outset, as in the case of the Neoclassical, Olympian agent.

The evolving, taste is combined with the constraint that Hugo's vision – both for intrinsic organic reasons and extrinsic structural reasons – is limited and therefore his vision of the alternatives from any bifurcation is more or less constrained. However, if his vision permits the sight of menus, then Hugo knows the way to reach the food. Hugo has to satisfy hunger and thirst for purely survival purposes which, presumably, is signaled by internal biological mechanisms and there is a maximal number of moves he can make after eating before his energy runs out. It is not clear whether or how exactly he learns these constraints, but learn he does and these 'loose ends', in the novelette, allow for the kind of imagination that the Borges story caters for, copiously.

There is no wonder, then, that Simon, when he read *The Library of Babel* (around 1960/61), felt a strong affinity with the richness of the possibilities of indefinite paths, indeterminate ageing, uncountable infinities and other surreal imagined realities that enriched the Borges story. The obvious difference between the two, of course, was that Borges left these imagined realities in the realm of the magic of the mind; Simon spent the rest of his life trying to tame them by modelling the many indeterminacies, indefiniteness and infinities with imaginative mathematics, for the most part those that Turing devised, with other – yet equally mind-boggling – inspirations at its bases.

To a few of them, I now turn.

## Turing's *Librarian* in Borges' *Library of Babel*[10]

> Like all men of the Library, I have traveled in my youth; I have wondered in search of a book, perhaps the catalogue of catalogues: now that my eyes can hardly decipher what I write, I am preparing to die just a few leagues from the hexagons where I was born.
>
> – Borges (1964, p. 52)

In his *paean* to Bloch's sustained, almost lyrical, mathematical rendering of *The Library of Babel*, the extraordinary magic realistic essay by Borges, formally written as a book review, Dan King (2010, p. 418), perceptively observed,

> In more unchartered terrain, Bloch closes his mathematical analysis of [*Library of Babel*] by weaving connections to the works of Turing and Gödel. He argues that the combined lives of the librarians endlessly searching the volumes of the Library can, in a sense, be regarded as homomorphic to the operations of a Turing Machine.

Bloch's characterization of the activities of a single librarian[11] – there is, obviously,[12] a *countable infinity* of them, since there are *at least* a countable infinity of hexagons and, according to the *Library of Babel* (footnote 1, p. 54), 'there was a [librarian] for every three hexagons'[13] – as those of the computation by a Turing Machine are persuasively described (*ibid.*, p. 124, last paragraph). The characterization is schematized as a formal (symbolic) computational procedure by a Turing Machine, with a defined halting state – that is, death ('by suicide and pulmonary diseases'!).

However, the Turing Machine interpretation of the life and times of a Borgesian librarian, in the *Library of Babel*, remains *incomplete* (sic!) without the addition of the following 'lemma':

> *Lemma*: It is (algorithmically) undecidable when (and *whether*) any particular librarian will expire.
>
> *Proof*: Due to the *undecidability*[14] of the *halting problem for Turing Machines*.[15]

I should add one 'surreal' (*pace* Knuth, 1974) mathematical note to substantiate some of the implicit mathematical assumptions in the notes above. The existence of a *countable infinity* of hexagons, in finite space, is easily formalized within one or another form of nonstandard analysis,[16] as clearly indicated by Bloch (see, in particular, pp. 53–4, *ibid.*).

Two other, distinctly *non-surreal*, notes refer to possible *non-consistencies*[17] in Borges, one, when he refers to the books in the *Library of Babel* having been composed using only *twenty-five orthographical symbols* (*ibid.*, p, 53), ruling out the use of 'digits or capital letters in the original manuscripts'. Yet, on the same page he observes,

> One [book] which my father saw in a hexagon on circuit fifteen ninety-four was made up of the letters MCV, perversely repeated from the first line to the last.

The second possible non-consistency is when he claims that the number of books, since they are 'made up of the same elements: the space, the period, the comma, the twenty-two letters of the alphabet' are 'not infinite' (ibid., p. 54). However, this has to be an *impossible* conclusion, given the premises! An elementary enumeration, even constructively enabled, would convince a reader, in particular, of Borges and Bloch, that the *listable* combinations of the 'twenty-odd orthographical symbols' is, in fact, countably infinite.

However, an important observation by Bloch[18] should be taken into consideration here:

> My guess would be that [Borges] meant something like, 'The number of volumes with *distinct orderings from the finite alphabet is itself finite*, due to the fact that each volume has a prescribed number of symbols in it.' This would entail a finite number of distinct volumes; the $25^{1,312,000}$ calculated by many besides myself. *If one allowed multi-volume sets of books with unlimited repetition*, then you are, of course, correct.

These non-consistencies and ambiguities are absolute trivialities in Bloch's lyrical rendering of *The Unimaginable Mathematics of Borges' Library of Babel*.

### Mathematising imagined worlds

> It is not uncommon for a scientist to be interested in Borges . . . Deep and varied connections sprang out as we read about *aleph* – the *cardinality* of infinity[19] . . . – about *forking paths* that lead to parallel universes. . . . Or about *an infinite library* that in the end turns out to have the same contents as a single 'book of sand,' whose number of pages is a *continuum*.
>
> – Quiroga (2012, pp. 4–5; italics added)

Quiroga's fascinating book lists an impressive number of scientists – including mathematicians[20] – who have read and interpreted the imagined unimaginable entities and structures in Borges's many stories.[21]

Do we – are we able to – encapsulate the Borgesian world of imagined unimaginable in any kind of formal mathematics? It is clear from the remarks and substantiated observations in Bloch, Odifreddi, Quiroga and Simon that Borges had more than a nodding acquaintance with at least some aspects of the foundations of mathematics and mathematical philosophy. But he moulded the deep mathematical concepts he worked with, predominantly for purposes of constructing and representing literary paradoxes, from which to extract lessons for the mind – and to represent deep and difficult ambiguities.

As far as I am concerned, the role of *paradoxes* and *ambiguities* in pushing the frontiers of economic formalizations have been less than felicitous. They have been confined to what I consider trivial examples, predominantly characterized by work in Modern Behavioural Economics, which I have also referred to as a field indulging in 'anomaly mongering', resolved *by ad hoc* appeals to a plethora of mathematical concepts. They play, at best, the role of counter-examples in mathematics, but without the discipline provided by an *Ansatz* or a clear understanding of the function of *thought-experiments* in dissecting and 'repairing' paradoxes or clarifying ambiguities.

I believe Simon's understanding of the vision that was behind the narratives Borges constructed is the best available, at least for now (Simon, 1991, p. 179; italics added):

> So Borges denied that there was an abstract model underlying 'The Library of Babel' or 'The Garden of Paths that Fork'. *He wrote stories; he did not instantiate models. He was a teller of tales.*

The message, then, at least for economics, seems to be that we, too, should try to 'write stories', be 'tellers of tales', without this mad rush into 'instantiating models.'

## Notes

1  For most of my conscious life, ever since the earliest years of my childhood, three activities have preoccupied my mind: logical puzzles (e.g., the *Tower of Hanoi*), the construction of *meccano* set models and solving for maze paths in *labyrinths*. These three activities – and these days also LEGO construction of a functioning Turing Machine – are predominant in the way I spend time with my children, whose curiosities, inspired by them, have – I think, in any case, I hope – prevented my mind from death by atrophy. The 'narrative' in this appendix is based on the fascination, and constructive inspiration, generated by puzzles, mazes in labyrinths and solving problems generated by them, on the minds and work of three of 20th-century's great thinkers: *Jorge Luis Borges, Herbert Simon* and *Alan Turing*, who, each in his own way, have made my intellectual life an unceasing adventure.

2  *Only* the part of the dialogue referring to the topic of labyrinths is reproduced in Simon (1991). The full dialogue appears in Simon (1971).

3  Interestingly one of the more accessible English translations of this fascinating story appears in a book titled **Labyrinths: Selected Stories and Writings** (Borges, 1964).
4  Earlier an undergraduate student of Herbert Simon at the then Carnegie Institute of Technology (cf. ch. 6, pp. 165–182, in Klahr & Kotovsky, 1989).
5  I am not, here, referring to facile references to deterministic chaos and its possibilities of encapsulating a study of apparently 'random' motion.
6  As Nozick so very perceptively wondered, so many years ago (perhaps influenced by Herbert Simon!),

> In what other way if not *simulation by a Turing Machine*, can we understand the *process* of making *free choices*? By making them perhaps.
>
> (Nozick, 1981, p. 303; italics added.)

7  It was still at least 20 years before Phelps and Lucas spoke – somewhat ignorantly and pompously – of an information 'revolution' in the microeconomic foundations of macroeconomics, itself a chimera, and of agents as signal processors. Neither of them, or their modern followers, have ever acknowledged or incorporated the notions of a channel's capacity – hence an agent's capacity – to transmit and process information, agents as information processing systems and, in general, any of the pioneering work of Turing, Shannon and Simon on these and related issues of *information theoretic complexity.*
8  I hope the discerning reader is now strengthened in his appreciation of the caveat I added in the previous footnote!
9  It is this that gave me the initial impulse to think about heuristics, a la Newell and Simon (1972), as a process that was independent of the Church–Turing Thesis. Turing's original statement is (*ibid.*, p. 18; 52; italics added):

> Let us suppose that we are supplied with some *unspecified means* of solving number theoretic problems; a kind of *oracle* as it were. We will not go any further into the nature of this oracle than to say that *it cannot be a machine* (call them *o-machines*), having as one of its fundamental processes that of solving a given number theoretic problem.

I read 'it cannot be a machine' to mean, exactly, '*it cannot be a Turing Machine*'.
10  I am using James Irby's translation in Borges (1964).
11  I do not think, contrary to King's interpretation of Bloch, that this characterization is about 'the *combined lives* of the librarians', but that of *one* arbitrary librarian. I am happy that Professor Bloch confirms my interpretation in an e-mail to me of 13 December 2012.
12  I am not sure 'obviously' is completely warranted here; I suspect there is some ambiguity in the original Borges text which makes it possible to think otherwise.
13  Although Borges adds the caveat (*loc. cit.*) that

> [s]uicide and pulmonary diseases have destroyed that proportion', this does *not* mean the existence of *any less than* a countable infinity of librarians, since only the 'proportions' are 'destroyed', not annihilated.

14  I add this 'lemma', invoking also the use of the words incomplete and undecidable to substantiate Bloch's otherwise seemingly unnecessary reference to Gödel (ibid., p. 121).
15  See Velupillai (2017) for a finessed discussion of the *Halting Problem for Turing Machines*. This paper was only very recently completed, although a first version was presented at the Turing Centennial Conference, organised by the *late Barry Cooper*, held at the Royal Society's Chicheley Hall, more than half a decade ago. The paper

was – is – dedicated (with permission) to the great Martin Davis, whose 1958 book (in the reprint edition of 1982) was an important source of my education in computability theory (see Chapter 1 of this book).

16 My own preference in this regard, particularly for reasons of easy mathematical compatibility with the computability requirements above, would be via *'Smooth' Infinitesimal Analysis*, with its underpinning in both intuitionistic logic and category theory (cf., e.g., Bell, 1998).

17 I choose this word, avoiding the more familiar 'inconsistency' because, in the spirit of Bloch's lyricism and King's paean, I do not want to imagine Borges being subject to ordinary strictures, mathematical or otherwise.

18 In a personal note to me.

19 I am not sure this is a rigorously correct assertion.

20 Odifreddi's wonderful thoughts (Odifreddi, 1997) emphasizes the role of self-referencing in many of the Borges stories, interpreted metamathematically. In particular, in **Tlön, Uqbar and Orbis Tertius**. I have myself used **Kafka and his precursors** for years in my economic writings.

21 On New Year's Day 2013, Ming Hai, my former student at the People's University of China (more than a quarter of a century ago), wrote me wondering whether I should not also consider the relevance of the story of *The Circular Ruins* for my philosophy of economics! Quiroga's book is a sustained study of the relevance of **Funes the Memorious** for his own field of research, broadly conceived as the neurosciences.

## References

Bell, John L. (1998), *A Primer of Infinitesimal Analysis*, Cambridge University Press, Cambridge.

Bloch, William Goldbloom (2008), *The Unimaginable Mathematics of Borges' Library of Babel*, Oxford University Press, Oxford.

Borges, Jorge Luis (1964), *Labyrinths: Selected Stories & Writings*, New Directions, New York.

Kao, Ying-Fang & K. Vela Velupillai (2012), Origins and Pioneers of Behavioural Economics, *Interdisciplinary Journal of Economics and Business Law*, Vol. 1, No. 3, pp. 47–73.

King, Dan (2010), *Book Review* of Bloch (2008), *The College Mathematics Journal*, Vol. 41, No. 5, November, pp. 416–418.

Klahr, David & Kenneth Kotovsky (eds.) (1989), *Complex Information Processing: The Impact of Herbert A. Simon*, Lawrence Erlbaum Associates, Publishers, New Jersey.

Knuth, Donald E. (1974), *Surreal Numbers: A Mathematical Novelette*, Addison-Wesley Publishing Company, Inc., London.

Newell, Allen & Herbert A. Simon (1972), *Human Problem Solving*, Prentice-Hall, INC, Englewood Cliffs, NJ.

Nozick, Robert (1981), *Philosophical Explanations*, Clarendon Press, Oxford.

Odifreddi, Piergiorgio (1997), Un Matematico Legge Borges, Text of a Lecture delivered at a conference on *Science and Art*, held in Trieste, November, 1996.

Quiroga, Rodrigo Quian (2012), *Borges and Memory: Encounters with the Human Brain*, The MIT Press, Cambridge, MA.

Simon, Herbert A. (1956), Rational Choice and the Structure of the Environment, *Psychological Review*, Vol. 63, No. 2, pp. 129–138.

Simon, Herbert A. (1957), *Models of Man*, John Wiley & Sons, Inc., New York.

Simon, Herbert A. (1971), Primera Plana va más lejos con Herbert Simon y Jorge Luis Borges, *Primera Plana*, Vol. 414, No. 5, Gennaio, pp. 42–45.

Simon, Herbert A. (1983), *Reason in Human Affairs*, Basil Blackwell, Oxford.

Simon, Herbert A. (1991), *Models of My Life*, The MIT Press, Cambridge, MA.

Simon, Herbert. A (1994), Herbert. A Simon: Thinking Machines: Interviewed June 1994 by Doug Stewart, *OMNI Interview*, June.

Turing, Alan (1939), System of Logics Based on Ordinals (a dissertation presented to the faculty of Princeton University in candidacy for the degree of Doctor of Philosophy), pp. 31–140, in: *Alan Turing's Systems of Logic: The Princeton Thesis*, edited and introduced by Andrew W. Appel, Princeton University Press, Princeton.

Velupillai, K. Vela (2017), Algorithmic Economics: Incomputability, Undecidability and Unsolvability in Economics, pp. 105–120, in: *The Incomputable: Journeys beyond the Turing Barrier*, edited by Barry Cooper & Mariya I. Soskova, Springer-Verlag, New York.

# Appendix 2
## Herbert Simon's pioneering methodological work in confirming public predictions

Unlike every other concept or framework Simon pioneered, the methodological application of a topological fixed-point theorem in one of the (many) fields of his expertise – political science, in this particular case – was 'one-off'. Although the mathematics underpinning the Hawkins-Simon Theorem may have a similar appearance, it is not so. That theorem, through notions of decomposability and unilateral coupling, had important ramifications in Simon's powerfully lasting work on causality, near-indecomposable evolution and so on.[1]

This is the main reason for treating this topic in an appendix, and also fairly briefly.

Today – in July 2017 – it is commonplace to be excited about the public predictions associated with polling by so-called representative sampling of, say, a voting population.[2] It is, however, little known, and even less acknowledged, that Herbert Simon contributed to the mathematical methodology of unravelling the circularity inherent in looking for consistency between the confirmation of a prediction and the prediction itself. He used a topological fixed-point argument, long before it became a bread-and-butter tool (at least) of a particular kind of mathematical economics. In this brief appendix I give a concise summary of the way Simon used the topological fixed point and the possibilities of generalizing his method and vision along recursion theoretic lines.

In standard mathematical economics, topological fixed-point theorems have been used fruitfully to encapsulate and formalize self-reference (rational expectations and policy ineffectiveness), infinite regress (rational expectations) and self-reproduction and self-reconstruction (growth), in economic dynamic contexts. This is in addition to, and quite apart from, their widespread use in proving the existence of equilibria in a wide variety of economic and game theoretical contexts.

The mathematical foundations of topology are, in general, sought in axiomatic set theory. Set theory, however, is only one of (Wang, 1981, pp. 3–4) four branches of mathematical logic, the other three being model theory, proof theory and recursion theory.[3] One can associate, roughly speaking, real analysis, nonstandard analysis, constructive analysis and computable analysis with these four branches of mathematical logic. Economists, in choosing to formalize economic notions almost exclusively in terms of real analysis, may not always succeed in capturing the intended conceptual underpinnings of economic notions with the required fidelity. However, the use of topological fixed-point theorems to formalize rational expectations does not capture the two fundamental *behavioural* notions that are crucial in its definition: self-reference and infinite-regress. The idea of self-referential *behaviour* is, for example, formalized by considering the action of a programme or an algorithm on its own description. Infinite regress is, of course, short-circuited, in the usual way, by a fix-point theorem, as Simon did more than sixty years ago.

An aside may be in order, here. All recursion theoretic formalizations and results come, almost invariably, open-ended in meaning, even when uniqueness results are demonstrated there will be, embedded in the recesses of the procedures generating equilibria and other types of solutions, an *indeterminacy*. This is because of a generic result in computability theory called the *Halting Problem for Turing Machines*. It is a kind of generic *undecidability* result, a counterpart to the more famous, Gödelian undecidability results. It is this fact that makes it possible to claim that seeking economic theoretic foundations for policy may not be an easy task. To be categorical about policy – positively or negatively – on the basis of formal mathematical models could be a dangerous sport.

A critical discussion of the use of the Brouwer fixed-point theorem, which was initiated by Herbert Simon (1954), that presaged its decisive use in general equilibrium theory, mathematical economics and the definition of a rational expectations equilibrium (particularly in Macroeconomics), Karl Egil Aubert, a respected mathematician, suggested that economists – and political scientists – were rather cavalier about the domain of definition of economic variables and, hence, less than careful about the mathematics they invoked to derive economic propositions. I was left with the impression, after a careful reading of the discussion between Aubert (1982, 1982a) and Simon (1982, 1982a), that the issue was *not* the use of a fixed-point framework but its nature, scope and underpinnings. However, particularly in a rational expectations context but also in proving the existence of a Walras–Arrow–Debreu equilibrium or a Nash equilibrium, it is not only a question of the nature of the domain of definition but also the fact that there are self-referential and infinite regress elements intrinsic to the problems. This makes the appropriate choice of the fixed-point theorem within which to embed the question of any kind of equilibrium – general equilibrium, Nash or rational expectations – is (or should be) particularly sensitive to the kind of mathematics and logic that underpins it.

Now, how did this topological fixed-point rational expectation tradition, in particular, come into being? Not, as might conceivably be believed, as a result of Muth's justly celebrated original contribution (1961), but *from the prior work of Herbert Simon* on a problem of predicting the behaviour of rational agents in a political setting (1954) and an almost concurrent economic application by Emile Grunberg and Franco Modigliani (1954).

Simon, in considering the general issue of the feasibility of public prediction in a social science context, formalized the problem for the particular case of investigating how the publication of an election prediction (particularly one based on poll data) might influence [individual] voting behaviour, and, hence – . . . – falsify the predictions. Simon, as he has done so often in so many problem situations, came up with the innovative suggestion that the self-referential and infinite-regress content of such a context may well be solved by framing it as a mathematical fix point problem:

> Is there not involved here a vicious circle, whereby any attempt to anticipate the reactions of the voters alters those reactions and hence invalidates the prediction?
> In principle, the last question can be answered in the negative: there is no vicious circle.
> . . . .
> We [can prove using a classical theorem of topology due to Brouwer (the fix point theorem)] that it is always possible in principle to take account of reactions to a published prediction in such a way that the prediction will be confirmed by the event.
>
> (Simon, 1954, pp. 82–4; italics added)

Grunberg and Modigliani recognized, clearly and explicitly, both the self- referential nature of the problem of consistent individually rational predictions in the face of being placed in an economic environment where their predictions are reactions to, and react upon (*ad infinitum*; i.e., infinite regress), the aggregate outcome, but also were acutely aware of the technical difficulties of infinite regress that was also inherent in such situations (cf. in particular, pp. 467 and 471).

In his or her setting, an individual producer faced the classic problem of *expected* price and quantity formation in a single market, subject to *public prediction* of the market clearing price.[4] It was not dissimilar to the crude cobweb model, as was indeed recognized by them (Grunberg & Modigliani, p. 468, footnote 13). Interestingly, what eventually came to be called rational expectations by Muth was called a warranted expectation[5] by Grunberg and Modigliani (ibid., pp. 469–70). In any event, their claim that it was formally possible to prove the existence of at least one correct public prediction in the face of effective reaction by the agents was substantiated by invoking Brouwer's Fixed-Point Theorem (ibid., p. 472). To facilitate the application of the theorem, the constituent functions and variables – in particular, the reaction function and the conditions on the domain of definition of prices – were assumed to satisfy the necessary real number and topological conditions (continuity, boundedness, etc.).[6]

Thus, it was that the tradition, in the rational expectations literature, of *solving* (*sic!*) the conundrums of self-reference and infinite-regress via topological fixed-point theorems was etched in the collective memory of the profession. And so, four decades after the Simon and the Grunberg–Modigliani contributions, Sargent, in his influential Arne Ryde Lectures (1993), was able to refer to the fixed-point approach to rational expectations:

> A rational expectations equilibrium is a fixed point of [a] mapping.
>
> (*ibid.*, p. 10)

Now, sixty plus years after that initial introduction of the topological fixed-point tradition by Simon and Grunberg–Modigliani, economists automatically and uncritically accept that this is the *only* way to solve the general equilibrium, Nash equilibrium and rational expectations equilibrium existence problems – and they are not to be blamed for the engendered complacency, but this is *not* true – I mean a fixed-point formulation of the equilibrium existence problem is not the only way to 'solve' the problem. Because of this complacency, the existence problem has forever been severed of all connections with the problem of determining – or finding or constructing or locating – the processes that may lead to the non-constructive and uncomputable equilibrium. The recursion theoretic fixed-point tradition, to which Simon adhered, often implicitly in his approach to Human Problem Solving, not only preserves the unity of equilibrium existence demonstration with the processes that determine it, but it also retains, in the forefront, the self-referential and infinite regress aspects of the problem of the interaction between individual and social prediction and individual and general equilibrium.

## Notes

1 Except in his sustained critique of Cournot-type game theoretic equilibria, where the problem of infinite regress is pervasive (see Simon's letter to me, reprinted in Appendix 4).
2 Despite the spectacular failures of almost all pollsters in predicting the outcome of the UK general elections of 2015!
3 Some add the higher arithmetic (i.e., number theory) as an independent fifth branch of modern mathematical logic.
4 The relation between a market price and its predicted value was termed the reaction function:

> Relations of this form between the variable to be predicted and the prediction will be called *reaction functions*.
>
> (Grunberg & Modigliani, p. 471; italics in original)

5 I am reminded that Phelps, in one of his early papers that introduced the concept of the natural rate of unemployment in its modern forms, first referred to it as a warranted rate. Eventually, of course, the Wicksellian term 'natural rate', introduced by Friedman, prevailed. Phelps and Grunberg–Modigliani were, presumably, influenced by Harrodian thoughts in choosing the eminently suitable word warranted rather than natural or rational, respectively. Personally, for aesthetic as well as reasons of economic content, I wish the Phelps and Grunberg–Modigliani suggestions had prevailed.
6 As became the tradition in the whole general equilibrium, game theoretic and rational expectations literature, the functional form for the reaction and other functions were chosen with a clear eye on the requirements for the application of an appropriate topological fix point theorem. The self-reference and infinite-regress underpinnings were thought to have been adequately subsumed in the existence results that were guaranteed by the fix point solution. That the twin conundrums were not subsumed but simply camouflaged was not to become evident till all the later activity on trying to devise learning processes for *identifying*, for example, rational expectations equilibria.

## References

Aubert, Karl Egil (1982), Accurate Predictions and Fixed Point Theorems, *Social Science Information*, Vol. 21, No. 3, pp. 323–348.

Aubert, Karl Egil (1982a), Accurate Predictions and Fixed Point Theorems: A Reply to Simon, *Social Science Information*, Vol. 21, No. 4–5, pp. 612–622.

Grunberg, Emile & Franco Modigliani (1954), The Predictability of Social Events, *The Journal of Political Economy*, Vol. 62, No. 6, December, pp. 465–478.

Muth, John F. (1961), Rational Expectations and the Theory of Price Movements, *Econometrica*, Vol. 29, No. 6, July, pp. 315–335.

Sargent, Thomas J. (1993), *Bounded Rationality in Macroeconomics*, Clarendon Press, Oxford.

Simon, Herbert (1954), Bandwagon and Underdog Effects of Election Predictions (1954, [1957]), chapter 5, pp. 79–87, in: *Models of Man: Social and Rational*, John Wiley & Sons, Inc., Publishers, New York.

Simon, Herbert (1982), Accurate Predictions and Fixed Point Theorems: Comments, *Social Science Information*, Vol. 21, No. 4–5, pp. 605–626.

Simon, Herbert (1982a), Final Comment, *Social Science Information*, Vol. 21, No. 4–5, pp. 622–624.

Wang, Hao (1981), *Popular Lectures on Mathematical Logic*, Van Nostrand Reinhold, New York.

# Appendix 3
## Professor Herbert Simon: an obituary

*The Independent*, 13 February 2001 (very slightly revised)

'The learned man and the wise man are not always the same person,' wrote Herbert Simon to Bertrand Russell in 1957. 'Of course this has been known for a long time, but it is nice to have such definite evidence to bring against the pedant.' In Simon the learned man and the wise man were judiciously mixed and his lifelong battles with the pedant made him one of the most interesting, astonishingly successful, exceptionally productive and innovative inter-disciplinarians of the second half of the 20th century.

No other single person has won the Nobel Prize for Economics, the Turing Award of the Association for Computing Machinery and the Orsa/Tims John von Neumann Theory Prize – not to mention countless other awards, distinctions and prizes straddling the behavioural sciences, the cognitive sciences, computer science, economics, psychology, philosophy of science and applied mathematics.

In a virtuoso academic life and career spanning more than six decades, Simon managed, almost single-handedly, to create the wholly new disciplines of behavioural economics and the cognitive sciences and nurture through to growth and prosperity one of the great academic institutions, the Graduate School of Industrial Administration at the Carnegie Institute of Technology (now the Carnegie-Mellon University) in Pittsburgh, where these disciplines challenged orthodoxies with the pugnacious visions and solid theoretical and experimental foundations that had been provided by their courageous and visionary creator.

Simon was born in 1916 in Milwaukee, Wisconsin, the son of Arthur Simon, a German émigré, and Edna Marguerite Merkel, a second-generation descendant of immigrants from Prague and Cologne. He was wholly Jewish on his father's side; partly Lutheran on his mother's ancestry (an important remembrance on this, the 500th anniversary of the revolution the Augustinian Friar wrought).

From the public elementary and high schools in Milwaukee, he won a full scholarship ($300 per year) to the University of Chicago, taking the exam in Physics, Mathematics and English. An early intellectual influence was his maternal uncle Harold Merkel, "an ardent formal debater [whom] I followed in that activity too", who had died young, at the age of 30, in 1922. Uncle Harold had graduated with distinction in Law from the University of Wisconsin, having also studied economics under the legendary John R. Commons and leaving behind copies of The Federalist Papers and William James's Psychology in the family library, both of which were devoured by the young Herbert, leaving indelible impressions on the future civil libertarian, economist and psychologist.

The "ardent debater" championed unpopular causes, "but from conviction rather than cussedness", in high-school discussions: the single tax, free trade, unilateral disarmament, strengthening the League of Nations. Indeed, his first publication, whilst still in grade school, was a letter to the Editor of the Milwaukee Journal, defending atheism.

To buttress his debating skills he began to read widely in the social sciences. Two books in particular were decisively influential: Richard T. Ely's Outlines of Economics (1893) and Henry George's Progress and Poverty (1882). By the time he was ready to embark upon a university career, he had developed a clear sense of the general direction he intended to take in his studies. He would devote himself to becoming a "mathematical social scientist".

He obtained his BA in Political Science from Chicago in 1936 and a PhD in 1943. He decided to major in Political Science because his first choice of major, Economics, required him to take an obligatory course in accounting, which he detested.

The undergraduate-term paper, written for graduation with a BA, led to a research assistantship at the Milwaukee City Government in the field of Municipal Administration, which in turn led to a Directorship at the Bureau of Public Measurement in the University of California at Berkeley, from 1939 to 1942. For Milwaukee he undertook a study of how the municipal employees made budget decisions, for example, when deciding between planting trees and hiring a recreation director. From this work grew his PhD thesis that, subsequently, became one of the fountainheads for the whole field of organization theory: Administrative Behavior, published first in 1947 and is still in print.

Simon's main intellectual impulses during the Chicago years came from Henry Schultz in mathematical economics and econometrics (still in their early years), who was also a mentor, from Rudolf Carnap in the philosophy of science, from Nicholas Rashevsky in mathematical biophysics and from Harold Lasswell and Charles Merriam in political science.

Simon observed, when writing an appreciation for his almost lifelong collaborator and co-Turing prizewinner Allen Newell, that the four great questions of human intellectual endeavour are those on the *nature of matter*, the *origins of the universe*, the *nature of life* and the *working of the mind*. There is little doubt that he himself devoted the whole of his professional life to various aspects of the problem of the working of the mind. How does the mind perceive the external world? How does perception link up with memory? How does memory act as a reservoir of information and knowledge in interacting with the processes that are activated in human decision-making, in individual and social settings? In short, *human problem solving* (the title of his 1972 book with Newell): in the face of internal constraints emanating from the working of the mind; and constraints, imposed on its workings, by the external, perceived, world.

An early and startling awareness that he was colour-blind, learned whilst picking strawberries as a child (strawberries are red and leaves are green and a colour-blind person cannot differentiate between the two), had taught Simon that the perceived external world was not necessarily identical to the "actual" world out there, whatever that meant.

George Polya's influential little book How to Solve It? (1945) introduced generations of students to *heuristics – the art of guided search*. Simon and Newell had both read it, before they met each other in 1952 (today – in July 2017 – I might even say that this is analogous to the mode of operation of *Turing's O – Machine*). They felt that the Polya framework provided a starting point for investigating, experimentally, the creative aspects of the workings of the mind in one formally and rigorously definable area – human problem solving. From lessons that could be learnt in understanding the formal aspects of human problem solving they felt they could move on to more ambitious tasks: to an understanding of human thinking, in general. From there it would, then, be a natural step, even if not an easy one, to a formal understanding of the underpinnings of human decision-making in general.

They set about building a framework to realize, formally and experimentally, such a research programme. This entailed the need to formulate precise hypotheses on the nature of information, its representation and its processing. Mechanisms of the mind that could be expected to seek out relevant information, to store it and to process it, had to be postulated in such a way that their implications could be experimentally investigated – in the rigorous senses that had been codified by the 'hard' sciences: repeatable, refutable, revisable systematically. The seeking out of information by the mind necessitated some hypothesis on the process of search: was it to be one thing at a time or would it be 'parallel'?

They had no preconceptions that the one hypothesis was more realistic than the other; the *principle of Occam's razor* guided them, at least in the initial stages, and they opted for the serial model, to which they remained faithful for the rest of their lives simply because it never failed them experimentally.

These tentative initial conditions led them to organize evidence on human problem solving within an explicit framework of a theory of information processing. This, in turn, led to 'a general theory of human cognition, not limited to problem solving, and a methodology for expressing theories of cognition as programs'. The last and, by now, the natural step was to use the stored-programme computer, just coming to life as the *Johnniac* in their part of the world, to stimulate human thinking. Thus was born the fertile and sometimes misunderstood field that came to be called *the theory of cognitive sciences*; and among their undisputed founders were Herbert Simon and Allen Newell. From this, and the Dartmouth conference of 1957, the steps towards artificial intelligence were almost inevitable.

Simon's thinking (wo)man, who emerged from the dim beginnings of the problem-solving (wo)man, was a more general construction than the economist's rational (wo)man. In constructing, for experimental investigations, the thinking (wo)man Simon and his co-workers stressed one, refutable, empirical fact: that there exists a basic repertoire of mechanisms and processes that the thinking (wo) man uses in all of the domains in which intelligent behaviour is exhibited.

This is, for many of us, a simple and powerful restatement of what in recursion theory – computability theory – is called *Church's Thesis* (or the *Church–Turing Thesis*). In more traditional ways and practice one would refer to it as a "working hypothesis". Instead, misunderstandings have bedevilled the rich and powerful empirical methods and results that Simon and his co-workers generated over a sustained period of research on human decision-making within organizations and in society – as economic, behavioural, social and political agents.

Simon was a member of the Cowles Foundation for Economic Research in its early Chicago days, before its decisive move to Yale in New Haven; he was also a member of the Rand Corporation in its glory days, the early 1950s. The former nurtured, in Simon's own words, the econometric 'mafia'; the latter fostered the mathematical economics 'mafia'. To his considerable distinction he preserved the courage of his convictions and remained a gadfly inside these citadels of orthodoxy whilst enjoying the respect, perhaps even the envy, of his distinguished and eminent peers.

His contributions to formal and traditional economic theory – both to micro and macro variants – and to econometric theory were fundamental and path-breaking. At a very early stage in the mathematization of economics he deduced, in joint work with the mathematician David Hawkins, conditions for stability, which came to be known as the *Hawkins–Simon conditions* in the folklore of the subject, for linear multisectoral models of the economy. This led to an amusing episode with the House Un-American Committee hearings, during the "McCarthy era", because Hawkins – whom Simon had *never* met and with whom he had written the famous paper entirely by corresponding – was a paid-up member of the Communist Party.

During the Depression Simon had seen a chart on the walls of his father's study, tracking the dismal progress of a faltering American economy. This chart was constructed on the basis of a model of the macroeconomy and its flows built on the principles of servomechanism theory, using hydrodynamic analogies. It had been devised by an imaginative engineer, A. O. Dahlberg, but the theory underlying the model was palpably false. Thirty years later, A.W. Phillips, who had trained as an electrical engineer, was to construct the hydrodynamic '*Phillips Machine*', based on Keynesian theory, and built on the basis of the theory of servomechanism.

Independently of the Phillips constructions, Simon had begun to look at the economy, particularly the macroeconomy, from the point of view of the theory of servomechanisms and feedback control. This line of research led him to his celebrated results on certainty equivalence in the devising of optimal policy in decisions on production scheduling in firms. He did not pursue the servomechanism metaphors for too long, because he did not feel that they gave additional insights or empirical levers that could not be got by the mathematical analysis underlying their structures. He also felt, by then, that analogue simulations were a distinct second best to the digital possibilities he was pioneering.

The origins of the inspiration that led to the influential work with his eminent Japanese student Yuji Ijiri on the size distributions of the growth and decay of business firms and organizations are narrated with humour and candour in his charming autobiography, *Models of My Life* (1991). It is also a tale of academic bloody-mindedness, recounted without rancour, and revisited with nostalgia and regrets on the fallibility of memory.

In 1946 Richard Goodwin had begun his own lifelong research programme of interpreting economic agents, markets and the economic system as (nonlinear) oscillators. His earliest paper on this subject analysed markets as coupled oscillators with hierarchies of coupling strengths: some markets weakly coupled; others strongly coupled. All of them linked by economy-wide, common, expenditure impulses. In a remarkable series of papers, extending over half a century, Simon exploited this simple idea in all sorts of fertile ways: to study causality in economic models; to formalize causality and link it with identifiability in econometric models; to theorize about aggregation in economic models; to formalize the idea of near-decomposability in hierarchical organizations and, most recently, with colleagues in the University of Trento, on using the idea of near-decomposability to study biological evolution.

In *Models of My Life*, he takes this particular example of the inspiration he got from Goodwin's remarkable attempt to represent markets interacting with delayed responses as hierarchically coupled oscillators to wonder about the kinds of representations scientists use in thinking about research problems: where do the metaphors for scientific representations come from? How are they represented and retained in the human mind? How are they recalled – and when and why at that particular juncture? What are the triggering mechanisms and the catalysts? He has answers, tentative, testable and, as always, interesting and provocative.

In recent years, and most eloquently and passionately, in his *Raffaele Mattioli Lectures* of 1993 (published as *An Empirically Based Microeconomics*, 1997), he made the case for study of economies in terms of organizations as the basic unit rather than the traditional device of markets. His case is many-pronged and based on solid empirical and theoretical results. He felt – but, again, justified by empirical and experimental data and results – that the reliance on markets led to the unnecessary and false claims for their optimality properties (true only in one of many possible mathematical worlds and false in all others) as well as the propagation of the false dichotomy between the virtues of decentralization and the vices of centralization, without forgetting the merits of the former and the disadvantages of the latter.

But he was optimistic about the future of economics and even more so of computer science and the interaction between the two and psychology. In a recent letter to a distinguished colleague of mine he wrote that he thought that 'the battle has been won, at least the first part, although it will take a couple of academic generations to clear the field and get some sensible textbooks written and the next generations trained'.

Herbert Simon did not accept criticism willingly – not often even gracefully. He felt that he had reached his convictions, beliefs and the stands he was taking at any time after deep theoretical studies, and seriously and carefully designed experiments to harness empirical data to substantiate those theories on which he was betting. The least he expected from his critics and detractors was an equal commitment to the scientific enterprise. On the other hand, he was exceptionally generous to junior colleagues and graduate students – with his time, with his advice and with his patronage. He was a passionate liberal and debunked any and every kind of pretense – in scholarship, in manners, in attitude and in interpersonal relationships.

At the time of his death he was the Richard King Mellon Professor of Computer Science and Psychology at Carnegie-Mellon University, a post he has held since 1966. He was the recipient of numerous prizes and distinctions. Winning the Nobel Prize in 1978, he was perhaps, with Leonid Kantarovich, the only Economics Nobel laureate not to have a degree in Economics or Management and never to have held a Chair in either of these subjects. He shared the Turing Prize with Allen Newell in 1975 and won the John von Neumann Theory Prize in 1988, the Distinguished Scientific Contribution Award of the American Psychological Association in 1969 and the National Medal of Science in 1986.

Herbert Alexander Simon, economist and social scientist: born Milwaukee, Wisconsin 15 June 1916; Assistant Professor, then Professor, Illinois Institute of Technology 1942–49, Head, Department of Politics and Social Science 1946–49; Professor of Administration, Carnegie-Mellon University 1949–67, Associate Dean, Graduate School of Industrial Administration 1957–73, Richard King Mellon University Professor of Computer Science and Psychology 1967–2001; Nobel Prize for Economics 1978; married 1937 Dorothea Pye (one son, two daughters); died Pittsburgh, Pennsylvania 8 February 2001.

# Appendix 4

## Letter from Herbert Simon

**Herbert A. Simon**
Carnegie Mellon
Department of Psychology
Carnegie Mellon University
Pittsburgh, PA 15213–3890
(412) 268 2787
(412) 268 2798 FAX
has@cs.cmu.edu

25 May 2000
Professors Axel Leijonhufvud
and Kumaraswamy Velupillai

Dear Friends,

I want to share some first impressions on my reading of 'Computable Economics.' (I confess that 'reading' did not include going through all the proofs.) I was delighted and impressed by the mileage you could make with Turing Computability in showing how nonsensical the Arrow/Debreu formulation, and others like it, are as bases for notions of human rationality. Perhaps this will persuade some of the formalists, where empirical evidence has not persuaded them, of what kinds of thinking humans can and can't do – especially when dealing with the normative aspects of rationality.

As the book makes clear, my own journey through bounded rationality has taken a somewhat different path. Let me put it this way. There are many levels of complexity in problems, and corresponding boundaries between them. Turing computability is an outer boundary, and as you show, any theory that requires more power than that surely is irrelevant to any useful definition of human rationality. A slightly stricter boundary is posed by computational complexity, especially in its common 'worst case' form. We cannot expect people (and/or computers) to find exact solutions for large problems in computationally complex domains. This still leaves us far beyond what people and computers actually CAN do. The next boundary, but one for which we have few results except some of Rabin's work, is computational complexity for the 'average case', sometimes with an 'almost everywhere' loophole. That begins to bring us closer to the realities of real-world and real-time computation. Finally, we get to the empirical boundary, measured by laboratory experiments on humans and by observation, of the level of complexity that humans actually can handle, with and without their computers, and – perhaps more important – what they actually do to solve problems that lie beyond this strict boundary even though they are within some of the broader limits.

The latter is an important point for economics, because we humans spend most of our lives making decisions that are far beyond any of the levels of complexity we can handle exactly; and this is where satisficing, floating aspiration levels, recognition and heuristic search, and similar devices for arriving at good-enough decisions take over. A parsimonious economic theory, and an empirically verifiable one, shows how human beings, using very simple procedures, reach decisions that lie far beyond their capacity for finding exact solutions by the usual maximizing criteria. A recent example that I like is the work of Shyam Sunder (now at Yale, alas) and his colleagues on the equilibrium of markets with 'stupid' traders, and the near indistinguishability of such markets from those with optimizing traders. When we have remade economic theory on that model, we will be able to write honest textbooks.

So I think we will continue to proceed on parallel, but somewhat distinct, paths for examining the implications of computational limits for rationality – you the path of mathematical theories of computation, I the path of learning how people in fact cope with their computational limits. I will not be disappointed however if, in the part of your lives that you devote to experimental economics, you observe phenomena that seduce you into incorporating in your theories some of these less general but very real departures from the rationality of computational theory. This seems to me especially important if we are to deal with the mutual outguessing phenomena (shall we call them the Cournot effects?) that are the core of game theory.

I am sure that you will be able to interpret these very sketchy remarks, and I hope you will find reflected in them my pleasure in your book. While I am fighting on a somewhat different front, I find it greatly comforting that these outer ramparts of Turing computability are strongly manned, greatly cushioning the assault on the inner lines of empirical computability.

Once again, thank you very much for sending your fine book. Please continue to keep me in touch with your work. I'll send along some recent reprints of mine.

Cordially,

Herbert A. Simon
Professor of Computer Science and Psychology

# Author Index

# Subject Index

A *Subject Index*, unlike an *Author Index*, cannot even try to be *exhaustive* – whatever that may mean, in context – but can, at best, be a 'scaled map' of a terrain, projected accordingly. The terrain might well be 'rough' or 'unfamiliar' and it is the task of a *Subject Index* to achieve some semblance of smoothness to the purpose of a Journey